COMMONPLACE CULTURE IN WESTERN EUROPE IN THE EARLY MODERN PERIOD
III

Legitimation of Authority

GRONINGEN STUDIES IN CULTURAL CHANGE

GENERAL EDITOR
H.W. Hoen

EDITORIAL BOARD
J.N. Bremmer, J.J.H. Dekker, G.J. Dorleijn,
A.A. MacDonald, B.H. Stolte, A.J. Vanderjagt

Volume XLI

COMMONPLACE CULTURE
IN WESTERN EUROPE IN THE
EARLY MODERN PERIOD
III

Legitimation of Authority

EDITED BY

Joop W. Koopmans and Nils Holger Petersen

PEETERS

LEUVEN - PARIS - WALPOLE, MA

2011

Illustration on cover: State carriage of King John (João) V of Portugal (r. 1706-1750). (Museu Nacional dos Coches [National Coach Museum], Lisbon, Portugal; with assistance of the Nationaal Rijtuigmuseum [National Carriage Museum], Leek, the Netherlands).

A catalogue record for this book is available from the Library of Congress.

D/2011/0602/17

ISBN: 978-90-429-2476-5
© Peeters, Bondgenotenlaan 153, 3000 Leuven

CONTENTS

PREFACE AND ACKNOWLEDGEMENTS

In 1999, the local Groningen Research School for the Study of the Humanities, and the Groningen members of the national Netherlands Research School for Medieval Studies succeeded in obtaining a grant for an innovative, large-scale, collective research programme entitled *Cultural Change: Dynamics and Diagnosis*. Supported by the faculties of Arts, Philosophy and Theology and financed by the Board of the University of Groningen, the *Cultural Change* programme constitutes an excellent opportunity to promote multidisciplinary approaches to phenomena characteristic of transformation processes in the fields of politics, literature and history, philosophy and theology. In order to enhance programmatic cohesion, three crucial 'moments' in European history were selected: 1) Late Antiquity to the Early Middle Ages (*c*.200–*c*.600), 2) Late Medieval to the Early Modern period (*c*.1450–*c*.1650), and 3) the 'Long Nineteenth Century' (1789–*c*.1918). In 2000 and 2002 further grants were obtained for *Cultural Change: Impact and Integration* and *Cultural Change: Perception and Representation* respectively. Several international conferences and workshops have already been organised and are planned for the coming years.

One focus of the *Cultural Change* programme has been a project entitled 'Authority and Persuasion: the Role of Commonplaces in Western Europe (*c*.1450-*c*.1800)'. This project was launched by scholars from the universities of Copenhagen, Durham and Groningen and generously funded by the Danish National Research Foundation, the British Academy and the Netherlands Organisation for Scientific Research (NWO). In the project the notion of commonplace was broadened to include means of persuasion in all kinds of texts as well as the visual arts, theatre, music and other media.

This is the third volume from the resulting *Commonplace Culture series*. It offers the papers presented at a workshop, organised in Groningen, 18-19 September 2008. The contributions focus on the eighteenth century, an era in which many new political groups appeared, challenging and confronting existing rulers and elites, who in turn were forced to find alternative ways of legitimating their authority. Although the traditional commonplace books went out of fashion, the ten contributions in this volume demonstrate that practices of quotation as well as persuasive uses of stock material did not disappear.

We thank the Board of the University of Groningen for the financial support given to the *Cultural Change* programmes.

The editors are particularly grateful to Marijke Wubbolts for helping to organise the workshop which was the inspiration for this volume, and Gorus van Oordt for preparing the texts for publication.

Herman W. Hoen, General Editor

1. State carriage of King John (João) V of Portugal (r. 1706-1750). The construction is attributed to the brothers José de Almeida (sculptor) and Félix Vicente de Almeida (wood carver). The Portuguese royal family used this carriage until the beginning of the twentieth century. (Museu Nacional dos Coches [National Coach Museum], Lisbon, Portugal; with assistance of the Nationaal Rijtuigmuseum [National Carriage Museum], Leek, the Netherlands).

INTRODUCTION

Joop W. Koopmans and Nils Holger Petersen

For centuries the horse-drawn carriage was used as a means of transport by people from various levels of society. Particularly from the sixteenth century on, closed carriages were favoured by the elite, as they were, of course, more comfortable and luxurious than cheaper uncovered coaches (see for example, the coach on the cover of this volume, also fig. 1).[1] As is made clear in Carsten Meiner's chapter in this volume, a whole range of different social encounters could take place in and around such closed carriages, also taking advantage of the doors connecting the secluded space of the carriage to the outside world. Inside, occupants could hold conversations, negotiate, flatter, court or make love, quarrel or be silent, all in various degrees of privacy which would change rapidly from one situation to another; in many cases such encounters could even take place anonymously. However, violent incidents such as robberies or accidents could also interrupt such encounters from without, sometimes with terrible consequences, although sometimes helping to bring happy endings to difficult situations. As Meiner points out, by the eighteenth century the carriage had become a typical meeting place in early modern higher society and for the same reason it was employed as a well-known *topos* or *locus* in European literature, a setting to be used in various narrative contexts, supporting different themes and arguments. A general question with much wider ramifications to which this volume is dedicated, however, is to what extent such a *locus* may also be considered to be an extended *locus communis*, or commonplace. This question has been the subject of debate in recent discussions about the use of commonplaces in early modern Europe. It is also the focus of a collaborative project to which this volume as well as two previous volumes in this series bear witness.

The project 'Authority and Persuasion: the Role of Commonplaces in Western Europe (*c.*1450-*c.*1800)' was initiated by Martin Gosman (University of Groningen, the Netherlands) several years ago. Together with his colleagues Philiep Bossier and Joop Koopmans, Gosman launched the project in cooperation with colleagues Mette Bruun and Nils Holger Petersen from the University of Copenhagen, Denmark, and Kathryn Banks and David Cowling from Durham University in the United Kingdom. The pro-

---

[1] See, for example, Libourel, *Voitures hippomobiles*.

ject – generously funded by the Netherlands Organisation for Scientific Research (NWO), the British Academy and the Danish National Research
Foundation – has held workshops in Copenhagen, Durham and Groningen
over the period 2006-2008, each one giving rise to a volume in the Groningen Studies in Cultural Change series. This third volume, which presents
the results of the final workshop of the project, predominantly deals with
the eighteenth century, while the previous two volumes focused mainly on
the sixteenth and seventeenth centuries respectively, in each case examining
themes particularly relevant to the specific historical period.[2]

The point of departure for the project was the use of commonplaces as
a means of persuasion in the early modern world. Commonplace as a term
refers to the late medieval and early modern commonplace books, studied
by Ann Moss in her *Printed Commonplace-books and the Structuring of
Renaissance Thought* (1996), a most valuable introduction to these collections of generally accepted authoritative quotations. In this work, Moss
studied many commonplace-books that were produced by humanists in
Western Europe for educational and pedagogical reasons during the Renaissance and up until the end of the seventeenth century. They contained
mostly Latin quotations which by virtue of their normative status provided
the user with a general systematised philosophical and rhetorical knowledge, as was deemed intellectually necessary. Moss also explained why
public printed commonplace-books – as well as private written collections
of commonplaces – became less popular by the end of the seventeenth century, although the commonplace-book remained marginally in use as a
study tool until the twentieth century. However, the philosophical scepticism of René Descartes, together with the general rise in practical scientific
and philosophical empiricism during the seventeenth century, meant that
traditional commonplace-books lost authority and popularity. Meanwhile,
during the same period in which newspapers originated, vernacular literature in general increased in popularity, with these other means of propagating ideas and knowledge becoming increasingly important.[3]

Generally speaking, the aim of this research project has been to study
ways in which late medieval or early modern authorities or authorities *in
spe* persuaded or attempted to persuade society or particular groups within

---

[2] See Cowling and Bruun, eds, *Commonplace Culture in Western Europe in the
Early Modern Period I. Reformation, Counter-Reformation and Revolt*; Banks and
Bossier, eds, *Commonplace Culture in Western Europe in the Early Modern Period
II. Consolidation of God-Given Power*.

[3] Moss, *Printed Commonplace-Books*, pp. 273-276. See, for example, the articles by
Andreas Musolff, Jan Clarke and Rina Walthaus in Banks and Bossier, eds,
Commonplace Culture in Western Europe in the Early Modern Period II. See also
the contributions by Alicia Montoya and Thomas Wynn in this volume.

society of their authority, or convey more particular agendas which required some degree of social acceptance. In other words, the project focuses on how authority could be asserted in various contexts and how particular political, religious or other agendas were launched with the aim of generating general support from the relevant groups. Importantly, and from the outset, the project intended to include persuasive strategies that were not only expressed in verbal argumentation and through traditional commonplaces but also by way of other media. Acts of public persuasion often and very obviously included the staging of, for example, public processions, architectural grandeur, theatrical performances and other displays manifesting authority, truthfulness or other characteristics which it was hoped would be accepted in the relevant contexts. As has been demonstrated in the two previous volumes resulting from this project, the use of different media in relation to public persuasion in the sixteenth and seventeenth centuries was quite extensive, and although the emerging picture for the eighteenth century is quite different for a number of reasons − not least because Enlightenment thought and practice created a political environment critical to hitherto generally accepted political manipulations − the employment of media other than the spoken word for such purposes also remained widespread during this period.

As indicated in David Cowling's introduction to the first volume, the notion of commonplace was broadened during the project to include means of persuasion which may be seen as generalisations of the notion of commonplaces in the visual arts, theatre, music and other media: this broader notion regards 'material that enjoyed both a history of use in a given society or language community and a wide currency in that society'.[4]

Thus, the project studies how various kinds of authorities employ such generalised 'commonplaces' to convince or influence their public or a specific audience. In some cases the audience was uneducated or even the illiterate masses, with a narrow knowledge of past events and highly dependent on oral or visual information, susceptible to hearsay or able to be influenced by expressions of majesty or other displays of power. In other cases, it was educated and even sophisticated groups within society which authorities nevertheless still hoped to manipulate, win over, or simply convince by some kind of 'commonplace' means. Within the project, 'authority' has been understood in a very broad political, religious and cultural sense, not only as institutional or individual, and not only seen from the perspective of existing rulers but also from opposing groups and individuals. Authority can be derived, of course, from a powerful position, from intellectual or moral ascendency and also from a combination of all three. Authority is very clear

---

[4] Cowling, 'Introduction', p. x.

and visible when a leading person has charismatic qualities, but even such unquestionably authoritative persons may use all kinds of means to enhance their position. Thus, within the project, scholars from several disciplines have extensively studied the assertion of various kinds of authority but always in the context of the employment of traditional means of wielding power, although sometimes revealing how it was used in sophisticated and intellectually challenging ways.

One may ask how important a generalised notion of commonplaces can be for eighteenth-century European culture, considering the demise of commonplace-books as a generally important educational tool and the appearance of many new political groups who challenged and confronted existing rulers and elites, who in turn were forced to find alternative ways of legitimating their authority. A significant part of the intelligentsia openly disputed the God-given status of the sovereign powers and replaced the authority of the Bible with the authority of reason. At the same time, increasing numbers of people were able to enter the public debate in Western Europe due to the rise of new printed media and a better infrastructure for dispersing information. Thus, the authorities of Western Europe had to cope with a society that was made up of better informed and more educated groups and they needed new persuasive tools and arguments that matched the changing times. Nevertheless, the practice of quotation as well as the persuasive use of stock material in all media, which, as mentioned above, could all be classified under the broader notion of commonplaces, did not disappear. Indeed, such practices are still common to the present day.

The question that remains to be considered is whether such a broad definition of the notion of commonplaces is precise enough to be useful or whether it is so general that it could refer to any kind of persuasive discourse. Is it possible to distinguish the use of materials belonging to the broad generalised category of commonplaces from adherence to and the employment of traditionally accepted wisdom or discourses? In his retrospective overview of the Groningen workshop of 18 and 19 September 2008, Frans Willem Korsten pointed to the dangers involved in a broad definition of commonplaces: citations, the notion of a *topos* – for example, the above-mentioned early modern use of the carriage as a notion with particular associations and expectations – conventions and metaphors may all seem to fall under such a broad category and may thus lead to a blurring of important distinctions, at least within certain fields. This is indeed a relevant criticism and while it has seemed worthwhile within the commonplace project to explore such a generalised notion of commonplaces all the way into the eighteenth century, we realize that the disadvantages of the broad notion may in the end carry greater weight than the advantages. This volume stands as an attempt to approach persuasive rhetorical devices in different media to create a basis for exploring the potential analogies between such rhetorical strategies. One fundamental common feature of all the present case studies is the conscious use of conventional material in them. What creates a commonplace (in the extended notion) out of a topos, a citation, a metaphor, or a convention is not something intrinsic to those particular notions or expressions but their conscious authorial use with the aim to persuade. In spite of the diversity of the employed strategies, it seems to us that those studied in this volume warrant further comparison and thus justify the present experiment. It is our hope that this may at least help determine to what extent such a generalised notion of commonplaces might be a fruitful heuristic tool in studying how various types of discourse – in different media and genres – employ conventional materials and rhetorical devices with persuasive purposes.

As in the previous two volumes, the authors represented in the present one have studied the use of such generalised commonplaces in different sources and genres and in various media, to be more precise, they have examined political rituals and symbols, news sources, reference books, literature and also theatre and music.

In the first volume, the order of articles followed the development of commonplaces, starting with articles about commonplaces in the educational context, broadening the view to the use of figures in vernacular texts and ending with articles about commonplaces in other media. Such an order would no longer work for the eighteenth century, for the simple reason explained above that traditional commonplaces did not hold an important place in eighteenth-century society. The articles in this volume cover a geographical cluster, roughly speaking from Denmark to the Netherlands, Great Britain and France, and finally the Holy Roman Empire mainly in the form of the Viennese court. Some articles span the whole century whereas others explore only a particular period within it. The articles have been thematically grouped; the first four deal in a variety of ways with the negotiation of political authority, whether with the purpose of its legitimation or subversion. The next group of articles deals with extended philosophical, literary and political commonplaces, exploring the *Encyclopédie* and some literary genres. Last but not least, the final three articles are concerned with theatre, again in various ways, including as an instrument for the propagation of virtue, and not least an extended notion of commonplaces discussed in relation to opera, both from a literary angle and also regarding musical composition.

The articles by Ulrik Langen, Marcel Broersma, Joop Koopmans and André Hanou together form a cluster in which political themes are predominant or at least play an important role. The volume opens with Ulrik Langen's contribution on the representation of the Danish king Christian VII (r. 1766-1808), that is, on the way he was displayed as a public figure through images or in person. Eighteenth-century royal representation could convey many subtle political references, immediately recognisable by the contemporary public. Langen discusses the various representations of Christian VII, in particular how he represented himself as a sovereign while representing royal power in a number of different ways, and in spite of his mental illness. Being the sovereign was, in itself, a commonplace.

Broersma takes up the idea that newspapers must be truthful and trustworthy as a kind of commonplace concerning the early modern news service at a time in which printed newspapers were becoming increasingly important media. Although everybody knew that many specific items of news were based on vague rumours or inventions, with notable criticisms of journalism and also attempts to disparage the news service – for example, Ben Jonson's *The Staple of News* – being common, the idea that news had to be true prevailed. Broersma further argues that this idea was necessary to establish the authority of the press and that – as a recognisable statement about the character of journalism – it became a commonplace understanding of this medium (in the most generalised sense of being well known and generally accepted).

Koopmans addresses the use and reinforcement of memories of the sixteenth-century Dutch Revolt – which became part of the Eighty Years' War (1568-1648) – against the Spanish Habsburgs during the political struggle between the Orangists and Patriots in the Dutch Republic that occurred in the 1780s. From the time of the Revolt, one of the constantly repeated images had concerned the disputed Spanish tyranny. This image was not only tied to the concept of 'tyranny' – or 'despotism' and 'slavery' – but also with the names of the abused king and 'tyrant' Philip II and his representative Alba, as well as their institutions, particularly the Inquisition and Alba's Bloody Council. Authors used these keywords and names in a metaphorical way, to compare the supposed bad authority of their own times with the supposedly well-known harsh policy of the Spanish Habsburgs. Because of the historically repeated use of these terms all layers of Dutch society immediately understood such authorial intentions, which, of course, embroidered the situation in this way. Koopmans' article also shows that opposing groups used the same catchwords or commonplaces to abuse their opponents.

While Koopmans analyses public political documents – a pamphlet and a petition to a local authority – and fictitious rhymed letters, Hanou focuses on a text from the classical literary genre of the fable, *The Grumbling Hive* or *The Fable of the Bees*, written by the Dutch Londoner Bernard Mandeville in 1705 and republished in 1714. In this fable, one commonplace wisdom, 'virtue must be', is replaced by its opposite, 'vice leads to well-being'. Hanou argues that Mandeville presents a generally subversive politico-religious message in the form of a fable. Apparently intentionally, Mandeville, in the context of the fable, basically transmits what can be seen as a potential commonplace, which is to say, a commonplace piece of wisdom expressing the idea that at least a certain amount of selfishness is necessary for a society to function optimally. As in all of the articles, the point is not so much to establish that one particular piece of wisdom was propagated, but how this happens by way of generalised commonplace formulations and rhetorical strategies.

Rebecca Ford's article concerns philosophical commonplaces in the *Encyclopédie*. In particular, she focuses on the notion of common sense and to what extent this notion may be understood as an extended commonplace, exploring the relationship between common sense and reason. Common sense was seen by the encyclopaedists as an innate human capacity apparent throughout the whole history of humankind, and was also accepted by them as a tool for progress. Although the role of the notion of common sense was less conspicuous in the *Encyclopédie* than that of 'reason', and not sharply separated from it, Ford argues that the notion of common sense was a key element in the Enlightenment project, not least as a corrective force which limited excessive philosophical and theological speculation as well as guarded against superstition and vice.

Alicia Montoya and Carsten Meiner also deal with literature, although they explore genres other than the moral political fable. Montoya explores the literary letters of two authors: the published letters of Marie de Rabutin-Chantal, Countess of Sévigné, to her daughter Françoise de Grignan at the very beginning of the eighteenth century, and the epistolary novel *Julie, ou la Nouvelle Héloïse* by the well-known philosopher Jean-Jacques Rousseau towards the end of the century. Montoya introduces the concept of 'pseudo-commonplaces' to emphasise how a practice of Latin humanist commonplaces drawn from classical literature was transformed into a practice of quoting canonical vernacular fiction. Both authors made particular use of Torquato Tasso's Italian-language Renaissance epic *Gerusalemme Liberata*. Montoya also points out that although Madame de Sévigné wrote at the beginning of the Enlightenment and Rousseau at the end, both idealised nature. The so-called book of nature seems to have replaced the commonplace-book as a source for inspiration and authority.

Meiner explores the typical early modern *topos* or fixed cliché of the carriage in several European literary texts in order to reveal the de-rationalisation of movement. Discussing its relationship to the classical literary *topoi*, Meiner maintains that the carriage is different, being a concrete material item giving rise to topical conventional treatments in the eighteenth-century novel. This is demonstrated through a number of examples in which unforeseen and fortuitous events are associated with a carriage.

Just as Broersma investigates the claimed truthfulness of printed newspapers as a commonplace, so Thomas Wynn explores another, already traditional *common place* of the public sphere in the eighteenth century: the commonplace of the theatre as a shared school of virtue. Wynn discusses Voltaire's successful tragedy *Tancrède*, which was performed on stage for the first time in 1760, and explains how Voltaire confirms the idea of the theatre and virtue as a commonplace in this play. However, Wynn also raises the question of how differently this may have worked when the play was read privately as opposed to performed publicly.

The last two articles, by Carlo Caruso and Ståle Wikshåland, also bring us into the world of theatre, this time the opera in the Holy Roman Empire and the Habsburg court in Vienna. Both authors focus on the meaning of commonplaces in music. Caruso studies the numerous librettos by the admired Italian poet and librettist Pietro Metastasio, who resided at the Viennese court for decades, clarifying the prominent role of commonplaces and other kinds of formulaic expressions in Metastasio's works. He pays special attention to Metastasio's production *La clemenza di Tito* from 1734.

In the final paper, Wikshåland explores the famous Da Ponte operas of Wolfgang Amadeus Mozart, works which are received today as masterpieces, thus seemingly far removed from the banal and from any use of commonplaces. Wikshåland, however, points out how Mozart employed many commonplace musical elements and how the subtlety of Mozart's composition consists not primarily in the originality of the individual musical elements as such but in the virtuosity with which he could and would combine such elements, and how he recontextualised them in order to establish a most effective form of theatrical entertainment for his audiences. Mozart used musical commonplaces and conventions, thereby creating new meanings by way of extended and refined play with the individual elements as well as the expectations of the operatic audience.

The articles in the present volume do not pretend to be an exhaustive collection of topics relevant to the extended notion of commonplaces for the eighteenth century. While touching upon various discourses in different media which were important for the propagation of authority through employment of such (extended) commonplaces, other areas and other similarly relevant topics could have been treated as well. The main objective of this volume has been to present a range of different case studies in order to exemplify how an extended notion of a commonplace might be a fruitful point of orientation for a study of negotiations of authority in various strands of society in the eighteenth century.

CONTRIBUTORS

Marcel Broersma is Professor of Journalism Studies and Media, University of Groningen

Carlo Caruso is Professor of Italian, University of Durham

Rebecca Ford is Lecturer in French, University of Nottingham

André Hanou is Emeritus Professor of Old Dutch Literature, Radboud University Nijmegen

Joop W. Koopmans is Senior Lecturer in Early Modern History, University of Groningen

Ulrik Langen is Lecturer of History and Civilization, University of Southern Denmark, Odense

Carsten Meiner is Research Fellow, University of Copenhagen

Alicia Montoya is Rosalind Franklin Fellow / Assistant Professor, French Literature, University of Groningen

Nils Holger Petersen is Lecturer of Church History and Leader of the Centre for the Study of the Cultural Heritage of Medieval Rituals, University of Copenhagen

Ståle Wikshåland is Professor of Musicology, University of Oslo

Thomas Wynn is Lecturer in French, University of Exeter

A CRISIS OF ROYAL REPRESENTATION?

REPRESENTATIONS OF KING CHRISTIAN VII OF DENMARK-NORWAY (1749-1808)

Ulrik Langen

In this volume, the notion of commonplaces has been drastically expanded from a more or less specifically sixteenth-century mode of discourse to refer to the diverse cultural practices of the eighteenth century. However, the opening definition by Ann Moss in her introductory article on the traditional conception of commonplaces is still valuable as a defining framework even in the context of the more complex perception of commonplaces presented in this volume:

> Commonplaces are cultural material with both past and present currency within a given language community. Their reference is to opinions commonly accepted as valid (…). Furthermore, commonplace propositions have a ritualised character that makes of them recognisable modes of communication coded for universal reception (…).[1]

If the meaning of 'cultural material' is broadened to include different kinds of transmittable cultural statements, many political references would be considered commonplaces by eighteenth-century spectators, with the representation of the king being the most universal. This brings us to the use of commonplaces in the legitimation of authority, which is highlighted in this volume.

One of the fundamental constituents of royal power in early modern Europe was the representation of the sovereign. The court, as well as numerous media such as portraits, coins, hymns and ceremonies, continuously confirmed the divine nature of royalty. A number of studies have focused on this aspect of royal power, including the classic works by Marc Bloch and Ernest Kantorowicz which investigated the medieval traditions of royal ceremony and inspired further research into the various characteristics of

---

[1] Moss, 'Power and Persuasion', p. 1.

royal representation.[2] In addition, as a contribution to the history of communication, Peter Burke analysed the 'making' of Louis XIV of France,
while Jeroen Duindam and several others have discussed court societies
with reference to the work of Norbert Elias.[3]

One main contribution to this continuously expanding field of research
is Louis Marin's *Le portrait du roi*. Dealing with royal representation,
Marin examined, among other things, the distinction between two kinds of
representation, turning to the definition of the word in an early eighteenth-
century dictionary. Evidently, representation meant showing an 'absent object', which could be a thing, a concept or a person, and substituting for this
an image which represented it in a satisfactory way. However, there was
more to the notion than mere substitution. 'Representing' could also mean
'to appear in person and exhibit things' – that is, the public presentation of a
thing or person. It would then be the thing or person that constitutes its own
representation rather than being represented by another object. The referent
and its image become conjoined, although still presenting two aspects of the
same thing. This notion led Marin to emphasise the reflexive dimension of
representation, whereby every representation not only represents its referent, but can also be considered as the act of a referent representing itself.[4]
The difference concerns either representing something absent or present. It
could also be argued that this distinction transforms the role of the spectator, who is no longer merely a distant viewer/interpreter but an engaged wit-
ness/performer.

When a king was represented – either by image or in person – he embodied power. However, what exactly made this incarnation recognisable as
power? Evidently, the monopoly of violence and the martial staging of the
absolutist monarch had a direct effect on his subjects. The display of raw
military power was accompanied by elements such as drums, trumpets and
guards so that there would be no doubt where power lay. However, the display of military power was also accompanied – and in some ways replaced
– by the increasing production of signs which represented the power of the
king, the purpose of which was to facilitate compliance and submission

---

[2] Bloch, *Les rois thaumaturges*; Kantorowicz, *The Kings Two Bodies*. See also Giesey, 'The King Imagined', pp. 41-59; *idem*, 'Models of Rulership', pp. 41-64; Jackson, *Vive le Roi!*.
[3] Burke, *The Fabrication of Louis XIV*; Duindam, *Myths of Power*. On the transformation of royal portraits during the second half of the eighteenth century, see e.g.
Rosenblum, ed., *Citizens and Kings*. The changing representation found in royal
Danish portraits from the period of the reign of Christian VII was recently analysed
in Johansen, *Den skiftende maktrepresentasjon*.
[4] As explained by Chartier, *On the Edge of the Cliff*, pp. 91-93.

without actually resorting to violence.[5] The splendour of the monarch and the divine nature of monarchy – and from the mid-eighteenth century the 'natural' ground (as in natural law) of monarchy – were concepts which could not be consolidated merely by the flaunting of arms. The question that thus arises is what strategies were used to represent the king in times of change and how were these representations interpreted? Also, how did the official *mise en scène* and enactment of power contrast with the different kinds of observations and comments from the spectator's point of view? And how was the royal representation maintained as a popular commonplace?

In January 1766, the not quite seventeen-year-old Crown Prince Christian became King Christian VII of Denmark and Norway. Over the following six years, a string of dramatic incidents took place in the court of Denmark. Intrigue ruled, statesmen rose and fell continuously, and the king threw himself into increasingly dissolute forms of entertainment. During a journey through Europe in 1768, the king became close friends with his new physician, Johann Friedrich Struensee. Upon returning to Denmark, the doctor's influence on the king grew steadily. At this point, the increasing mental illness of the young king became apparent to those closest to him. Struensee took advantage, seizing power and embarking on an affair with the queen. He was ultimately the victim of a coup d'état, leading to his execution in the spring of 1772. From this time it became increasingly evident that the king was suffering from a mental illness, which many years later was diagnosed as schizophrenia.

How did Christian manage to represent himself as the personification of royal power and divine right? How did his efforts match the representations displayed in such events as ceremonies, staged spectacles, written ovations and portraits? First of all, it is necessary to look at the occasions where the king – in person – *did* come to represent royalty. Dealing with the practice of historical agents (for example, a king) demands another approach to that used when interpreting political treatises, royal portraits, buildings and other kinds of media and *mise en scènes* used to represent royalty. Using a situational approach, I have constructed a few themes – using them as clusters of meaning and signification. Within the framework of these themes, I have tried to detect the contrasts and contradictions deriving from the specific situation – or sometimes series of situations. The title of each theme evokes an image which is not an actual description of the king, but a mix of commonplace conceptions stemming from the period as well as investigative considerations of my own. These themes should not be considered as

---

[5] *Ibidem*, p. 96.

fixed analytical categories but rather as malleable and fragmentary tools of deliberation.[6]

The Promising Prince

Most Danish historians have characterised the intellectual capacity of the indisputably intelligent Christian VII as a superficial and witty ripple on the surface of the king's mad mind.[7] Every sign of independent enlightened thought has been regarded as merely a reflection of the influence of the people surrounding him. Danish historiography has been obsessed with characters such as Doctor Struensee and Elie-Salomon-François Reverdil, a Swiss intellectual who became a teacher of eleven-year-old crown prince Christian. Reverdil in particular has been considered to be a reliable witness when it comes to characterising the skills – or the lack of skills – of the young king.

Without a doubt Christian had more than a superficial knowledge of a considerable part of the literature of the times. This knowledge was originally inculcated by a much less flamboyant figure than the likes of Struensee or Reverdil. When Christian was provided with his own royal household at the age of six, the 45-year-old court employee Georg Nielsen was selected as the prince's main teacher. Nielsen was the son of a priest and had grown up on the small island of Als in southern Denmark. He had studied at the universities of Jena and Halle, and on his return to Denmark began giving private lessons to young nobles in Copenhagen. Shortly afterwards, he became Master of the Royal Pages and in 1755 was promoted to become the prince's main teacher. An assistant teacher, the Swiss Paul-Henri Mallet, was hired to teach history and French.

An instruction, which stated in general terms how the teacher should approach his task, was written by members of the State council and signed by Christian's father, King Frederic V. The instruction set out how Nielsen should strive to gain the confidence and love of his pupil so that the prince would find pleasure in learning. The teaching was to be carried out in an entertaining manner through conversations with the pupil. Naturally, it was to be based on Christianity, but this was not to be learned by rote through grinding out biblical quotations repetitiously. Rather, it should involve the explanation of the hidden meanings of the texts using examples that could be related to the personality and actions of the prince. In this way Christian

---

[6] Unless otherwise mentioned, documentation and source references to the following examples are to be found in Langen, *Den afmægtige*.

[7] See for instance Bregnsbo, *Caroline Mathilde. Magt og skæbne*; Amdisen, *Til nytte og fornøjelse*; Holm, *Danmark-Norges Historie*, vol. 4.

was to 'gain a true knowledge of himself, a naked faith and a pure and truthful love of God'. The instruction highlighted several times that it was essential that the prince's education built on 'everything that is virtuous and Christian'.[8]

How then did Nielsen seek to comply with the demands of the instruction? He was a man of fairly liberal religious beliefs, a freemason who actually founded the first Masonic lodge in Denmark in 1743, and was influenced by the rationalism of the period. It is obvious that Nielsen (and Mallet) must have had intentions and plans for the education of the prince which went further than the generalised stipulations of the instruction. So, what did the prince read and what influence did it have? I have gone through all the records for the books purchased for Christian during his education, however the list is too extensive to go into detail here. Also, of course, book titles in themselves do not tell us if the books were read or how they were used. Nonetheless, the titles can tell us something about the perspective and the intentions behind his tuition.[9]

During the first years of Christian's education (from around 1755 to 1760), the curriculum mainly consisted of Latin classics: Virgil, Cicero, Tacitus, Cornelius Nepos, Pliny, Seneca, Lucretius Carus, Lucanus, Valerius Maximus, Herodotus and Titus Livy. The purpose was to introduce Christian to antiquity as well as teach him Latin. Among these works we also find Quintilian's influential *Institutio Oratoria* as well as Petronius' *Satyricon*. Of course, religious works made up a considerable part of the collection but not to the extent that might be expected. They mainly consisted of collections of sermons and different kinds of devotional literature. More comprehensive was the body of books on natural law. Names such as Grotius and Pufendorf appear on the purchase account, and the fact that Nielsen had some of them translated, including *Principes du droit naturel* by Burlamaqui with which the prince became familiar at the age of eight, suggests that these works of natural law were actually read by Christian.

Natural science and philosophy were well represented. The *Encyclopédie* was bought on subscription and works of Montesquieu and Voltaire are common features on the lists of purchases. Even Rousseau's *Du Contrat Social* was bought shortly after it was published in 1762, although it is explicitly stated on the account that the book was to be delivered to the

---

[8] Quotations from the instruction: Høst, *Geheimekabinetsminister*, vol. 1, p. 50. Also available in German: J.K. Høst, *Der Dänische Geheimecabinetsminister Graf Johann Friedrich Struensee und sein Ministerium. Nebst Darstellung der nächst vorhergehenden und folgenden Begebenheiten in Dänemark*, vols. 1-2 (Copenhagen, 1826-1827).

[9] Rigsarkivet (Danish National Archives), Copenhagen: Chamber of Finances: Frederick V's children: Crown Prince Christian: accounts, invoices, etc. 1755-65.

prince's Lord Chamberlain. Perhaps he wanted to examine this already famous and notorious book before it was used in the education of the prince.
Considered as a whole, the collection covered a wide range of literature. In
addition to the books, literary journals such as *Choix litteraire* were bought
to keep Christian informed about the intellectual currents of the day. Furthermore, Nielsen ordered different kinds of recently published treatises and
pamphlets from a supplier in Hamburg.

One of the works of pedagogical interest is Jeanne Marie le Prince de
Beaumont's *Magazin des enfans*, which comprises a series of conversations
between a governess and seven girls aged five to thirteen. The book was
written with the purpose of teaching the French language as well as providing a common introduction to geography, history and moral philosophy.
The conversations in the book consist of edifying tales and discussions
about knowledge, duties, friendship, fear of God, inner beauty, truth and
lies, but also descriptions of more tangible skills such as being able to read a
map, being able to resist drinking too much wine and keeping one's finances in order. All of this is delivered in dialogues between the wise governess and the inquiring girls. *Magazin des enfans* was immensely popular
in Europe at the time and was also translated into Danish. We must presup-
pose that *Magazin des enfans* was used directly in the education of Prince
Christian.

Despite this rather broad range of literature it is possible that it did not
fulfil Nielsen's requirements. Perhaps that is why in 1760, when Christian
was eleven years old, Nielsen wrote a still unpublished treatise which was
to be used in the education of the prince entitled *Abriss der Sittenlehre. Zum
Gebrauch des Unterrichts Seiner Königlichen Hoheit der Kronprinzen
Christianus*. This *Abriss der Sittenlehre* is a systematically constructed treatise of 300 handwritten pages, providing information and advice on many
aspects of princely conduct as well as human life in general. As far as I
know this work has never been subject to any kind of detailed study even
though it is of great importance when trying to understand the nature of
Christian's education.[10]

The treatise is practical and informative but also has a philosophical
dimension. For example, it provides an introduction to the world of politics,
explaining what a society is and how it is formed. Nielsen writes quite
openly about human rights and about the need for an affable relationship
between ruler and ruled. The nature of war and peace is also discussed, taking the principles of international law as a starting point.

---

[10] Det Kongelige Bibliothek (Royal Danish Library), Copenhagen: New Royal
Manuscript Collection 77: Nielsen, *Abriss der Sittenlehre*.

On a more personal level, Nielsen explains the conditions and obligations connected with different types of human relationships, such as those between master and servants, between spouses, and between adults and children. In his review of the relationship between master and servant Nielsen writes that there is no such thing as a relationship of dominion between men that is based in nature. In the natural state, humanity is free. If one human being chooses to submit to another human being, it can only happen by explicit consent and must be based on a contract between the parties. This is quite a progressive statement if one keeps in mind that it is the future absolute ruler who Nielsen is teaching.

Regarding the relationship between men and women, Nielsen also presents quite modern views. He writes how carnal lust is connected with the sexual act for the sake of reproduction. However, Nielsen makes clear that the satisfaction of the natural sex drive can lead to *extinctio libidinis*, and without being evasive he straightforwardly explains promiscuity, fornication and polygamy. Furthermore, he describes to his pupil how divorce can be obtained on the grounds of adultery or denial of conjugal duty. None of these explanations are condemnatory and they are written in a manner that is dry and matter of fact.

Reaching a more philosophical level, Nielsen distinguishes between obligatory and free acts. Obligatory acts are grounded in nature, or what Nielsen describes somewhat imprecisely as 'the natural power of the soul and in love of mankind'. Obligatory acts are external to the will, while free acts depend on the human will. In this context, humanity is manifest through 'free deeds and doings'.

While it is the free acts with which Nielsen's *Sittenlehre* is concerned, he considers that humanity is placed under obligation by the possibility of free actions. One has obligations towards oneself as well as others in general. In this way, Nielsen distinguishes between 'the moral nature of man' as something immanent, and humanity's obligation to lead a respectable and decent life. This manner of conducting one's life partly finds expression in an inner harmony which is created through correct and humane conduct and also through communion with one's fellow human beings. To achieve personal harmony, one has to fulfil the obligations towards oneself. Here Nielsen once again turns to the practical aspects of life. For example, one must eat healthy food, get plenty of fresh air and always have a good night's sleep.

How do Nielsen's ideas relate to the demands of the instruction? Where is God in Nielsen's treatise? Everywhere and nowhere in fact, and it seems that Nielsen had created a system for the prince composed of natural law and deism. Nielsen's ideas are directly connected to mainstream northern European Enlightenment – especially the moderate German version repre-

sented by Christian Wolff. It could be said that revelation and divine provi-
dence are omitted in favour of natural law, with the predominant religious
ideas being an invisible God, humanity's obligation to lead a life based on
moral duty and retribution in the hereafter. Morality thus becomes the core
of religion, with virtue and the notion of the decent life of the individual being decisive factors. This is where Nielsen's *Sittenlehre* has its role, as it is
clear that Nielsen made an effort to assist Christian to gain 'true knowledge
of himself', as mentioned in the instruction. However, this 'true knowledge'
was based on suppositions that were quite different from those intended in
the instruction.

It could easily be argued that Nielsen taught the prince a mechanical
observance of Christianity. Prayers and the performance of devotions were
of course not to be neglected. However, when it came to the important questions about life, as well as the daily routine, religion was omitted and the
Sittenlehre took its place. In this way, the Enlightenment was present early
in the prince's education in the guise of profane moral philosophy, with
Nielsen representing the quiet Enlightenment – an implicit Enlightenment
wrapped in moral philosophy and esoteric freemasonry.

The confirmation of the sixteen-year-old crown prince occurred at
Easter in 1765 in the Palace Church of Christiansborg.[11] The prince shone,
appearing to be a brilliant incarnation of a promising future. Foreign diplomats and local eyewitnesses alike praised the young prince for his ability to
hold the audience spellbound during the lengthy ceremony. Immediately
after the confirmation, enthusiastic treatises on the eloquence and skilfulness of the prince were published. It would not be mistaken to say that the
reactions of the foreign observers and the admiration expressed in private
letters of the time actually exceeded expectations, which are attested to in
the official accounts of the confirmation. Christian presented himself as a
representation of the future absolute ruler, well versed in theological dog-
mas. However, a contradiction could be detected beneath the surface of the
ceremony. As we have seen, Christian had been brought up and educated in
the spirit of moderate Enlightenment and had been taught that his power
was based on natural law rather than divine right. The contrast was very
evident when Christian stated his self-composed confession of faith at his
confirmation.[12] Nonetheless, the representation of the king subtly played on

---

[11] For the confirmation, see Guldberg, *Tale til sine Landsmænd*; Harboe, *En hellig
og høitidelig Bekiendelse aflagt*; Von Schmettau, 'Kammerherre'; Suhm, *Hemmelige Efterretninger*. A number of diplomatic reports have been published in Wittich,
Struensee and Von Raumer, *Europa vom Ende*.
[12] The confession is preserved in Rigsarkivet (Danish National Archives), Copenhagen: Archives of the Lord Stewart: Sager vedr. Kongelige nedkomster og andre fa-
miliebegivenheder, 1761-1770, 'Kronprins Christians konfirmation'.

this ambiguity. At one and the same time, Christian represented himself as a modern Enlightened prince and a traditional princely defender of Christianity.

The promises for the future that were made at the confirmation were reinforced on Christian's first appearance as king. A few hours after the death of his father, Frederick V, Christian was proclaimed king from the balcony of the royal castle of Christiansborg. Many observers, as well as the jubilant crowd in the square in front of the castle, expressed heartfelt enthusiasm following their initial encounters with the new king. However, some conservatives were offended by the fact that when presented on the balcony Christian waved to the crowd with a smile on his face. Had he forgotten that he was supposed to be mourning the death of his father? Furthermore, on the day after the proclamation the new king rode around town viewing the many buildings covered in black drapes and affixed with temporary inscriptions marking the demise of the Crown. This behaviour was considered a serious breach of ceremonial etiquette and the protocol of mourning. As usual at the accession of a new king, rumours concerning changes to the royal household were rife among the common Copenhageners: the Promising Prince had become the New King.

The first signs of his displeasure with or even resentment of the role of representing royalty became evident at Christian's coronation, which took place on 1 May 1767. The ceremony started with a procession which required the participation of a great number of the citizens of Copenhagen as well as the traditional group of courtiers, men of the Church and high-ranking State officials. Christian was also accompanied by his queen, Caroline Mathilde, whom he had married the year before. As the inhabitants of the city performed their duty as the cheering crowd, they also witnessed a representation of the monarch which seemed to be a little more awkward than was expected after the confirmation and accession. More than one witness reported that Christian looked troubled and burdened by the weight of his massive coronation costume and the heavy regalia.

Christian was clearly uncomfortable during the ceremony which followed the procession. While sitting in church listening to the bishop, he became restless and started playing with the royal regalia. Suddenly he dropped the golden 'Apple of the Realm', which fell to the floor with a bump and rolled away. The audience was clearly worried by this incident, as well as with the prospect of being subjects of a king who explicitly expressed his indifference towards the ceremonial staging of the royalty which he personified. Though Christian had trouble presenting the image of himself as a firm ruler, the bishop's speech presented an oratorical representation of a modern enlightened ruler – a prime example of the theory of enlightened absolutism, with small dashes of natural law. Even though the New King had suddenly become the Restless King, the bishop, as a devoted servant of absolutism, confirmed the representation of the king that had been created over the previous ten years.

One reason why Christian seemed indifferent during the coronation could have been that his mind was elsewhere. At the same time as he was preparing for the coronation, he was also rehearsing for the role of Orosman in *Zaire*, a play by Voltaire, which he staged with a handful of his courtiers, giving private performances in one of the halls of the royal castle. Not surprisingly, the role of the fictional Orosman – a handsome, courageous and high-minded ruler – was more attractive than the role of an actual sovereign bullied by his ministers and besieged by scheming courtiers.

The coronation was also the occasion for the use of a traditional medium of royal representation, the royal portrait. Portraiture changed radically during the second half of the eighteenth century, and it is possible to detect some of these changes in the traditional parade portrait of Christian from 1767, painted by the Danish artist Peder Als for the occasion. While this *portrait d'apparat* differed little from the standard design of royal portraits established by Hyacinthe Rigaud in his famous portrait of Louis XIV from 1701, some of the neo-classical elements present in Als' portrait, as well as the posture of the king, deviate from Rigaud's model. Nonetheless, the portrait still presents the political body of the king – to use one of Ernest Kantorowicz' notions. The painting still follows the old tradition of representation, and it is not an enlightened prince but an absolute ruler who is represented (fig. 1). Within a few years this representation – as we shall see – underwent a remarkable transformation.[13]

In the autumn of 1767, Christian changed his routine. During the day he went hunting, attended military parades, worked with his cabinet and met with the State council twice a week. However, at night Christian started undertaking excursions into the city with a small entourage. He visited pubs and wine houses, got drunk and had fights with the night-watchmen, who at first did not know they were dealing with the king. At this time Christian was introduced to Anne Cathrine Benthagen – also known as 'Støvlet-Cathrine' (Bootee-Cathrine or Boots-Cathrine) – a woman of dubious reputation who became Christian's mistress and joined him in his nightly escapades. Although Christian and his entourage were more or less disguised during their nightly raids, there was no doubt about the identity of the group. What the citizens of Copenhagen witnessed was a delinquent youth in the company of a renowned prostitute, a footman and a handful of shady officers, roaming around town smashing up bordellos and wine houses. One morning a group of street urchins followed Christian all the

---

[13] This transformation is also discussed in Johansen, *Den skiftende maktrepresentasjon.*

way from the house of his mistress to the gates of the castle shouting insults at him. At the gate the king was saluted by the guard as he entered the castle, escaping his pursuers. In a remarkable development, the Restless King took restlessness to another level and became the Debauched King.

The court, as well as the professional producers of signs of monarchical grandeur, had a hard time maintaining the dignity of the royal representation. It seemed as if Christian insisted on breaking every rule of etiquette. The debauchery finally came to an end when the king was forced to sign an order expelling Anne Cathrine from the city. A few days later Caroline Mathilde bore an heir to the throne.

The Travelling King

In the early summer of 1768 Christian began his 'grand tour', accompanied by his most important ministers and a retinue including a number of courtiers and officials, doctors, a pastor, secretaries, bursars, chamberlains, footmen, chefs, a dresser and a barber as well as others. The travel journals and newspapers of the day record an eventful trip with a comprehensive and often stressful programme whereby Christian rushed from one place to another, being entertained at balls and theatrical performances en masse. It was very unusual for a reigning king to travel through Europe for several months and considering the previous month of royal excesses, ministers and civil servants could not be blamed for harbouring serious concerns about the possible consequences that such a journey might have on policy and prestige. During a trip abroad all eyes would constantly be on the king and the least deviation in his conduct would be registered and interpreted by an international audience that would not hesitate to make use of the opportunity to dishonour the Danish throne.

Worries and objections concerning the journey were many and varied – clearly illustrated by, for example, the foreign minister J.H.E. Bernstorff in his letters, written in the months preceding Christian's departure. One of the minister's objections broached the consequences that the moral conditions of southern Europe might have on the king:

> (...) j'ajoutois [to the king] que je ne me permettois pas de lui dissimuler que l'oubli d'un quart d'heure ne seroit pas oublié dans l'histoire, que de certains amusements mettroint sa vie et sa personne en danger, et que les femmes infectées estoint bien plus dangereuses et plus mortelles à la santé dans des pays chauds que dans les nôtres.[14]

---

[14] Friis, *Bernstorffske Papirer*, pp. 499-500.

[I added [to the King] that I could not allow myself to hide from him the fact
that the negligence of a quarter of an hour would not be neglected by history,
that certain amusements could bring his life and person into danger and that in-
fected women were much more dangerous and harmful to health in warmer
climes than our own.]

Despite the minister's concerns, Christian's representation of the travelling
king was to be very successful. Although several observers noted the haste
with which Christian visited sights and objects of interest, he nevertheless
impressed his hosts with his wit and conversation. Furthermore, there was
no indication of any escapades such as those of the previous autumn. In
Paris, Christian presented himself as the enlightened monarch, and in this
guise met the famous *philosophes* of the period. At five o'clock in the after-
noon, 20 November 1768, eighteen of the most prominent philosophers, authors and scientists in France assembled at the York Palace in Paris for an
audience with King Christian VII.[15] The Duke of Duras, who had been appointed by the King of France to act as Christian's official escort and *maître
de plaisir* during his stay in Paris, had carefully avoided any contact between the *philosophes* and the Danish king in his extensive programme. Duras was ostensibly not very enamoured of these freethinkers, believing that
Christian was best served by not meeting them, and the French people best
served by not being represented by such figures.

However, Christian felt otherwise and, perhaps recognising Duras' re-
luctance, had his own emissary to the French court, Baron C.H. von Gleichen, make preparations for an audience. Von Gleichen had good contacts
among the *philosophes* and quickly made preparations for a dinner party at
his own residence. A letter inviting the *philosophes* to dinner on 19 November was circulated. The king planned to make his entrance once everyone
was gathered around the table, with the idea apparently being that he would
meet the *philosophes* informally in order to promote lively, free-ranging
conversation over dinner. One could assume that Von Gleichen may have
had the philosophical dinner parties of Frederick the Great in mind while
making the arrangements. Everything was prepared for the dinner, but un-
fortunately it was cancelled at the last moment when Christian caught a cold
and was forced to remain indoors. In lieu of the dinner party, the *philoso-*

---

[15] Those present were Mairan, Cassini, Duhamel, d'Alembert, Duclos, Abbé
Barthelemy, d'Holbach, Crébillon, Condillac, Abbé Morrelet, Grimm, Bernard,
Diderot, Saurin, Helvétius, Marmontel, Watelet and de la Condamine. Christian had
leased York Palace prior to his arrival in Paris and used it as his base throughout his
stay. The following description of the audience is based upon Petit de Bachaumont,
Mémoires secrets pour servir a l'historie and Grimm, *Correspondance littéraire*.

phes were invited to an audience in the king's apartments which was to take place the next day.

There they stood, eighteen *philosophes* and scientists, gathered together by circumstance in a circle in the king's receiving room. Christian entered from his study and began to make his rounds. One by one, Von Gleichen introduced those present to the king, the latter addressing himself to each guest with a remark that had some connection to either the individual's work or his reputation. After the first introduction, the king chatted with select *philosophes* – among them d'Alembert and Diderot, in an audience that lasted just over half an hour. The scene is unique and striking, and one's historical imagination cannot help but be captivated: the nineteen-year-old Danish king in the company of a handful of the eighteenth century's greatest thinkers and scientists.

A few days later, Christian attended a session at the French Academy of Science, where d'Alembert gave a speech in his honour. In essence, the speech dealt with the great mutual advantages princes and *philosophes* can derive from one another.[16] D'Alembert began by stating that philosophy has a need for powerful and respected protectors, and that it is the prerogative of princes to provide this service to philosophy – and people in general. What greater satisfaction could there be for the learned than that those whom the people have made their lords and examples take an interest in the work of philosophers, encourage them with their esteem and inspiring them with their regard? D'Alembert also mentioned that both Louis XV and Peter the Great achieved this by visiting the Academy, and it was an honour now to add Christian to their company. This young prince, he claimed, after showing the French nation his pleasant and estimable qualities, had also demonstrated a solid appreciation of reason and enlightenment.

Rassasié, et presque fatiqué de nos fêtes, il vient dans cet asile de la philosophie se dérober pour quelques momens aux plaisirs qui le poursuivent; et les amusement dont on l'accable augmentent son empressement à connaître cette partie de la nation que les étrangers et souverains semblent honorer particulièrement de leur estime.

[Sated and almost fatigued by all our festivities, he comes to this haven of philosophy in order, for a short time, to escape the amusements that pursue him. These pleasures heaped upon him only promote his eagerness to become acquainted with this part of the nation, which strangers and princes to a particular degree seem to honour with their esteem.]

---

[16] The speech is printed in D'Alembert, *Oeuvres complétes*, vol. 4, pp. 321-325.

The French encyclopaedist complimented the Danish monarch on his enlightened views and for his support of science and literature, as well as his hunger for knowledge.

> Quoique déjà tres-instruit, quoique jeune, et quoique prince, (que de titres pour la présomption!) il croit qu'il lui reste encore à apprendre, et qu'on ne peut être trop éclairé quand on tient les rênes d'un grand empire.

> [Despite his already great learning, his youth and his princely status (and presumptuous titles), he believes he still has something to learn and that one can never be too knowledgeable, when one holds the reins of state.]

D'Alembert concluded that as a prince of a kingdom in which science flourished Christian had without doubt no need to leave his own land to find enlightened thought. However, knowing that nature does not gather every talent into a single person, nor gather all enlightenment into a single people, the king travels in order to add new riches to those he already possesses, which he can then pass on and disseminate throughout the States under his care. The representation of the king could not have had a better medium than the famous Frenchman.

The Absent King

On his return to Denmark, J.F. Struensee, who had accompanied Christian on the tour, was appointed Physician in Ordinary. Over the next two years Struensee strengthened his influence over the king and became de facto ruler of the kingdom, introducing sweeping reforms which were launched in the name of the king. The innumerable orders flowing from the cabinet were presented as the true will of the king, contrary to the earlier practice of issuing resolutions deliberated on by the royal council. Most of the cabinet orders were in fact dictated by Struensee and as the king grew increasingly disinterested Struensee finally started giving orders without royal approval.

During 1771, the king was mainly represented in public by the tremendous number of edicts coming from the cabinet. The person of the king was kept from a number of public appearances and if he did appear he was heavily guarded by soldiers. The restriction of Christian's public appearances was actually a far more serious blow to the efficacy of royal representation than the nightly raids undertaken by the king and his entourage during the autumn nights of 1767. If the king could not be seen, it mattered little that thousands of orders appeared with his signature and seal, as speculation and apprehension were bound to overtake the city. Why did he not appear at public celebrations as promised? Who was responsible for his absence?

One of Struensee's most critical mistakes was to disband the royal guard. In his opinion there was no reason to maintain an expensive and privileged guard when the regular troops could guard the king as well as any other regiment. However, disbanding the royal guard, which contributed so much to the splendour of royal representation, as well as to the martial effect associated with royal display, was a symbolic act, the meaning of which was obvious to even the most ignorant observer. Furthermore, the act nourished many of the rumours already circulating which suggested that Struensee and the queen were about to seize the throne by forcing the king to abdicate. Dispensing with the royal guard was considered one step closer to the realisation of this. Another mistake was to isolate court life to the castle of Hirschholm, a four hour ride north of Copenhagen. Traditionally, the royal family left Copenhagen for the summer, but in 1771 Struensee kept Christian away from the city until Christmas.

Christian's behaviour in the streets of Copenhagen four years earlier seemed to have been forgotten. The absence of the king from the public space gave rise to serious concern. In this context, general discontent prevailed and the threat of open rebellion became increasingly evident. The image of the Travelling King was replaced by that of the Absent King.

On the night of 17 January 1772, the Queen Dowager and her son, the Hereditary Prince (Christian's stepmother and half-brother), led a coup d'état which put Struensee in prison. The new rulers were very aware that the first essential step in legitimising the change of government was to present the king to the public. The following morning Christian was forced into a royal coach with his half-brother to ride around town in order to show his person to the euphoric crowd. Indeed, Christian certainly presented himself as the king. However, while the crowd shouted and pressed towards the coach in mindless celebration, some of the more observant noted with concern the undisguised terror displayed on the face of the king.

The significance of showing Christian to the general public at every imaginable occasion to legitimise the new regime was intertwined with the importance of communicating the coup as sheer deliverance. Although well-paid pamphleteers praised the change, the Church was the prime medium for this. On the first Sunday following the coup every church in the kingdom held a thanksgiving service. The events of the night of 17 January were described as a liberation of the king from captivity by evil and immoral persons who had held him prisoner against his will. These sinful criminals were presented as having taken control of the kingdom and as being well on their way to destroying society as a whole. Fortunately, the sermon contin-

ued, God had intervened to help the Queen Dowager and her son free the
king and re-establish the natural order.[17]

As loyal spokesmen of the absolutist State, the priests communicated
the true interpretation of the events to the population. Royal representation
was now shared between the king, the Queen Dowager and the Hereditary
Prince. The Absent King had now become the Liberated King.

The Static King

As mentioned above, the new rulers ensured that Christian appeared in public at every necessary occasion. From now on there was no change in the
way that Christian was represented or in the way he represented himself. He
was never left unsupervised but always accompanied by the Queen Dowager or the Hereditary Prince during his many public appearances. By and
large Christian participated in all of the court's activities during the last 36
years of his life – from the daily royal tables to the formal reception of foreign diplomats and the annual grand opening of the Supreme Court. Nonetheless, he was kept on a short leash, though as time went by his tics and
increasingly odd behaviour did not pass unnoticed. Despite this, many witnesses also remarked that his appearance and manners were very dignified:
royal to the bone, as one foreign observer wrote in his diary. The more dy-
namic representation of royalty was handed over to Christian's half-brother
the Hereditary Prince Frederick, and from 1784, to his son, Crown Prince
Frederick. The Crown Prince effectively ruled as an absolute sovereign
while Christian was a mere figurehead, although the illusion of Christian's
absolute sovereignty was maintained until his death in 1808. Every order or
resolution still had to be co-signed by the king. Every act was still undertaken in the name of King Christian VII of Denmark and Norway.

Let us briefly return to the medium of royal portraits to glance at a portrait painted less than 15 years after that produced by Als. In this painting,
the ruler does not embody the State in the manner of the earlier painting. He
is presented from the chest up, showing – more or less – his actual physical
features. He has been demystified, becoming an individual. The dignity of
royalty has been toned down – nothing tells us that we are looking at the
absolute ruler of the kingdom of Denmark and Norway – no devices, no attributes. It is the king's physical body that is represented, rather than the political body of the king as seen in Als' portrait.[18] In a way, Christian has become anonymous (fig. 2).

---

[17] Bregnsbo, *Caroline Mathilde*, pp. 160-163.
[18] Johansen, *Den skiftende maktrepresentasjon*.

The transformation detected in this representation of the king in the royal portraits is very significant with respect to the alterations of royal representation as a commonplace. Returning to Ann Moss's ideas about commonplaces, it becomes clear that the 'cultural material' – such as portraits and the king's physical presentation of himself – had 'both past and present currency within a given language community'.[19] The images and representations of royalty, however changing and ambiguous they may have been, referred 'to opinions commonly accepted as valid' and were indeed 'coded for universal reception'. This is evident in the way that the changes in royal representation were actually perceived or interpreted by the king's subjects.

The different images of the king – the enlightened prince, the travelling king, the liberated king – refer to commonplace conceptions of kingship and authority. Although these images were challenged by the king's own physical presentation of the restless king, the debauched king and the absent king, to a certain extent they were never considered empty. It seems that the representations of the king, despite the momentary excesses and his enduring illness, were generally accepted as meaningful images, although 'everyone' knew, at least from 1770 on, that he no longer actually ruled the kingdom. I suggest that this characteristic may be regarded as a form of *compliance*, which is somewhat similar to what theorists of ritual call 'misrecognition' – that is, a voluntary, irreversible, delayed and strategic play that establishes the meaning of the ritual. 'Misrecognition' in the case of King Christian entailed deliberately ignoring the 'not so royal' features and actions of the king and an acceptance of the contrasts between the representation of the king and the king's – to some extent failed – representation of himself. The analytical problems emerge when we are trying to describe this seeming contradiction. The description could easily miss the point – it could remove the very conditions that allow misrecognition (or compliance) and the social efficacy of accepting the representational power of the king – whether illusory or not.[20] It is precisely this characteristic that makes the representation of the king a commonplace.

Epilogue

What his Danish subjects witnessed during the last 30 years of Christian's reign was a king who danced the old minuets to perfection, receiving ambassadors with dignity and occasionally even engaging in witty conversation. Admittedly, they also saw him talking to himself, unable to control his

---

[19] See footnote 1.
[20] On this particular reading of the concept of 'misrecognition', see Bell, *Ritual Theory*, pp. 82-83.

movements and his face troubled with tics. Nevertheless, he still represented royalty, or rather, he presented himself as the representative of *l'ancien régime* royalty, while in fact not 'ruling'. The 'misrecognition' that this entailed was actually a way of accepting that while the king had no power, he still represented a particular world, albeit lost. His dance – regardless of how perfect he danced – was outdated, while his dignity was old-fashioned and his wit a rococo attribute no longer in vogue. Christian was more or less regarded as a living anachronism, but was still considered to be 'the real king'. Several memoires and letters of the day confirm this impression, with many foreign observers noting how 'kingly' Christian appeared despite his illness.[21] Politics may have been taken care of by statesmen or by his son, the Crown Prince, but the very essence of kingship – true royalty – could only be represented by the king himself – whether a madman or not. The representation of the king was most certainly a commonplace.

---

[21] See e.g. Von Holten, *Af en gammel Hofmands Mindeblade*; Von der Marwitz, *Friedrich August Ludwig v.d. Marwitz, ein Edelmann*; Matthisson, *Briefe*.

1. Christian VII in his anointment costume painted by Peder Als in 1767. (Rosenborg Castle, Copenhagen).

2. Christian VII at the age of 32 painted by Jens Juel in 1781. (The Museum of National History at Frederiksborg Castle, Hilleroed).

A DAILY TRUTH

THE PERSUASIVE POWER OF EARLY MODERN NEWSPAPERS

Marcel Broersma

> For when news is printed, it leaves, sir, to be news. While, 'tis but written –
> Though it be ne'er so false, it runs news still.[1]

In *The Staple of News*, written in 1625, the playwright Ben Jonson satirised the burgeoning news trade of his day. In the first act the main figures visit a newly opened office in which all kinds of news is brought in, examined and filed, before being published 'under the seal of the office as staple news, no other news be current'.[2] Information on current affairs is sold here like a commodity. In the office, the news reports are registered as 'authentical' or 'apocryphal' but whether they are true or false is not a criterion of their commercial value. Jonson clearly states that the last category of 'news of doubtful credit' outnumbers the true accounts.[3] In his play he gives multiple examples of false reports: the king of Spain chosen as pope and emperor, the Dutch navy possessing an invisible eel that has sunk the fleet in Dunkirk and the invention of perpetual motion, just to name a few.[4]

> Is't true? As true as the rest.[5]

It does not matter as long as people will buy it.

The public must have recognised Jonson's sketch of the news industry that was emerging in Great Britain and the rest of Europe. In the early 1620s printed newspapers were a very new, 'hot' medium in England.[6] In his play Jonson repeatedly hinted at actual persons and events. The Gossips, four ladies Jonson introduced during the scene changes to comment on the play, for example, consider the above-mentioned reports as 'too exotic; ill cooked, and ill dished! They were as good yet as Butter could make them.

---

[1] Jonson, *The Staple of News*, p. 79 (Act I, Sc. v, 48-50).
[2] *Ibidem*, p. 79.
[3] *Ibidem*, p. 93.
[4] *Ibidem*, pp. 157-158, 162.
[5] *Ibidem*, p. 163.
[6] Black, *The English Press*, pp. 4-5.

In a word, they were beastly buttered!'.[7] In this comment they refer to Nathaniel Butter, one of the first and best-known publishers of London *corantos* in the 1620s.[8] Butter here functions as a *pars pro toto* for the newspaper business and its dubious practices.

Due to severe censorship, the first London newspapers, just like other European papers, mainly, or merely, published foreign news. At first sight it seems that the Gossips reject these reports because they are of less interest than the local London news they hear from their maid 'Joan Hearsay' or other fellow townspeople. However, on closer examination it appears that Jonson had these women oppose the dissemination of printed news for two other reasons. Firstly, as Catherine Rockwood has pointed out, Jonson takes a political stand. The playwright supported Jacobean royal policy, which enforced censorship to prevent the dissemination of international news that might stir up public sentiment in favour of England becoming involved in the Thirty Years War. The conflict between the king and Protestant opposition about whether or not to enter the war was a catalyst for the introduction of the newspaper in England.[9] Secondly, Jonson rejected the novelty of printing news because it thus seemed to acquire the same status as literature and scholarship. These genres were all now available in print, rather than in the more exclusive handwritten form, but according to Jonson the public should not make the mistake of valuing them equally.[10]

However, I would argue there is more to his position than a concern about propaganda for the Jacobean cause or cultural criticism. By criticising both the dissemination of news and the veracity of the reports in the papers, Jonson exposed the political-philosophical implications of the new *corantos* which brought the world to England and England to the world. He considered them, as Anthony Parr has observed, 'a threat to civilised communication' because they considered news, whether true or false, as a commodity.[11] Editors presented their representation of reality as truth, while their motives were to gain commercial and political profits from the exploration of current events, with no concern for the consequences. However, by disseminating news they challenged the God-given order which Jonson supported. Ordinary people could now obtain all sorts of information which was previously unavailable. They were confronted with various interpretations of what was happening in the social world and were encouraged to think for themselves. By doing so, newspapers stimulated the rise of scepti-

---

[7] Jonson, *The Staple of News*, p. 187.
[8] Grant, *The Newspaper Press*, pp. 32-33; Griffiths, *Fleet Street*, pp. 6-7; Sherman, 'Eyes and ears', pp. 32-33.
[9] Rockwood, '"Know Thy Side"', pp. 137-139.
[10] Parr, 'Introduction', p. 23.
[11] *Ibidem.*

cism and public debate. Jonson opposed this, believing that such a debate was undesirable because it would only lead to trouble. Relying on corrupt information supplied by the papers was no way for people to begin to think for themselves.

Jonson not only criticises the 'producers' of the news who sold their buyers what they ask for, but also the people who paid money for these fabrications. A customer who asks for 'any news o' the saints at Amsterdam' is answered: 'Yes, how much would you?', and is then given his 'six penny-worth' commodity. Anyone who pays is given anything they want and the more bizarre the news items, the better they sell.[12] The main character seems to voice Jonson's argument in a nutshell when he states: 'Why, me-thinks, sir, if the honest common people will be abused, why should not they ha' their pleasure in the believing lies are made for them, as you i'th'office, making them yourselves?'. When you leave communication up to businessmen and public demand you will end up with lies, and that will lead to social agitation: nothing but trouble, according to Jonson.

The Staple of News can be considered a very early example of press critique. I chose this example to illustrate how newspapers have been inextricably bound up with issues of truth since the day of their invention. Jonson satirised the deficiencies of the newspapers of his times. Following in his footsteps, many press critics would do the same (Pierre Bayle, for example, said the papers furnished a new comedy every day) and to this day the alleged untruthfulness of newspapers raises much debate.[13] However, while criticising the press for veiling the truth, Jonson and other critics also implicitly confirmed the standard for newspaper writing which has passed down through the ages: news must be true to be a civilised form of communication which serves society.

The claim to truth was a distinctive characteristic of the newly invented genre of the periodical newspaper which entered the European media landscape around 1610. The belief that newspapers had to preserve the truth became a broadly shared principle in both seventeenth and eighteenth-century newspaper writing and laid the ideological foundation for the development of modern journalism. Newspaper writers and their public agreed on this commonplace – which I will define as an idea or a phrase that is commonly accepted.[14] In its universality, a commonplace thus also becomes trivial, as it does with respect to the notion that news is or should be true. In this contribution I will explore the use and constant reconfirmation of this commonplace as a strategy to establish cultural authority.

---

[12] Jonson, *The Staple of News*, p. 166; cf. p. 178.
[13] Quoted in Dooley, 'News and doubt', p. 280.
[14] Cf. Jennifer Phillips, '"Vox populi, vox dei"', p. 23.

I will first analyse the discourse in which newspaper writing defined itself as a practice that had the ability to present a representation of reality
that was 'true', that is, that reflected what had happened in the 'real world'.
In their statements of aim in the first issues of their papers, almost all printers and editors promised to give truthful accounts of real events. This explicit claim to truth seems as obvious from a popularist point of view as it is
questionable from a scholarly perspective. Contemporaries were, as we
have seen with Jonson, all too well aware of the fact that newspapers presented a disputable, if not false, image of social reality. However, rather
than debunking the newspapers' claim to truth we should study this claim as
a discursive strategy which helped journalism to establish itself as a distinct
and more or less autonomous field within society. In the course of the seventeenth and eighteenth centuries editors developed specific discursive
practices which had to secure a truthful representation of events. As I will
show, we have to interpret the 'invention' of these conventions within a
broader context of a 'culture of fact', in which the gaze was shifted from a
divine Truth to an enlightened appeal to human rationality.

I will argue that the commonplace idea that news had to be true provided newspapers with authority and underpinned their appeal for both
commercial success and press freedom. Truthfulness as the central argument in journalism discourse, at first functioned at a practical level as a
unique selling point for a new intellectual product – the newspaper – while
later on this moved onto a more philosophical level. It then legitimised the
special position of the press and newspapers in society as the Fourth Estate,
as described by the British historian and MP Thomas Macaulay in 1828.[15]

A discourse of truthfulness

From their inception in 1605 printed newspapers have claimed to tell
the truth about the social world. They have assured their readers that the
events reported really took place and had been represented correctly and
without bias in the columns of their paper. However, this claim presented,
as frequent criticisms indicated, an epistemological difficulty, if not an im-
possibility. News does not neutrally reflect social reality or empirical facts
at all. It is a social construction. As newspaper writer Daniel Defoe wrote as
early as 1702: 'Nothing is more common than to have two Men tell the
same Story quite differing from one another, yet both of them Eyewitnesses to the fact related'.[16] No story fully maps out an event. Furthermore, news is the result of a process of selection. Events and facts do not

---

[15] Macaulay, *Essays*, p. 97.
[16] Quoted in Woolf, 'News, history and the construction', p. 107.

have 'intrinsic importance' but become important because they are selected by newspaper writers who adhere to a culturally, ideologically and commercially determined set of selection criteria. That is why journalism has to be studied not as a descriptive but as a performative discourse. In every issue, the public must be persuaded that what was written actually happened in 'real' life. Early modern newspaper writing (which is in my opinion a better term than journalism when discussing the period before the nineteenth century) developed textual strategies to achieve this reality effect. When it succeeded it transformed an interpretation into truth – into a reality upon which governments and citizens could act.[17]

To distinguish themselves from gossip, pamphlets, written newsletters and other early modern news products, newspaper editors promised their readers a supply of reliable information rather than opinion or fictional stories. When Haarlem city printer Abraham Casteleyn, for example, announced the opening of his own newspaper in 1656, he wrote that the 'extremely fabulous' character of current news had forced him to organise a network of informants from all parts of Europe whom he considered trustworthy. This regular correspondence cost him much 'effort and money'. However, he believed citizens would prefer his paper to his competitors because of the truthfulness of his accounts.[18] Defoe was also unable to escape the assumption that news had to be true, and he promised the readers of his London *Daily Post* in 1719 that they would be given 'just accounts of facts in plain words'. He stated that the 'business' of a newspaper writer was 'to give an account of the news, foreign and domestic, in the best and clearest manner we can'.[19] The editor of the Dutch *Leeuwarder Courant* also emphasised the importance of reliable correspondents in the first issue of his paper (1752). He considered that the main reason for the public reproach of newspapers was that they did not always report truthfully. Therefore, he promised his readers that he would provide the most recent news, but also emphasised that he would always and above all print truthful reports (fig. 1).[20]

Newspaper writing's claim to truth is the most important characteristic of its discourse, in which it establishes itself and claims authority. It is the alpha and omega of its existence and the basis of a social code shared by journalists and their public. The claim to truth by journalism today is an implicit one which underlies news coverage, but in early modern times this code had to be declared openly and repeatedly, as Daniel Woolf has noted:

---

[17] Cf. Broersma, 'Journalism as performative discourse'.
[18] Van der Meulen, *De Courant*, pp. 27-28.
[19] *Daily Post*, 6 October 1719.
[20] *Leeuwarder Courant*, 29 January 1752; cf. Broersma, *Beschaafde vooruitgang*.

'The early modern mind, with its deep distrust of anything new and unsanctioned by authority, needed reassurance that what was contained in the newsbook was not idle rumour, or fancy'.[21] Editors explicitly and implicitly emphasised how faithful they were. The British journalist Nathaniel Mist, for example, declared in 1721 that 'a love of truth' was a necessary ingredient for a newspaper, while Daniel Border of the *Faithful Scout* in 1651 promised to use 'the sword of truth' to counter falsehood.[22] Other printers also added 'true', 'faithful' or 'sincere' (*opregt* or *oprecht* in Dutch) to the title of their paper, or chose names such as 'The Mirror' to recall their claim to truth.

News consumers considered truthfulness to be more important than speed, the other selling point used by publishers to recommend their papers. In 1666, a citizen wrote to an acquaintance to tell him about the news from the Haarlem newspaper, the *Oprechte* [sincere] *Haerlemsche Courant*, 'because we do hear many matters, but without knowing if they are certain, and I consider the *Haerlemsche Courant* the most reliable [newspaper]'.[23] In business terms, truthfulness was a unique selling point, which distinguished newspapers from literature and polemic. It provided them with a unique place on the seventeenth-century market for information. This discourse of truthfulness helped printers, as Stephen Ward has argued, to rationalise the role of the newspaper in society.[24]

However, this discourse of truthfulness obviously had to mask an awkward reality which was known to publishers and at least suspected by their public. Printers and editors were not always very conscientious. They often published reports that they knew, or may have known, were incorrect. 'To make their news sell', the London *Protestant Mercury* wrote in the late seventeenth century, the papers 'take many things in trust from the first reporter'.[25] Sensational news about political affairs, murders and marvels attracted readers. The focus of these stories differed from country to country. In Britain, for example, there was a strong emphasis on blood and crime, especially that of a sexual nature, while in the Dutch Republic the stories seem to have been a bit more innocent. Deformed animals, such as a sheep with two heads, or family tragedies (for example, a pig eats the baby, the

---

[21] Woolf, 'News, history and the construction', p. 103.
[22] Black, *The English Press*, p. 31; Ward, *The Invention of Journalism Ethics*, p. 106.
[23] Van der Meulen, *De Courant*, p. 45.
[24] Ward, *The Invention of Journalism Ethics*, p. 101.
[25] Dooley, *The Social History of Skepticism*, p. 75.

mother then kills herself and the father goes crazy) were remarkably popular.[26] After all, publishing was a business.

Furthermore, politics complicated the publishing of truthful accounts in at least two ways. Firstly, periodical publications such as newspapers were vulnerable to censorship and other government measures. They could be fined or even be banned from publication, which occasionally happened in both Great Britain and the Dutch Republic as well as other European countries.[27] Most newspapers therefore were careful not to publish news which could antagonise the authorities and they also avoided taking sides. As the editor of the *Leeuwarder Courant* asked his correspondents in the midst of the Dutch conflict between the so-called Patriots and Orangists in 1785: 'Since a newspaper is meant to publish news events, and print official documents, and is not designed to be a collection of contesting articles, we kindly request our contributors not to bother us with this kind of copy'.[28]

Secondly, the relationship between the press and politics could also be the other way around. In early modern Europe, press and politics were to a large extent intertwined. Editors needed new and reliable information about political affairs and were thus dependent on governments, which tried to prevent them from publishing certain stories and encouraged them to publish others. In times of turmoil printers and editors used their paper to voice political views and to protect political interests. In most cases authorities bribed them or their correspondents. As early as 1631 Richelieu supported the *Gazette de France* of Théophraste Renaudot to circulate news both nationally and internationally that was favourable to his government, while at the end of that century Louis XIV established a sophisticated propaganda system. Governments even launched their own newspapers and propaganda campaigns.[29]

All of this was hidden, however, behind the openly voiced discourse of truthfulness. A German guidebook to the newspaper, written in 1695 by Kaspar Stieler, stated that newspaper publishers earned their reputation through the truthfulness of their reports. He refuted the common critique that newspapers were unreliable and untruthful: 'One buys and reads newspapers because one is told what is true and can be passed on. Lies have short legs and never live to be old'. He argued that most of the reports were

---

[26] Cranfield, *The Development of the Provincial Newspaper*, pp. 78-80; Broersma, *Beschaafde vooruitgang*, pp. 78-80.

[27] Weekhout, *Boekencensuur*, pp. 79-83.

[28] Broersma, 'Constructing public opinion', p. 227. See also Koopmans' article in this volume.

[29] Burrows, 'The cosmopolitan press', pp. 32-34; Popkin, *News and Politics*, pp. 36-37.

true and asked whether a writer should blamed for making a mistake now and then: 'There is no face so beautiful that it is without blemish'.[30]

A Dutch guide for newspaper readers, written by the botanist Johann Hermann Knoop and published in 1758, also emphasised that one should keep in mind that newspapers intended to tell the truth about events: 'Because it is unthinkable that a newspaper writer or a correspondent will knowingly spread lies'. The author chose an apt motto for his book: *Relata refero* (I am telling it as it was told to me). It was possible that an editor might be falsely informed, but he was obliged to correct this mistake in a new report in a subsequent issue. However, according to Knoop, this was not lying deliberately: 'the newspaper recounts what others have recounted or reported; if others lie about an event, so the newspaper inevitably does the same'.[31] Editors believed that this basic principle allowed them to provide an accurate representation of an event, even when their newspaper was partisan and they, or their correspondents, were biased themselves.

Editors emphasised their attachment to truth and their good intentions but they tended to apologise in advance for making mistakes. They underlined how difficult it was to obtain reliable correspondence and to judge the information it contained. 'I can assure you, there is not a line printed nor proposed to your view, but carries the credits of other Originals, and justifies itself from honest and understanding authority', the editor of the London newsbook *Weekely Newes from Italy, Germanie, Hungaria, Bohemia, The Palatinate, France and the Low Countries* wrote in 1622. 'So that if they should faile there in true and exact discoveries, be not you too malignant against the Printer here, that is so far from any invention of his owne, that when he meets with improbability or absurdity, he leaves it quite out rather than startle your patience'.[32] In early modern Europe a single 'true' account of events seemed impossible, and both of the guidebooks mentioned above warned newspaper readers not to believe everything that was written in the papers. They were encouraged to form their own opinion, and judge the facts clearly for themselves, as did the editors.

A culture of fact

Barbara J. Shapiro has shown how a culture of fact was established in England between 1550 and 1720. She argues that in the early sixteenth century, the term 'fact' was used to a limited extent and mainly in law courts. In a

---

[30] Stieler, *Zeitungs Lust und Nutz*, pp. 32, 56, 58. Cf. Popkin, 'New Perspectives', pp. 7-12.

[31] Knoop, *Kort onderwys,* p. 12. Cf. Schneider, 'Hoe de krant lezen'.

[32] Griffiths, *Fleet Street*, p. 6.

law suit, satisfactory evidence had to be presented to the jurors to convince them that a fact, that is, 'a human deed or action which had occurred in the past', was 'true'. This kind of legal system, which was not based on rituals or religious convictions but on rational argument, required 'faith in the possibility of reaching adequate and reasonable belief about such events and a mode of thinking about what is knowable, who can know it, and under what conditions it is knowable, as well as institutional arrangements and processes for knowing'.[33] The events under consideration could not be observed or replicated in court; however, a firm belief was established that it was nevertheless possible to know the truth about them.

Law developed routines for finding facts. It relied on documents whose authenticity had to be examined, and the credibility of eyewitnesses was also central to the system. In an ideal case, a witness would have been present when an event happened, have no interest in the case themselves and would be educated and of irreproachable conduct. They had to be faithful and consistent in their testimony and, ideally, multiple witnesses would give the same account of an event. The judge and the jurors for their part had to be impartial.[34] These principles and routines were subsequently adapted by other disciplines such as history, science and news reporting.

We should judge the newspapers' discourse of truthfulness within this framework. Editors emphasised their impartiality and faithfulness. While this was a rhetorical necessity designed to persuade their readers to believe that newspapers mirrored social reality, it was also a normative methodological position. To persuade readers to believe their coverage – and to gain authority thereby – they developed textual conventions which had to demonstrate that their reports were reliable. They attempted to give news a sound basis in facts and aimed to attribute news to written sources or to eyewitnesses if they had not witnessed the event themselves. News writers used a set of standard phrases to indicate the dependability of the news in their articles. By doing so they enabled their readers to make a judgement of their own.

The dateline of an article stated where and when it was written. 'Harwich, Jan. 30', 'Dublin, Jan. 20', 'Kingsale, Jan. 23', 'Marseilles, Jan. 17', and so on. This convention was used by almost all European newspapers from the early seventeenth century onwards. To underline the reliability of their article, news writers would specify the time and place in the first sentence. 'On Saturday last here arrived (…)', 'Wednesday last was burried here (…)', 'On Sunday last, three small vessels came into this harbor

---

[33] Shapiro, *A Culture of Fact*, pp. 11, 208.
[34] *Ibidem*, pp. 12-26.

(…)'.[35] However, it did not always mean that the article was actually about these towns or the events that occurred on these days. Letters from central places on European postal routes could also mention events that happened earlier in other countries. An account from Vienna could give news about events in Constantinople some weeks before. The dateline and first sentence would then read like this: '*Leghorn, March 30.* On the 21st, the King of Sardinia and the Prince Hereditary of Piedmont, arrived at Placentia, where he has fixed his Head Quarter'.[36]

The most reliable information was probably that which was based on official documents and government publications. To avoid political measures newspapers tended to print documents related to domestic politics in their entirety. In most cases these were released for publication by the government. It was safer not to make alterations. It was less of a problem to print foreign secret documents in summary. In January 1759 the *Leeuwarder Courant*, for example, wrote that it had postponed a story about a conspiracy against the Portuguese king because it lacked official documents: 'Now we have received the concessions and sentences which were published by the Court itself we are able to compile a concise history of this outrageous incident based upon the most important matters which are in them'.[37] The public enjoyed both the sense of truthfulness and the disclosure of State secrets. The number of official documents that were published rose extensively in periods of contestation and political troubles. It was much safer to print these than to interpret events. Moreover, it offered the opportunity to provide balanced reporting by publishing documents from opposing political factions. In this way, readers could make up their own minds.[38]

News from correspondents, people in different parts of the country or in foreign countries who were paid to regularly send updates of the news they obtained was almost always presented in the form of a letter. This made these accounts very personal, which was important in a society in which there was no formal system for the organisation and distribution of knowledge. Trust was therefore dependent upon the authority of the person who made the statement. It could happen that accounts from different towns and countries, for example in the diplomatic build-up to a war, contained con-

---

[35] Examples from *London Gazette*, 1 February 1666.
[36] Example from *London Gazette*, 6 April 1742.
[37] *Leeuwarder Courant*, 10 March 1759. The Dutch text: 'Nu wy de Consessien en Sententien, door het Hof zelf gepubliceerd, magtig geworden zyn, zullen wy uit den voornamen inhoud der zelven, eene beknopte Historie van dit voorval formeeren (…).'
[38] Broersma, 'Constructing public opinion', pp. 230-231.

tradictory statements. In such cases editors tended not to weigh pros and cons, and readers were again expected to judge for themselves.

Almost as reliable as official documents were those accounts in which the writer had been an eyewitness to an event. A letter from Paris in the *Leeuwarder Courant* of 18 August 1792, for example, stated: 'I have just a minute to write you that at this moment the Tuilleries are besieged; that the people are rolled back by the Swiss; that blood flows from all sides'.[39] The suggestion of action and involvement, and the use of expressive details caused a reality effect. In a story about a devastating fire in the prison of Leeuwarden the reporter emphasised that he had heard the shouting and seen a pall of smoke at night. He went to the building, saw the flames and heard the prisoners shouting and crying: '(...) one saw these poor people put their hands through the bars, when they were almost choked by the smoke they could not make a sound anymore, and shortly afterwards were burnt under the burning ruins'.[40]

When official documents were not available and the correspondent was not an eyewitness to an event, newspapers had to rely on second-hand information. In the text, editors attempted to convince their readers of the reliability of the information they presented by giving as much detail about the source of the account as possible. This resulted in phrases such as: 'A letter from Stockholm of the 3d instant mentioned (...)', 'By our accounts from Bavaria we learn (...)', or 'According to a private letter from a bombardier in the British train of artillery in Flanders, it consists at present of (...)'.[41] In many cases they explicitly stated that an account was true and why it could be believed: 'From a letter from Weymouth, written by a reliable person and dated December 15th, we learn that (...)'.[42] Or, 'We read the following account in the foreign newspapers which has been confirmed by private correspondence (...)'.[43]

Some editors mentioned the newspapers from which they extracted information. The editor of the London *Daily Courant*, which was first published 11 March 1702, assured his readers in the first issue that he would

---

[39] In Dutch: 'Ik heb slegts even tyd om u te melden, dat men op het oogenblik de *Tuillerien* belegert; dat het volk door de Zwitzers terug gejaagd word; dat het bloed reeds van alle kanten stroomd.'

[40] *Leeuwarder Courant*, 16 November 1754. The Dutch text: '(...) men zag die Rampzaligen hunne Handen door de Tralien steken, wanneer ze half verstikt in damp geen geluid meer konden geven, en kort daar op onder de glandige Puinhopen verbraden wierden.'

[41] Examples from *London Gazette*, 6 April 1742, 10 April 1742 and *Newcastle Courant*, 20 November 1742.

[42] *Leeuwarder Courant*, 6 January 1753.

[43] *Ibidem*, 3 February 1753.

'give his extracts fairly and impartially'. He promised to name the newspaper from which he had taken a news item at the beginning of each article. In this way, 'the public could, seeing from what country a piece of news comes with the allowance of that government, may be better able to judge of the credibility and fairness of the relationship'. He promised, furthermore, not to comment on the news but provide 'only matter of fact, supposing other people to have sense enough to make reflections for themselves'. Two months later he elucidated his statement by saying that 'the proper and only business of a news-writer' was, in addition to providing the latest news, 'delivering facts as they come'.[44]

To emphasise their faithfulness, correspondents also used conventional phrases when they doubted the quality of the information they provided. When news could not be attributed to a source, the account would start with the words, 'It is said that'. Readers were familiar with this phrase, which was also commonly used in personal letters and diaries. They would know then that it was a rumour that might be true but which was likely to be false. Furthermore, there was much space devoted to corrections. If an editor had faithfully copied news from a source and also attributed the information so readers could judge it, and then learned after some days that it was false, the honest editorial response was to correct the earlier account and apologise to the readers. For example, the *Northampton Mercury* wrote in 1721: 'We hope our candid readers will not condemn our Mercury for the many falsities that have of late been inserted therein, as we took them all out of the London Printed Papers, and those too the most creditable'.[45]

Newspapers as sites of knowledge construction

The introduction of the printed periodical newspaper in the early seventeenth century marked an important change in the construction of knowledge and its dissemination, as it was now much more regularly distributed and among a much broader audience. Information that came by word of mouth, the private letters of merchants and even written newsletters, only reached a small and in many cases select group. The same can be said of the scholarly journals, which began with the publication of the French *Journal des Sçavans* in 1665, which were aimed at a select academic public. Newspapers profited from the growth of the reading market. In the eighteenth century especially, their number rose rapidly in various European countries. Many of them were purely commercial enterprises, but newspapers also

---

[44] *Daily Courant*, 11 March 1702, 19 May 1702. Cf. Black, *The English Press*, p. 88.
[45] Smith, 'The long road to objectivity', p. 157.

cherished their aura as heralds of progress and of benefit to the people through their working for the common good.

Many newspapers extensively covered discoveries in science and technology. In the second half of the eighteenth century, the *Leeuwarder Courant*, for example, dedicated almost six percent on average of its editorial space to science. 'Public writing (…), like our daily paper is the most suitable instrument to enlighten enthusiasts, to tell them how much progress other countries are making and inspire them to do useful experiments themselves as well', the paper wrote in 1776.[46] Less specifically, newspaper writing 'systematized the collection and organization of data' about the social world.[47] Publishers selected the most important or remarkable news from the flow of messages they found on their desk, and sometimes added comments. Subsequently, they presented their more or less connected representation of reality to their readers as the truth about social reality, even when they knew that the accounts were false, or were likely to be, or at the very least sensational or overstated. Be that as it may, by disseminating 'true' information, newspapers constructed a social reality that had potentially subversive powers of its own.

The commonplace idea that, on the one hand, news had to be true, but on the other hand, in demonstrable cases it was not – with critics even wondering if it even could ever be – stimulated the rise of pragmatic scepticism. Newspaper readers were confronted with discrepancies between reports. In the case of a peace treaty or a battle, for example, a reader would find, often in the same issue, letters from different European cities which said different things. A discouraged British reader in 1659 observed: 'We have every day several news, and sometimes contraries, and yet all put out as true'. This stimulated critical comparison of news items. Peter Burke points out that the habit of newspapers correcting false information in a subsequent issue would have stimulated news consumers to 'look at the news with a critical eye', while Brendan Dooley speaks of a 'common thread of doubt'.[48]

Newspaper reading stimulated the critical powers of an intellectual elite who understood how the process of news and meaning-making functioned. It enabled them to question the 'natural' social order. However, newspapers aimed to reach a broad public. Many people still believed that what was written in the papers was actually true, even in the case of advertisements.

---

[46] Broersma, *Beschaafde vooruitgang*, p. 75. The Dutch text: 'Publyke geschriften (…) gelyk ons dagpapier, zyn de geschikste werktuigen, om den liefhebberen te onderrichten, hoe ver men daar omtrent in andere landen vordert, en hen dus aan te moedigen insgelyks nuttige proeven te neemen.' *Leeuwarder Courant*, 31 August 1776.

[47] Popkin, 'Periodical publication', p. 205.

[48] Burke, *A Social History of Knowledge*, p. 202; Dooley, 'News and doubt', p. 276.

When, for example, in 1774 the *Leeuwarder Courant* published an announcement for a book which stated that the end of time was near, public fear in the Dutch Republic was so great that people stopped working and hid themselves under their beds, shaking and trembling.[49] Its power to move people, to construct opinions and form interest groups made newspapers into a subversive medium which would be of decisive importance during the social changes that took place in the late eighteenth century. They stimulated the idea that society did not have a closed God-given hierarchy in which everyone's life was predetermined. They stressed the conviction that the right to truth was not the prerogative of the elite.

Truth and freedom of the press

The concept of press freedom which developed during the eighteenth century was first and foremost a political invention.[50] The bourgeois who opposed the autocratic regimes needed the media to express their political views and to raise support for their position. Furthermore, contrary to a monarch who had God-given authority, they had to legitimise their actions by founding their authority on public opinion, another newly invented concept which was closely related to press freedom. To facilitate the necessary rational and critical debate in the public sphere, which eventually would lead to a political 'truth' (the best answer to a political question or problem), people needed facts, reliable information and true accounts of events. In 1702, the *Daily Courant*, for example, promised to report 'only Matter of Fact, supposing other people to have Sense enough to make reflections for themselves'.[51] Reading a newspaper became more than a personal affair that provided enjoyment or education, or satisfied a need for information. It became a means for citizens to participate in the public sphere.

   Although it might have been difficult to give 'true' accounts of reality – and editors willingly admitted that this was problematic – newspapers developed a discourse of truthfulness in the seventeenth and eighteenth centuries which aimed at building trust and authority. This discourse had both a rhetorical and a methodological character. They wanted to persuade readers to believe that events had actually happened as they were represented in the newspaper. Once the idea – or the promise – that news had to be true became commonplace, newspaper writers developed, or adapted from other professions, textual conventions which established a reality effect. The at-

---

[49] Broersma, *Beschaafde vooruitgang*, pp. 76-78.
[50] Baker, 'Public opinion as political invention', pp. 167-199; Broersma, 'Constructing public opinion'.
[51] Ward, *The Invention of Journalism Ethics*, p. 148.

tribution of information using well-known phrases gave news a semblance of truth.

The discourse of truthfulness that newspapers had developed initially as a commercial feature was remarkably successful. It was contested when actual cases of falsity were exposed, but from a more general perspective, as a commonplace, it was by then firmly rooted in public conscience: newspapers had to write the truth and they were able to do so, but they simply did not always do so because of practical problems and political considerations. In the late eighteenth century, however, this discourse of truth moved onto a philosophical level. Newspapers were no longer just a business but also had an important task within the political system. They had to deliver the ingredients necessary for the public to form its opinion. As Jeremy Bentham would later argue: they were 'the only regularly and constantly acting' distributors of public knowledge and truth.[52]

In one of the first treaties on press freedom, *Essai sur la liberté de produire ses sentiments* (1749), the Dutch scholar Elie Luzac stated that men are obliged to contribute to the general good. To do so the search for truth was essential. While this was only possible if all viewpoints could be known and examined, Luzac concluded that curbing the freedom of expression obstructed the prosperity of society.[53] As Velema has argued, Luzac's plea concerned the exchange of information and views of the elite: 'He was writing about the collective search for truth within an idealized Republic of Letters'. Furthermore, Luzac's essay was apolitical. He did not want, nor foresee, the creation of a vehicle of public opinion that could influence government policy as a result of press freedom.[54] However, ultimately, essays such as that by Luzac or David Hume's *On the Liberty of the Press*, as well as John Stuart Mill's *On Liberty*, contributed to the idea that newspapers were important instruments in the dissemination of the truth about the social world and in facilitating the development of public opinion.

This commonplace ideal of truthfulness shaped the development of the concept of press freedom. If the press was to be allowed absolute freedom it had to show that it was a responsible guardian of the common good. Newspapers had 'not only to give public intelligence', as the *Whitehall Evening Post* stated in 1718, but 'all intelligence' had also to be 'calculated for the public good'.[55] To obtain commercial and political autonomy they had to present themselves as impartial and independent registers. Readers, for their part, had to acknowledge that the news was a true account of what had hap-

---

[52] Boyce, 'The Fourth Estate', p. 21.
[53] Velema, *Enlightenment and conservatism*, pp. 16-17.
[54] *Ibidem*, p. 20.
[55] Ward, *The Invention of Journalism Ethics*, p. 146.

pened in the social world or at least that newspapers strove for a truthful representation of reality. They had to acknowledge the value of the press as a social institution. This mutual discursive embrace of newspapers as investigators of what was true and what was false, of the respectable motives or the selfish reasons of agents in the public sphere, helped to establish the notion of the press as the Fourth Estate. As a representative of the citizens it had to pursue the truth, confronting both the public and the government with the consequences of their actions, motivated by the need – to paraphrase Hume – to preserve society from tyranny.

LEEUWARDER  Saturdagfe Courant.

Eze Courant die men voornemens is alle weken uit te geven, zal volgens een byfonder en nieu plan geformeert worden, uit de volgende No. zal den Lefer het rechte denkbeeld van defelve kunnen formeeren, men zal defelve moet en meer trachten te verbeteren, en tot de uiterfte volmaaktheit brengen, geen moeite noch koften ontfien om die voor het algemeen van nut te doen zyn, het welke de ondervinding beter dan een cierlyk opgepronkte Voorreden zal aantonen: Defelve zal een veel groter menichte van voorwerpen in zig bevatten dan de ordinaire Nieuspapieren in 't gemeen behelfen, door dien het geenfints myn oogmerk zoude zyn om de myne op de ondergang der andere te vestigen, de lief hebbers van den ouden trant kunnen zig met de ordinaire Nieuspapieren vergenoegen, en men zal defe met veel nut en vermaak kunnen lefen, zonder de jaloufie van de Autheurs of Drukkers van de andere op den hals te halen.

De Couranten in 't algemeen aangemerkt, zyn niet zo zeer te verachten als zommige menfchen zig wel verbeelden, zy kunnen de Hiftori-Schryvers voor Memorien of Gedenkftukken verftrekken in alles wat de wefentlykheit en de rydt der gebeurteniffen betreft. Het verwyt dat men haar doet van niet in alles oprecht en na waarheit te zyn, fpruit dikwils voort uit een valfche Correspondentie: Maar het is de nootzakelyke plicht der Schryveren omme het gemeen van de begane misflagen te adverteren, dit is een point waar op in defe Courant een byfondere reflectie gemaakt zal worden: En hoewel wy aan den Lefer de eerfte en nieufte tydingen zo veel en mogelyk zullen mededelen, waar toe wy menen genoegfame middelen aan de hand te hebben; zo zullen wy nochtans als het eerfte en voornaamfte point de waarheit derfelve in 't oog houden.

Men heeft veel reden om te vermoeden dat geen Schryver van enige Nieuspapieren verwaantheit genoeg befit, om zig te verbeelden dat zyne Lefers eenvoudig genoeg zullen zyn, om te geloven, dat zyne Correspondentie hem het geheim van het ftaatkundig Çabinet kan doen doorgronden, en al hadde hy het geheim van defe of gene intrigue ontdekt, zoude hy wel zekerheit hebben om defelve op een veilige wyfe te divulgeren? Men belooft in defen opfichte niets, als het gene dat men mag en kan zeggen, zonder zig te exponeeren. Men zal met zo veel vrymoedigheit als ymand het Land der Conjecturen doorwandelen: Nochtans altoos een billyke onfydigheit en een gepafte welvoegelykheit in agt nemende: De grondregel is ons zeer bekent dat het onvoorfigtig is zig tegens de fterkfte party aan te kanten, Het zal zeer dienftig zyn met een woord uit te nodigen alle die gene die ons met hare Correspondentie gelieven te vereeren, al het gene dienen kan om het ware intereft en wezentlyk nut van de inwoonders defer Provincien te bevorderen, zal een nuttig en gefchikt onderwerp voor defe Courant verfchaffen. Indien ymand dierhalven eenige nieuwe ontdekking doet in enige kunft of wetenfchap, zo 'er iets zeldzaams en byzonders gebeurt waardig om tot de kennis van de nakomelingfchap overgebragt te worden, indien 'er iets voorvalt dat van enig nut kan zyn voor de Commercierende Inwoonders van defe Provincien; indien ymand in zyn functie of bediening deze of gene zaak uitgevonden heeft die voor het algemeen van nut kan zyn, in een woord alles wat het Politique, zo wel als den Koophandel of het Kerkelyke betreft, ja van alle byfondere takken waar uit het nut en vermakelyke kan hervoortfpruiten: Alle die gene die de Burgerlyke plichten der Maatfchappie weten en betrachten, worden uitgenodigt ons de by haar bekent zynde byfonderheden mede te delen, en die gene die het nodig oordeelt zal zyn Naam met de vereifte omzichtigheit gemeld zien.

Alle advertentien van wat Natuur defelve mogen zyn, zal men voor een zeer redelyke en gefchikte prys in deze Courant kunnen invoegen, mits defelve aan niemands goede naam, of affaires enige prejuditie toebrengen.

A

De-

SPANISH TYRANNY AND BLOODY PLACARDS

HISTORICAL COMMONPLACES IN THE STRUGGLE BETWEEN DUTCH PATRIOTS AND ORANGISTS AROUND 1780?

Joop W. Koopmans

In September 1781, the Dutch nobleman Joan Derk van der Capellen tot den Pol anonymously published his pamphlet, *To the People of the Netherlands*,[1] considered to be a core text of the Dutch Patriot Movement. During the final two decades of the eighteenth century, this group opposed the Orangists and their leader, Stadtholder William V of Orange-Nassau, contesting his authority and seeking to put an end to the abuses of what they considered to be a corrupt oligarchic system. They strove to reestablish old civil liberties and legal equality for all church denominations. A number of them also advocated the further democratisation of the Dutch political system.[2]

In this influential pamphlet Van der Capellen provides an interpretative commentary on Dutch history, clarifying how and when things had gone wrong in his country. He refers several times to the Dutch struggle for freedom from the Spanish Habsburgs during both the sixteenth century and the first half of the seventeenth. In a somewhat exaggerated manner, he describes Philip II, the prince to whom the rebellious Dutch renounced their allegiance in 1581, in the following manner:

> Philip, King of Spain and master of our country, was an ambitious Prince, who like his father [Charles V] and his other ancestors, had deprived his subjects in

* I wish to thank Edwina Hagen, Ton Jongenelen, Pim van Oostrum, Rietje van Vliet and Pieter van Wissing for their suggestions. My student Tim Huijgen inspired me to write the section about Joannes Nomsz.

[1] The Dutch title is 'Aan het volk van Nederland'. This pamphlet was soon translated into French, German and English. Quotes from the pamphlet in this paper are derived from *An Address to the People of the Netherlands, on the Present Alarming and most Dangerous Situation: Showing the True Motives of the most Unpardonable Delays of the Executive Power in Putting the Republic into a Proper State of Defence, and the Advantages of an Alliance with Holland, France and America* (London: J. Stockdale, 1782).

[2] See Van Dijk, *et al.*, eds, *De wekker*; Klei, '"Notre Wilkes"'; Kuijper, 'Van voorbeeld', pp. 158-159; Prak, 'Citizen Radicalism'.

Spain and his other dominions, of their liberties and privileges, and now intended to introduce slavery into our Netherlands.[3]

The message of these and similar phrases could not escape the readers of the time: the Dutch should not allow anyone to deprive them of their 'liberties and privileges' or 'slavery' would follow.

Van der Capellen was definitely not the first nor the only author using the images and events of the Dutch Revolt (1568-1648) to reinforce his argument. Quite the contrary, this had become common practice in the late sixteenth century and continued during the seventeenth.[4] References to the Dutch resistance functioned as examples that were immediately understood by the Dutch populace. Whenever Dutch freedom was threatened, the call to remember those who struggled against the 'Spanish yoke' and to follow their example returned with force. The idea that the earlier struggle had been in vain was unthinkable to the Dutch, and it was imperative that the freedom gained would be safeguarded for the future. In the Dutch Republic around 1780, friends and foes were agreed on this; however, Patriots and Orangists strongly disagreed on the course of the Republic's political future and the structure of authority. In the light of this struggle it is interesting to examine how the rival groups began to use the memories of the rebellion for their own political gain. What symbolic value did they attribute to the persons, events and concepts that were deemed important in the late eighteenth century?

Following a general introduction to the people, events and concepts involved, I will respond to the question above using three texts and some pertinent examples. The three texts are a political petition from 1770 by Orangist Elie Luzac, the pamphlet by Patriot Van der Capellen from 1781 and some fictitious rhymed letters from 1785 by the political opportunist Joannes Nomsz. My purpose is to argue that some historical comparisons with and references to the Dutch Revolt in these sources may be viewed as commonplaces, or at least have clear similarities with this form. As in other papers in this volume, the concept of commonplaces refers to 'cultural material with both past and present currency within a given language community. Their reference is to opinions commonly accepted as valid. And they are deployed primarily as tools for argument in discourse designed to promote and reinforce culturally sanctioned modes of thought.'[5] Obviously, the 'language community' in question is the Dutch population of the time.

---

[3] Van der Capellen, *An Address*, p. 9.
[4] Pollmann, *Het oorlogsverleden*, pp. 7, 12.
[5] Moss, 'Power and Persuasion', p. 1.

Interest in the Dutch Revolt around 1780

Collective memories of the Dutch Revolt have been shaped and encouraged in several ways since the days of the late sixteenth-century Republic. Examples include heroic stories transmitted through historical works, plays, poems, prints, paintings and songs, the minting of memorial coins and the erection of monuments, as well as the organisation of commemorations of important moments of the rebellion. One specific example is a well-known book from the seventeenth century, reprinted many times, called the *Spiegel der jeught, ofte een kort verhaal der voornaemste tyrannye ende barbarische wreetheden, welcke de Spangiaerden hier in Nederlandt bedreven hebben etc.* (Mirror of the youth, or a short story about the most important tyranny and barbaric cruelties which the Spanish committed in the Netherlands – see also fig. 1).[6] In this way, all members of the populace, including those with very little education, remained aware of the courageous struggle that supposedly had been waged against Spain. Some events became highly mythologised, such as the famine that was said to have been suffered during the 1574 siege of Leiden. Less pleasant events and painful experiences, for example Dutchmen denouncing one another or even murdering each other during the Revolt, were ignored.[7] Only the image of the 'obstinate War, to avert Spanish Despotism and protect Liberty and Conscience' was of interest and this basic message was repeated endlessly.[8]

Around 1780 several factors rekindled interest in the rebellion. They were in the first place the commemorations of important events that occurred in the struggle around 1580. In 1779, for example, it was the bicentennial anniversary of the Union of Utrecht, celebrating the agreement concluded by the regions of the Netherlands that had rebelled against Philip II. This document acted as the foundation of the Republic. New editions of the Union text had been published during the 1770s to encourage study of its content. New studies were also published, the best known being a four-volume study by the Patriot lawyer Pieter Paulus.[9] Other moments were

---

[6] For example, in 1614 (see Pollmann, *Het oorlogsverleden*, pp. 9-10, 12), 1631, 1663, 1680 and 1687. The Leiden University Library keeps a 19th edition copy from 1631, printed in Amsterdam. It is interesting to note that the French wars against the Dutch Republic at the turn of the seventeenth century led to the book *Nieuwe spiegel der jeught, of Franssche tyrannye, zijnde een kort verhael van den oorsponck en voortgangh deses oorloghs* (New mirror of the youth, or French tyranny, being a short story about the origin and progress of this war), printed in Utrecht in 1707, thus during the War of the Spanish Succession.

[7] Pollmann, *Het oorlogsverleden*, p. 8.

[8] Quote (in translation) from the Frisian *Leeuwarder Courant*, 3 January 1781.

[9] Schutte, 'Van grondslag', pp. 199-203. Paulus published his *Verklaring der Unie*

also commemorated, such as the capture of Brielle in 1572 by the Sea Beg-
gars – the start of the successful rebellion against the regime of Philip's
governor Fernando Alvarez de Toledo, Duke of Alba – and the relief of
Leiden in 1574, which always drew much attention. The commemoration of
200 years of the Act of Abjuration (*Acte van verlatinghe*), the Dutch declaration of independence, followed in 1781 with the Dutch Revolt remaining
a political theme of great currency.[10]

The Patriots used the commemorations to emphasise that the hard-
fought liberty was at risk of being lost, while the Orangists also used the
Revolt to display their patriotism. The latter praised the stadtholders from
the House of Orange-Nassau and in particular William of Orange (1533-
1584), who had emerged as the leader of the rebellion and had paid for this
with his life. Bullet holes in the Prinsenhof in Delft – now a museum – still
recall the moment of the Prince's assassination by Balthazar Gerards. In
contrast the Patriots drew attention to those who had criticised the policies
of the stadtholders. In other words, the interpretation of the past correlated
to a high degree with political orientation,[11] leaving the meaning of historical names and concepts equivocal and subject to change over time.

A good example is the changing meaning of the term 'patriot'. The
group calling themselves the Patriots during the 1780s, monopolised this
label, to the great displeasure of the Orangists. During the so-called Year of
Disaster in 1672 and during the threat of French invasion in 1747 those who
had wished for a return of the Orange dynasty had called themselves 'patriots'. However, around 1780 the labels were reversed. Opponents of the
House of Orange-Nassau now claimed the label 'patriots' and asserted that
they would prevent the decline of the fatherland.[12] Unsurprisingly, the
Orangists disagreed, hence the title of one of their periodicals: the *Ouderwetse Nederlandsche Patriot* (Old-fashioned Dutch Patriot).[13]

At the same time, imagery from the Revolt again became current. The
edicts of the Spanish Habsburgs against the Protestants had been called
'bloody placards'. Alba's Council of Troubles, the court of justice that pronounced sentences of heresy from 1567, had been popularly known as the
'Bloody Council'. The expression 'bloody placard' would later return, re-

---

van Utrecht in 1775-1778. See Vles, *Pieter Paulus*, pp. 25-34.
[10] See e.g. Sbarra, *Tieranny*, p.12; Le Francq van Berkhey, *Het verheerlijkt Leyden*,
and Adriaan Kluit's inaugural lecture *Inwijingsrede*. The last two authors belonged
to the Orangists. De Vries, *Beschaven!*, pp. 235-236.
[11] *Ibidem*, p. 235.
[12] Cf. Van Sas, 'De vaderlandse imperatief', pp. 278-279. In 1672, France, England,
Münster and Cologne attacked the Dutch Republic. Thus, the year is called
Rampjaar (the Year of Disaster).
[13] See Jongenelen, 'De *Ouderwetse Nederlandsche patriot*'.

ferring to other dramatic measures, such as the regulation against the Contraremonstrants, the opponents of the Arminians, drafted in 1616 by the
Rotterdam pensionary Hugo Grotius (1583-1645) for his city government.[14]
This measure was called the 'Bloody Placard of the New Inquisition'. In the
1780s, Patriots from Guelders used the term 'bloody placards' in reference
to regulations against publications critical of Stadtholder William V.
Meanwhile, Patriots from Friesland used the term to designate regulations
against Patriot civic guards and periodicals in their province. In Patriot circles this gave rise to great indignation, and a fake placard was circulated in
Friesland with the names of the members of the States of Friesland who had
voted in favour of these regulations written in red ink. All these cases referred to the 'Bloody Placards' of the sixteenth century.[15]

The Fourth Anglo-Dutch War also reinforced memories of the Revolt.
Starting in 1780, the war was caused by supposed Dutch support for the
American struggle for independence and it would last until 1784. Once
again, Dutch freedom had to be fought for. The Anglo-Dutch War generated
a flood of patriotic poems, pamphlets and also new political periodicals,
with criticism of the war as their main theme.[16] One of the new periodicals
was the pro-Patriot *De Post van de Neder-Rhijn* (The Post of the Lower
Rhine), which first appeared in early 1781. Alongside editorials and letters
to the editors this periodical contained poems by various authors, including,
for example, the Zeelander and man of letters Jacobus Bellamy (1757-
1786). In April 1782 he published 'Aan het Vaderland' (To the Fatherland)
under the name of Zelandus, which contained the following lines:

> Zie slegts den weg te rug van tweemaal honderd jaaren,
> Toen hebt gij 't Spaansch geweld van uwen hals gerukt.
> Thans wil America dier fierheid evenaaren,
> America te lang door Britsch geweld gedrukt.[17]

> [Just look back twice one hundred years
> When thou pulled the Spanish violence from thy neck
> Today America wishes to match that pride
> America, too long oppressed by British violence.]

---

[14] The phrase in Dutch is 'Bloedplakkaat van de Nieuwe Inquisitie'. Blok,
Geschiedenis, vol. 2, p. 451; Nellen, *Hugo de Groot*, p. 178.
[15] Smit, 'Mijnheer', pp. 121-122.
[16] De Vries, *Beschaven!*, p. 261.
[17] Theeuwen, *Pieter 't Hoen*, p. 147; Van Wissing, 'De post naar den Neder-Rhijn',
p. 50. In 1782-1783 Bellamy published his patriotic book of poetry, *Vaderlandsche
Gezangen van Zelandus*.

In the Orangist 'answer' to *De Post van de Neder-Rhijn*, called *De Post naar den Neder-Rhijn* (The Post to the Lower Rhine), this poem was parodied under the name of Zelandus, but this was ofcourse not Bellamy. It contains the following lines:

> Zie vrij den weg te rug van tweemaal honderd jaaren;
> Toen hebt g' U, dat is waar, GEWEETENSDRANG ontrukt,
> Dus, zou Amerika uw moed thans evenaaren,
> 't Moest dan, als gy, zyn door GEWEETENSDRANG gedrukt.[18]

> [Look freely back twice one hundred years; / When you,
> it's true, freed yourselves from OPPRESSION OF YOUR CONSCIENCE
> Hence, should America now match your courage,
> It must, like you, suffer from the OPPRESSION OF ITS CONSCIENCE.]

The authors agreed on the importance of the Revolt but disagreed on the situation in America. The Orangist Zelandus was of the opinion that it made more sense to make peace with the English than to recognise American independence, and this is what the Republic did between the publication of the two poems.[19]

In October 1781, the pro-Patriot newspaper in Leiden, the *Leydse Courant*, accused the English of hypocrisy by also comparing the Dutch Revolt to the American struggle for independence. It argued that England should not complain about Dutch support for the Americans because the English had, in a similar fashion, given support to the rebellious Dutch in the sixteenth century:

> Voormaals waren de *Hollandsche* Provincien aan *Spanjen* onderdanig, maar,
> door de dwinglandy van *Philips* den tweeden onderdrukt, stonden zy tegen hem
> op, verklaarden zig zelf onafhanglyk, en toenmaals handelde *Engeland* op de-
> zelfde wyze, als nu tegen haar gehandeld word en waar over zy zig nu zo zeer
> beklaagd. Zy ondersteunde die weerspannige Onderdanen tegen hen wettig Op-
> perheer.[20]

> [At the time, the *Dutch* provinces were subject to *Spain* but, suppressed by the
> despotism of *Philip* the second, they stood up against him, declared themselves
> independent, and at the time *England* had acted in a similar way to those who

---

[18] Quote from Van Wissing, 'De post naar den Neder-Rhijn', p. 51.
[19] *Ibidem.*
[20] *Leydse Courant*, 10 October 1781.

act against her now and about which she now so strongly complains. She provided support to those Subjects rebelling against their legal Lord.]

The *Leydse Courant* was clearly not unique in this respect. The Dutch Revolt and the American struggle for independence had been compared many times over the years, both within the Republic and beyond. The Americans were seen as victims of unlawful taxation and an army of occupation, just like the Dutch. The British king, George III, was found to resemble Philip II, and his General, Thomas Gage, was likened to the Duke of Alba. Also, Thomas Hutchinson, the governor of Massachusetts, was compared to Cardinal Granvelle, while George Washington was likened to William of Orange.[21] However, according to Pieter 't Hoen, the Patriot editor of *De Post van de Neder-Rhijn*, Washington and the Prince of Orange differed in that where Washington resisted all honours, William would have wanted to rule.[22]

Along with the commemorations of the Dutch Revolt and the Fourth Anglo-Dutch War we can therefore identify the American struggle for independence as a catalyst in its own right for the above-mentioned increased interest in the rebellion around 1780, within as well as outside the Republic. Friedrich Schiller and Johann von Goethe would, at the end of the 1780s, make an international contribution with their respective plays *Don Carlos* (1787) and *Egmont* (1789), in which they again focused attention on the 1560s, the first decade of the Revolt.[23]

Text one: the petition by the Luzac brothers (1770)

A petition by a group of Leiden booksellers addressed to their city government in 1770 is the first text presented here to investigate the extent to which a discourse of rebellion resonated in eighteenth-century reasoning. The petition is a request by three Leiden booksellers to the States of Holland to reject a proposal to appoint *censores librorum*, who were to be appointed in cities with five booksellers or more. We may assume that the petition was convincing, as the petitioners obtained what they sought. In the request, the authors did not openly attack their provincial and city governments, but rather provided critical commentary on their actions, in particular concerned with whether these governments would be imprudent enough to implement their plan.

---

[21] Dunthorne, 'Dramatizing the Dutch Revolt', p. 16. Antoine Perrenot de Granvelle was one of Philip's most influential councillors in the Netherlands.
[22] Theeuwen, *Pieter 't Hoen*, pp. 148-149.
[23] Dunthorne, 'Dramatizing the Dutch Revolt', p. 11-12, 18-20.

The substance of the request was drafted by two brothers from Leiden, Elie (1721-1796) and Isaac Elias (1727-1790) Luzac. The elder brother, the enlightened printer-bookseller and lawyer Elie Luzac, was well known.[24] He was a convinced advocate of freedom of the press and the search for truth, and as such a man of his time. In 1747 he clashed with his city government by publishing the materialist book *L'homme machine* by Julien Offray de la Mettrie. During the 1780s, Elie Luzac would emerge as an Orangist ideologue who came to be hated by the Patriots.[25] We must keep in mind, however, that the Leiden booksellers drafted their petition ten years before the struggle between the Patriots and Orangists escalated. It is not linked to the later political controversy and is a politically neutral document in the context of this contribution.

Nonetheless, the petition contains striking references to the Dutch Revolt, employed to convince the governing bodies. The authors subtly observe that their text originates from 'Citizens and Inhabitants of a City [Leiden] that was the first to halt and thwart Spanish tyranny'.[26] In other words, the Leiden ancestors of the petitioners had participated in the Dutch freedom struggle and their heroism was still reflected in their offspring. However, the authors misrepresent history, for it was Alkmaar not Leiden which, in 1573, was the first Dutch city to break a Spanish siege. It is true, however, that the Leiden siege of 1574 lasted longer and caused more suffering than that of Alkmaar. Leiden's pride in its long, heroic resistance being much greater was therefore acceptable.

At some later point in their text, the authors refer, without much explanation, to Philip II, Alba and his 'Bloody Council'. By referring to the past they wished to demonstrate that governments should do everything to protect society from harm but were not permitted to limit the natural freedom of their citizens. Were the sovereigns to possess this right, then the persecution of heretics by Philip II and Alba would have been fully legitimate. The petitioners did not expect, however, that the States of Holland would be of such an opinion.[27] If they were, they would then act in the same manner as Philip II, Alba and his Council of Troubles, which evidently, for rhetorical purposes, the authors refer to as the 'Bloody Council'. The authors use a very potent device here, for no Reformed Holland regent would want to be identified with Spanish tyranny.

---

[24] 'Memorie', pp. 809-896. Cf. Van Vliet, *Elie Luzac*, pp. 315-317.

[25] Van Vliet, 'Leiden and censorship', pp. 203-217; id., *Elie Luzac*, pp. 307-317.

[26] *Ibidem*, p. 840. The Dutch text: 'Burgers en Ingezetenen van eene Stad [Leiden], die de Spaensche tiranny het eerste gestuit en gefnuikt heeft.'

[27] *Ibidem*, pp. 863-864.

The authors also link the development of Dutch science to the expulsion of the Spanish Habsburgs: 'To what height have risen the various branches of Scholarship in this Province [Holland] since the enemies of the Reformed Religion, Suppressors of our freedom were driven out of the country.'[28] According to the authors, by contrast, the clergy in Roman Catholic countries barred free research in the sciences, the result being the martyrdom of Catholic believers such as Balthazar Gerards, who assassinated William of Orange in 1584:

> De Geestlyken duchten de vryheid van onderzoek; zy vreezen, dat, wanneer hunne zwakheden, gebreken en onkunde, bespeurd zouden worden, zy minder geëerd, geacht en gevierd zouden zyn. Dezelve grondbeginselen boezemen zy den Vorsten in; men eischt in Kerk en Staet eene blinde gehoorzaemheid; een blind geloof, een blind vertrouwen; geen menschen, maer slaeven. En wat is van die leere het gevolg? Dat men een Balthazar Gerhards de uiterste pynen hartvochtig ziet doorstaen, waenend, dat hy door den gepleegden moord de zaligheid zal verwerven.[29]

> [The Clergy fears freedom of research; they fear that if their weaknesses, shortcomings and ignorance could be traced, they would be less honoured, esteemed and celebrated. They feed the same principles to the Princes; one demands blind obedience to Church and State; a blind faith, a blind trust; no men, but slaves. And what is the outcome of that doctrine? That one sees a Balthazar Gerhards harshly suffer the most extreme pains, falsely believing that he will obtain salvation through the murder that he perpetrated.]

Strikingly, all explanation in this passage is again lacking, and the reference is not to Balthazar Gerards but to 'a Balthazar Gerhards'.[30] We may wonder if this name acts as a commonplace here. He represents the fanatical martyr of faith who blindly and in full surrender goes to the extreme, his name functioning as an 'enwrapped narrative'.[31] Furthermore, the reference to 'slaves' is telling in this context.

---

[28] *Ibidem*, p. 875. In Dutch: 'Tot welken top zyn de verschillende takken der Geleerdheid in deeze Provincie niet gereezen, sedert dat de Belagers van den Hervormden Godsdienst de Onderdrukkers onzer vryheid ten Lande zyn uitgedreven.'

[29] *Ibidem*, p. 880.

[30] His name has different variants. Today Balthazar Gerards is the most accepted.

[31] Thanks to Frans-Willem Korsten, who suggested this term to me. It implicates that the name encapsulates a story.

Text two: the pamphlet To the People of the Netherlands *(1781)*

The pamphlet *To the People of the Netherlands*, introduced at the beginning of this paper is the second text discussed here which references the Revolt. As indicated, the pamphlet was published anonymously, but it originated from the Overijssel nobleman Joan Derk van der Capellen tot den Pol (1741-1784), although this would only be proven at the end of the nineteenth century. Contemporaries therefore ignored the fact that the pamphlet originated from Dutch regency circles. In his opening, the author presents himself as an independent mind, but many readers would have understood from the content that the text was drafted by someone close to the political arena.[32]

Baron Van der Capellen drafted his pamphlet as an open letter. By opting for anonymity – even the place of publication was disguised in the original Dutch text – the author could present his criticism of the authorities, and the Stadtholder in particular, with candour, the letter being an unqualified contestation of authority. *To the People of the Netherlands* was one of many pamphlets published during the Fourth Anglo-Dutch War, in this case shortly after the Battle of Dogger Bank in the North Sea, in August 1781. This was the war's only significant sea battle and both Patriots and Orangists claimed it as a resounding Dutch victory. In reality, its outcome was undecided, with both parties suffering many casualties and great material losses.[33]

Van der Capellen was already known for his sharp criticism of nepotism within the clique of Dutch regents. He also agitated vehemently against old feudal practices in his province of Overijssel, which caused him to lose access to the provincial States. Van der Capellen admired the ideals and successes of the American independence fighters. Like them, he argued in favour of popular sovereignty and the bearing of arms by civilians, expressing such views in *To the People of the Netherlands*.[34] The impact of his pamphlet may be compared to that of Thomas Paine's *Common Sense* in America. It threw oil on the Dutch fire and mobilised vacillating Patriots into action against the regime of Stadtholder William V. The editors of a modernised edition of the pamphlet, published in 1981, liken both the structure and the sense of the text to a new 'Act of Abjuration'.[35] While this may be somewhat exaggerated, it is not without justification.

---

[32] The Orangist Rijklof Michaël van Goens was one of the contemporaries who presumed that Van der Capellen, or people around him, were responsible for the pamphlet. Van der Capellen tot den Pol, *Aan het volk van Nederland*, pp. 8-9.

[33] Koopmans, 'Oorlogen', pp. 115-120.

[34] *Ibidem*, pp. 9-14.

[35] W.F. Wertheim and A.H. Wertheim-Gijse Weenink in *Aan het volk*, p 8.

In his pamphlet Van der Capellen presents the Dutch Revolt as a purely political struggle for freedom and not as a conflict between Protestants and Catholics, as many before him had emphasised.[36] He writes for example:

> But the [Dutch] people soon perceived [Philip's] designs, and the Roman Catholicks as well as the Protestants (…) united like brethren, to repel the common danger.[37]

This view helped Van der Capellen enlist the support of the Catholic members of the population, who in 1781 still held a second-class position in the Republic. His implicit message was of course that Protestants and Catholics now needed to unite to fight Stadtholder William V, as they had done earlier against Philip II. He also favoured the emancipation of Catholics.[38]

Van der Capellen writes extremely negatively concerning the Habsburg landlords and their representatives. Concerning Philip II he states:

> [Philip II] entrusted the management of affairs to foreigners (…). And (…) he issued the most abominable edicts against those who embraced the reformed religion, and established the Court of *Inquisition*; which, without any regard to persons, rights, or privileges, was to enforce his laws by tormenting, hanging, or burning those conscientious and brave men, who were determined only to relinquish with life, their civil and spiritual freedom.[39]

The Duke of Alba was one of the 'foreigners' who were 'universally hated by all ranks of the people, and (…) generally considered as the cause of all our present misfortunes'.[40] The past, with prominent figures such as the despised Cardinal Granvelle of Franche-Comté and the Spanish Duke of Alba, who on behalf of Philip II operated in the Netherlands in the 1560s, had shown that government by foreigners always ended badly.

In the above passage, Van der Capellen also draws an implicit parallel with his own era. Around 1780 it was William V who was robbing the Dutch people of its liberties, as Philip II had done before him. In addition,

---

[36] This was the so-called Loevestein view, held by people such as the historian Jan Wagenaar. See, for example, Hagen, *Een min of meer doodlyken haat*, pp. 76-77.

[37] Van der Capellen, *An Address*, p. 11.

[38] *Aan het volk*, p. 16.

[39] Van der Capellen, *An Address*, p. 10. The Spanish Inquisition was never introduced into the Netherlands. However, the Papal Inquisition functioned here, and furthermore, Philip's governor, the Duke of Alba, created the so-called Council of Troubles in 1567 to try and to condemn the suspects of the previous Protestant uprisings.

[40] Van der Capellen, *An Address*, p. 12.

another foreigner acted as counsellor during Van der Capellen's era: Louis Ernest, Duke of Brunswick-Wolfenbüttel, who, according to the Dutch Patriots, caused great damage to the Dutch Republic.

Van der Capellen has a positive view of William of Orange due to the latter's campaign against Philip, however, his readers needed to be made well aware that the Prince of Orange also pursued his own self-interest and was not an advocate of democratic decision-making. He writes that the States of Holland had consented and decided in 1581 'that, for the future, the commons should not be consulted without their permission, which, it appeared afterwards, and still appears, they never had an intention to grant'.[41] His conclusion:

> We may learn from [this], that those nations who are zealous to preserve their liberties, should always be vigilant in their defence, and never place an unbounded confidence in any mortal.[42]

Van der Capellen reiterates the well-known image of 'slavery' which is linked to Philip II – as shown in the introduction above – when he turns against the English and introduces the French king as an ally of the Dutch rebels:

> The King of France, our old Ally, who had delivered us from the Spanish slavery; who during a course of eighty years had either privately supported us or openly fought on our behalf (…).[43]

This view concords with Van der Capellen's stance in favour of France and against England, which he shared with other Patriots during the period of the American struggle for independence and the Fourth Anglo-Dutch War. Van der Capellen therefore negatively portrays the support given to the Dutch rebels by Queen Elizabeth of England around 1580. He presents the English as a 'perfidious nation' seeking to usurp Dutch 'liberties' and for that purpose sending 'auxiliary troops' to the Netherlands under the command of 'the Earl of Leicester, a hypocritical villain'. Fortunately, he continues, the sage Grand Pensionary of Holland, Johan van Oldenbarnevelt (1547-1619), together with the young Stadtholder Maurice (1567-1625), found a way to remove Leicester in 1587. However, thirty years on, in 1617, in the ecclesiastical conflict between the Arminians and their oppo-

---

[41] *Ibidem*, pp. 16-17.
[42] *Ibidem*, p. 18.
[43] *Ibidem*, p. 49.

nents, Maurice chose the wrong path, eliminating the pro-Arminian Olden-barnevelt and turning the States of Holland into 'his slaves'.[44]

Van der Capellen ends his open letter with the expectation of its being censored. A ban, he states, could be expected from the authorities, who do not wish to hear the truth. He also emphasises this with an example from the Dutch Revolt:

> Remember that the King of Spain declaring our forefathers to be rebels, set a price on the life of Prince William I and ordered all the justifications, which that Prince and the States published in their defence, to be burnt by the hangman as infamous and seditious libels.[45]

The pamphlet was in fact almost immediately banned. The Orangist authorities found that the text undermined the State and severely insulted Stadtholder William V.[46]

Text three: Patriotic poetry by Joannes Nomsz (1785)

The third example comes from Joannes Nomsz (1738-1803). It consists of six letters in rhyme dating from 1785, entitled *Vaderlandsche brieven* (Patriotic letters), second part (fig. 2).[47] A prolific Amsterdam writer, Nomsz enjoyed great notoriety during his time and in his region through his historical plays and other literary works. He also translated several works by Voltaire, whom he greatly admired. Politically, Nomsz was an opportunist. Until the early 1780s he was an Orangist; however, during the turbulent revolutionary years that followed, his sympathy was with the Patriotic camp, probably for financial reasons. With the Orangist revolution of 1787 he returned to the stadtholder's camp, which allowed him to continue to operate within the Republic.[48] The *Vaderlandsche brieven* were published during

---

[44] *Ibidem*, pp. 18-21.

[45] *Ibidem*, pp. 131-132.

[46] Knuttel, *Verboden boeken*, pp. 124-125.

[47] I have chosen the six letters from the second part for the practical reason that they were available on the Internet at the time of my research (see <www.let. leidenuniv.nl/Dutch/Renaissance/Facsimiles/NomszBrieven1785/index.htm>). Moreover, discussion of all twelve letters would exceed the scope of this article. Furthermore, and more importantly, some letters in the first part are irrelevant because they deal with people from the Spanish side. Nevertheless, other letters in the first part contain some striking anti-Spanish examples, which confirm my conclusions based on the second part.

[48] Kalff, 'Jan Nomsz', pp. 476-484; Mattheij, *Waardering*, pp. 113-137; Smit, 'De vaderlandse epen', pp. 776-777; Van Wissing, *Stokebrand Janus*, pp. 177-179.

Nomsz's Patriot phase and this is clearly evident. It is also one of his many publications in which he kept memories of the Dutch Revolt alive.[49] One may question whether this was his main motive, for unlike Van der Capellen, Nomsz was primarily interested in making money from his publications.

All of the letters chosen here concern the first decades of the rebellion, including the Twelve Years' Truce (1609-1621). The author does not present his letters in chronological order, the first set of three concerns the Truce, and the second set the period around 1570. During the Truce, the religious quarrels mentioned above were played out between orthodox Calvinists (the Contraremonstrants) and the followers of Jakob Arminius (the Remonstrants). For political reasons, Stadtholder Maurice sided with the Contraremontrants, as his political rival, Grand Pensionary Oldenbarnevelt, who was undermining the stadtholder's military might, sided with the Arminians. Maurice eliminated his opponent by having him arrested and executed in 1619, accused of high treason.

Nomsz expresses his bewilderment over this political assassination by having the Grand Pensionary address the Prince in his first letter. The latter is presented as the valued commander who 'shattered Spain's hateful yoke (…)'.[50] However, Maurice is considered to have miscalculated when he entered the theological conflict, which led him into the same situation faced by the sixteenth-century Spanish princes, who had also opted for a single theology. Oldenbarnevelt – in the words of Nomsz – admonishes Maurice as follows:

> Wat toch heeft Spanjes grond van ketterbloed doen rooken?
> Een' Torquemadoos[51] drift voor de eer van Romes kerk:
> Die leeräar heeft zyn' vorst gedurig voorgesproken,
> Als waar' de kettermoord een heilverdienend werk.
> Zeg niet, doorluchte vorst! [Maurice] dat Romes priesterscharen
> 't Alleen zyn die door 't zwaard haar heerschzucht doen gestand;[52]

> [What made Spain's soil smoke with heretics' blood?
> The passion of a Torquemado for the honour of Rome's church:
> That teacher continuously spoke to his prince

---

[49] Mattheij, *Waardering*, passim. Nomsz was not the only author who chose this form. In 1784, *Vaderlandsche brieven* were published under the pseudonym Janus Ironicus, and letters under the same title from 1785 have been attributed to Elie Luzac.

[50] Nomsz, *Vaderlandsche brieven*, vol. 2, p. 5.

[51] Tomás de Torquemado (1420-1498) was the first Grand Inquisitor in Spain.

[52] Nomsz, *Vaderlandsche brieven*, vol. 2, p. 8.

As if the effort of killing heretics earns salvation.
Do not say, illustrious prince [Maurice] it's only Rome's priestly hosts
That satisfy her lust for power with the sword;]

In this passage Nomsz links the problems of the sixteenth-century Church with those of the Republic in the early seventeenth century. In this way he indirectly argues in favour of the separation of Church and State propagated by the Patriots, with the prince standing above all parties, because a sovereign who identifies with just one church becomes a tyrant. That, he believes, was the experience of the Dutch people, as is apparent from the following lines, where the Duke of Alba and the Inquisition are also mentioned without explanation:

Een volk dat om 't geloof zyne oudren had zien slagten,
Een volk door Alvaas voet, noch kort geleên, gedrukt,
Daar 't Inquisitievuur noch voor hun oog moest gloeijen,
Daar 't ketterdoodend zwaard in 't oog noch glinstren moest,[53]

[A people that watched its ancestors slaughtered for their faith
A people, only a short while ago, oppressed by Alba's foot,
While the Inquisition's fire still was to glow before their eyes
While the heretic killing sword still was to sparkle in their eyes.]

In his second letter, Nomsz chooses to write as Maria van Reigersberch, addressing the letter to her spouse, the scholar and politician Hugo Grotius, during his detention in The Hague from August 1618 to June 1619.[54] As someone who shared Oldenbarnevelt's thinking, he was also a victim of Maurice's coup against the Remonstrant regents. Nomsz sides with Grotius, as expressed in the following:

(...) Zo verr' gaat dwinglandy,
Die in dit vryë land met bloed haar stappen teekent,
En zelfs haar meesters slaat in 't juk der slaverny!
Haar meesters! naauwlyks 't juk des Kastiljaans [Philip II] onttogen!...[55]

---

[53] *Ibidem*, p. 10. The context of this quote is Nomsz's treatment of the intolerant Calvinistic regime in Ghent (1578-1584), under the Calvinist preacher Petrus Dathenus, who opposed William of Orange's tolerancy policy.
[54] Grotius was sentenced to life imprisonment and brought to Castle Loevestein, from which he escaped in a book chest in 1621.
[55] Nomsz, *Vaderlandsche brieven*, vol. 2, p. 19.

[(...) Despotism goes so far
That in this free country it marks its steps with blood
And puts even her masters under the yoke of slavery!
Her masters! scarcely freed from the yoke of the Castilian [Philip II]! ...]

Clearly, Maurice's regime was considered to be no better than the Castilian regime of Philip II:

Wat baat ons nu niet meer Kastiljes juk te dragen,
Wat baat de breking nu van Philips ontzind geweld,
Nu wy ons schandlyk zien in Nassaus juk geslagen?
Nu Maurits hovaardy dit volk de wetten stelt?[56]

[What use is it to us to no longer bear Castile's yoke
What use is it to us to have broken Philip's insane violence
Now that dishonourably we are put under Nassau's yoke
Now that Maurice's pride sets the law for this people?]

Nonetheless, he continued, the Dutch people would stand tall:

Neen! dat eer 't eerlyk bloed, ter schand' huns dwinglands, vloeij'!
Het week voor Philips geenszins, zou 't nu voor Maurits wyken?
 Zou 't wislen van tiran? noch naauw' van banden vry!...
Zo Maurits heerschen wil, hy heersch' hier over lyken[57]

[No! rather let honest blood flow and shame the tyrant.
It did not yield to Philip, would it yield now to Maurice?
Would it change tyrant? hardly freed from its ties! ...
Should Maurice wish to rule, he'll rule here over corpses.]

It should be clear by now that despotism, slavery and tyranny constitute the core concepts that Nomsz chooses – as did Luzac, Van der Capellen and many others – to forcefully support his argument.

For his third letter, Nomsz chose as author the Grand Pensionary of Utrecht, Gilles van Ledenberg (c.1550-1618), also in detention. The letter addresses Ledenberg's son Joost. Prince Maurice had sacked and then arrested Gilles van Ledenberg, a faithful partisan of Oldenbarnevelt, who then chose to commit suicide, an act which he justifies in this letter. He describes the court of justice that interrogated him as Nassau's 'Council of Blood'

---

[56] *Ibidem*, p. 20.
[57] *Ibidem*, p. 26.

(*Nassaus bloedraad*),[58] rather than Alba's Bloody Council. This choice of words immediately alerts the reader to the idea that Maurice should be considered to have behaved just as tyrannically as Alba.

In the fourth letter, Nomsz writes as Lamoraal, Count of Egmond (1522-1568). In the 1560s, this nobleman led the resistance against Philip II, together with Philip de Montmorency, Count of Horne, and William of Orange. Alba arrested Egmond and Horne and had them beheaded in Brussels in 1568.[59] In the minds of the rebels and their offspring this act would remain associated with Alba and it became one of the traumatic memories of the struggle. The drafting of the letter is set in the Brussels' prison, the author addressing his spouse, Sabina of Bavaria, shortly before his execution.

The negative characterisations of Alba in this particular letter are not surprising, for the Duke was responsible for Egmond's death sentence. Alba is depicted as a man 'who drenches the Netherlands in blood and flames' and 'haughtily turns his will into law'. He is the 'evil rot, the source of the misfortunes of the Netherlands'.[60] Egmond finishes his letter with imagery of Spanish despotism, while consoling his spouse:

Die eedlc vryheidszon is slechst een wyl verduisterd
Door 't zwart der donderwolk van Spanjes dwinglandy[61]

[That noble sun of freedom is darkened only for a while
By the blackness of the thunderstorm of Spain's despotism]

It is remarkable that in a rare footnote Nomsz distances himself from the 'new finders of historic truth', who in his time denied that Alba and the Spanish behaved cruelly.[62] It is unclear to whom Nomsz was referring. Possibly it was to the Patriots, who minimised the negative role of the Spanish

---

[58] *Ibidem*, p. 30 The famous Dutch author Joost van den Vondel had done the same in his poem 'Het Stockske van Joan van Oldenbarnevelt, Vader des Vaderlants' (The little Stick of Joan van Oldenbarnevelt, Father of the Fatherland) (1657) in the phrase 'Geknot door 's bloetraets bittren wrock' (Clipped by bloody council's bitter resentment).

[59] William of Orange had a lucky escape to Germany in 1567, from where he organised the resistance movement against Philip II.

[60] Nomsz, *Vaderlandsche brieven*, vol. 2, pp. 39, 41. See also the curious dream of 'Liberius Gelrus' in the Patriot periodical *De Haagsche Correspondent*, nr. 9 (1786), pp. 65-72, in which Alba is one of the ghosts who walks before the coffin of the regent or '*Volks-verdrukker*' (People's Oppressor).

[61] Nomsz, *Vaderlandsche brieven*, vol. 2, p. 45.

[62] *Ibidem*, p. 42.

in order to be able to paint a darker picture of Stadtholder William V. To
the Groningen clergyman and Patriot, Bernardus Bruins, for example, William V was even worse than Alba and the devil.[63] Nomsz possibly also
knew that at the performance of his play *Maria van Lalain, of, de verovering van Doornik* (Maria of Lalain, or, the conquest of Tournai) in 1783, the
Patriotic-minded Amsterdam audience had applauded when they heard the
words 'Nassau's prince, the pest of the Dutch states'. The subject was the
sixteenth-century Prince William of Orange, who was also respected by
most Patriots, but the audience evidently linked the words to Stadtholder
William V. The anti-Orangist spectators even continuously cheered the actor playing the part of Alexander Farnese, Duke of Parma – one of Alba's
successors and therefore the enemy of William of Orange.[64] In 1787,
Nomsz himself would write about *Willem den Vyfden* and his 'Partners in
curse' who 'exceed *Philip* and the *Duke of Alba* in Cruelty'.[65] However,
perhaps he was only paying lip service to his political friends of the time.

In the remaining two *Vaderlandsche brieven* from the second part,
Nomsz's characterisations do not differ from those in the preceding letters.
The penultimate letter is written in the name of Magdalena Moons (1541-
1613), who addresses the Spanish commander Francisco Valdez during his
siege of Leiden in 1574. Moons supposedly persuaded her dear Valdez to
delay his attack on the city in exchange for her hand in marriage and this
was said to have saved Leiden.[66] Valdez is characterised as the direct opposite of Alba:

> Waar was hy [Valdez] Alva ooit gelyk in landverwoesten?
> Waar was hy ooit een man van bloeddorst, of geweld?[67]

> [Where did he [Valdez] ever resemble Alba in destruction of the country?
> Where was he ever a man of bloodlust, or violence?]

According to Moons, the Dutch population could learn from Valdez that not
all Spaniards enjoyed 'the people's pain'.[68] Evidently, Nomsz was not
averse to differentiating between Spaniards.

---

[63] In 1788 he would be expelled from his province forever because of this view.
Regionaal Historisch Centrum Groninger Archieven, Huisarchieven Menkema en
Dijksterhuis, inv. nr. 409. I am grateful to Peter Kamminga for this example.

[64] Klein, *Patriots republikanisme*, p. 139.

[65] In no. 83 of the Patriot *Oprechte Nederlandsche Courant* from July, quoted in
Mattheij, *Waardering*, p. 122.

[66] Kloek, 'Moons, Magdalena'.

[67] Nomsz, *Vaderlandsche brieven*, vol. 2, p. 52.

[68] *Ibidem*, p. 55.

In Nomsz's last letter, set in 1572, Louis of Nassau writes to his oldest brother, William of Orange, from Mons in Hainaut while under siege. Louis had to surrender this city in the Southern Netherlands to Alba in that year, as Huguenot reinforcements failed to materialise from France as a result of the massacre on St Bartholomew's Day. In this letter, Alba is also portrayed as a cruel despot and tyrant who cares little for loyalty, word or oath. Louis' brother William of Orange in contrast is portrayed as seeking to protect the Dutch people from 'slavery' and wrest it from the 'Spanish coercion yoke'.[69]

In radical Patriot circles the imagery of 'slavery' would not be reserved solely for the Spanish princes. They considered that the Dutch Revolt had also brought about 'slavery' under the House of Orange-Nassau and its partisans, and they identified the Spanish yoke with Nassau's. To the Patriots the Union of Utrecht was no longer the Republic's ideal foundation, for it brought disorder in its statecraft and exchanged 'one despot' (Philip II) for 'a multitude of tyrants' (the Dutch Orangist oligarchy).[70]

Commonplaces and contested authority

The material from the last decades of the eighteenth century quoted above contains a great variety of text types and styles, and is written from several points of view. One finds documents, pamphlets, newspapers and periodicals, as well as prose and poetry in various forms. In addition, the material available includes fragments dating from before and throughout the Dutch revolutionary period of 1780-1787, and stems from authors belonging to several branches of society. As regards the revolutionary period, these authors belong to both the Orangist and the Patriot sides.

We may also distinguish between eighteenth-century texts that take the Dutch Revolt as a theme and printed material from the same period that discusses other themes. Regarding the eighteenth-century material on the rebellion we may further subdivide the sources into texts which discuss the first decades of the Revolt and material on the Twelve Years' Truce which may contain historical comparisons with the first phase of the struggle.

Understandably, the publications on the Revolt contain more qualifications and stereotypes of this struggle than those involved with the other themes. In the latter, the historical comparisons with the rebellion are more or less fortuitous. Yet both types of sources are of equal interest with respect to the issue of the characterisations and stereotyped images of the Revolt which are cited to strengthen and emphasise the argument. If we are to

---

[69] *Ibidem*, pp. 59-64.
[70] Schutte, 'Van grondslag', pp. 212, 215.

describe these images as commonplaces or similar concepts, they should occur in all sorts of texts and have unequivocal meanings.

This criterion is undoubtedly met in the case of the names of the opponents of the Dutch rebels that function as 'enwrapped narratives'. The hated Philip II and Alba are 'the villains' in nearly all types of texts and for all of the Dutch authors quoted. The Inquisition, the Bloody Placards and the Bloody Council represent 'evil' and poor government policy. In many cases all explanation of the historical context is lacking: simply uttering these names and concepts sufficed to create associations in the readers' minds with ruthless politics and politicians. The names of Philip II and Alba are in this way transfigured into commonplaces of a kind. The same process occurs with their institutions. In addition, references to the 'Bloody Council' and 'Bloody Placards' transcend the status of sobriquet since in later periods they are again chosen to mark comparable 'evil', as if they have become concepts in their own right.

In addition, the Spanish Habsburg enemy is continuously alluded to with the same words, in the form of both adjectives and nouns. Philip II and Alba are inevitably surrounded by the typically early modern words 'despotism' (*dwingelandij*), 'tyranny' (*tirannie*) and 'slavery' (*slavernij*). To the Protestant Dutch readership especially, these were familiar concepts, known from the Bible – referring to the people of Israel enslaved in Egypt – and the Calvinist insurrection doctrine in which the tyrant prince may be deposed. Because these concepts are continuously reused and because of their familiar historical meanings we may also describe the words 'despotism', 'tyranny' and 'slavery' as forms of commonplaces in this context.

The situation becomes more complex when we look at how the Orangists on the one hand and Patriots on the other describe the sixteenth-century rebels. Obviously for the Orangists, all members of the Orange-Nassau dynasty were 'heroes'. They did not identify Philip II with their Stadtholder William V and did not defy his authority, unlike the Patriots, for whom the rebellious personality, Johan van Oldenbarnevelt, was unconditionally good, while William of Orange and Maurice's virtues were considered to be limited. Here the two parties diverged, and unequivocal commonplaces and other concepts are absent. This leads to the fascinating conclusion that the phenomenon of commonplaces and similar concepts that were linked to the Dutch Revolt in the late eighteenth century must be limited to hostile images of foreign foes.

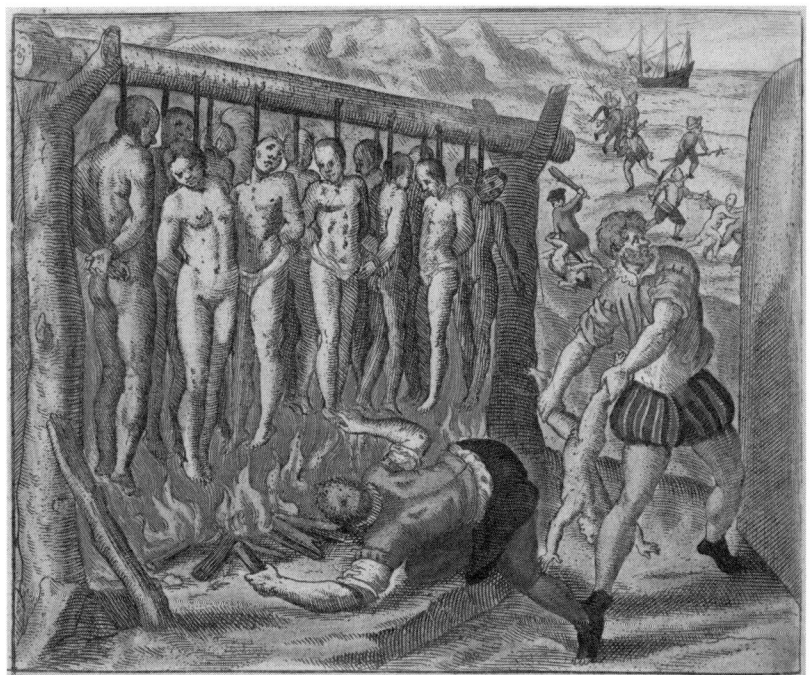

1. The alleged Spanish tyranny in the New World against the native Americans – the so-called Black Legend – intensified the ideas about the supposed Spanish tyranny in the Netherlands. This image comes from the Dutch version of Bartolomé de las Casas, *Den vermeerderden spieghel der Spaansche tierannye in Westindien etc.* (The increased mirror of the Spanish tyranny in the Westindies etc.), which was printed in Amsterdam in 1621. (Rotterdam, Atlas van Stolk).

VADERLANDSCHE

BRIEVEN,

DOOR

J. NOMSZ.

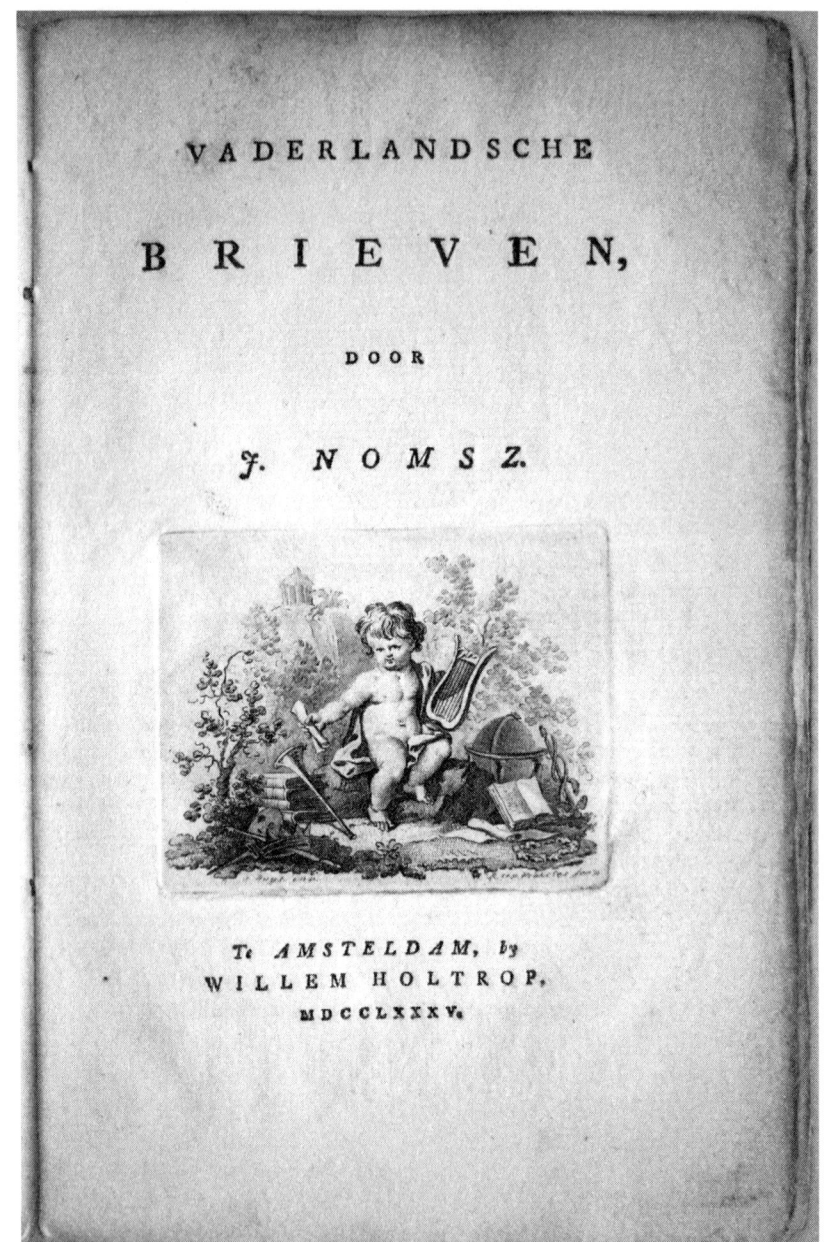

Te *AMSTELDAM*, by
WILLEM HOLTROP,
MDCCLXXXV.

2. Title page from the second part of Joannes Nomsz' 'Patriotic Letters' (1785).

COMMON SENSE AND COMMONWEALTH:
A NEW COMMONPLACE ABOUT VICE AND VIRTUE

BERNARD MANDEVILLE AND HIS *FABLE OF THE BEES* (1705/1714)

André Hanou

A fable about bees and their hive: it seems quite innocent.[1] In 1705, the Londoner, Bernard Mandeville (1670-1733), published such a tale under the title *The Grumbling Hive, or Knaves turn'd Honest*. In 1714, the text reappeared as *The Fable of the Bees, or Private Vices, Public Benefits*. This time Mandeville added 'An Enquiry Into the Origin of Moral Virtue', as well as a number of his own comments. In later editions he provided further supplements. In what follows, I not only have the fable of 1705 in mind, but also its embedded version in the 1714 edition.[2]

The title would have aroused some curiosity. Since antiquity, hives have been associated with industrious bees and a hard-working life, as well as with being engaged in virtuous and pure affairs: the production of honey and beeswax. Consequently, in literature, human society was often likened to a bee community. After all, in a good society each member contributes something to life in the hive and the life of the hive.

However, this title refers to *knaves*, scoundrels or criminals. How could it be? The reader will learn that the quest of these remarkable bees for virtue, and their wish to lead an honourable, industrious and sober life, impoverishes and weakens the hive. The moral of this story, in the words of the author is 'vice is beneficial'.

The story therefore seems to deal with the inversion of all values. The commonplace, 'virtue must be', which is, according to Church and State, a prerequisite for the greater good, is replaced by a new and uncomfortable truth: 'vice leads to well-being'. It is time to become acquainted with the content and powerful rhetoric of this tale. After a short overview of Mandeville's fable, a brief biography of the author of this dubious little piece will

---

[1] An expanded and slightly different Dutch version of this article was published in *Mededelingen van de Stichting Jacob Campo Weyerman* 31 (2008), pp. 89-106, under the title 'Mandeville en zijn *Fabel van de bijen*'. A new Dutch translation of the fable was published in 2008: Mandeville, *De fabel van de bijen*.

[2] When the *Fable*, in one of its versions, or the additions by Mandeville are quoted, I refer to the edition of all these texts by Kaye ed., *The Fable of the Bees*.

be presented, dealing with his life prior to his fable seeing the light of day.[3] Thereafter the contents of the fable will be discussed in more depth. In conclusion I will make some remarks about the genre and the cultural circumstances which led to the citizens of early eighteenth-century Britain being treated, through fable, to a strange morality and a new idea of society.

A brief outline of the fable

There is a hive, populated by the well-known industrious bees. There is no anarchy or democracy, no tyranny. The administration is bound by laws. In the hive one finds many activities and occupations, just as with human beings. The hive flourishes. What the rich bee gains through skilfulness is eventually beneficial to the poor in the form of employment and wages. In a similar fashion, the luxuries of the highly paid, such as some of the clergy, provide an income for swindlers and imposters. Legal bees earn money by blocking the legal process. Political bees ensure that as many subsidies as possible land in their own pockets or those of their followers. In short, hardly any activity is morally sound, but it all works, in spite of, or rather, due to the fact that everyone behaves like a scoundrel, a knave.

Suddenly, one bee, a shopkeeper, has an idea. He begins with a crusade against deceit and corruption. His ideas draw a response, and honesty becomes fashionable. Prices drop and the courts become empty. Doctors only prescribe medication that actually works. Politicians stop creating unnecessary perks for themselves and occupy themselves with important issues. No more money is spent on military adventures. Houses become cheap. However, in the construction industry there is unemployment. In pubs, only prior debts are paid. The clothing sector struggles because women dress simply and no longer care about luxuries or embellishments. The inhabitants are satisfied with the food that nature herself offers in season. Companies have to make cutbacks and retrench their workers. In no time, the economy collapses. The hive loses a large part of its population and can barely defend itself any longer. It becomes a sixth-rate hive.

The lesson is: do not behave morally. Ethical principles do not help a society that wants to flourish. The fable's contemporary reader, and perhaps even the reader today, is confronted with an unusual utilitarian and prag-

---

[3] Unless otherwise indicated, the biographical details in this section are based on: Christiaans, 'De Mandeville', pp. 118-125; Dekker, 'Schijnheilig atheïst', pp. 1-17; which appeared at the same time as 'Private vices, public virtues', pp. 481-498; Jansen, 'Het leven van Bernard Mandeville', pp. 329-257.
For a selective bibliography of books and articles by Mandeville, see the list compiled in 2004 by Charles W.A. Prior on the internet:
http://andromeda.rutgers.edu/~jlynch/C18/biblio/mandeville.html.

matic view of the essence of society. A cynical vision? It is indeed an empirical, and simultaneously irreligious approach to reality.

Did Mandeville need the widely accepted genre of the fable to challenge the old, self-evident wisdom with his new and much more dangerous insight? In the same manner as La Fontaine, whose readers intuitively understand that you will never be able to turn a cricket into an ant, even if you label cricket behaviour sinful and criminal.

Mandeville in the Netherlands

In spite of his growing fame, especially in Anglo-Saxon circles, little research has been done on Mandeville's life, possibly because he was a man of two worlds. His first world was the Dutch Republic,[4] in which his family, which had a medical background, can be traced back to the late sixteenth century. Bernard's father, Michael (1639-1699), was initially a physician in Nijmegen and thereafter in Rotterdam, where he was given an administrative position. Bernard, the middle child of five, was baptised into the Reformed faith in Rotterdam on 20 November 1670. He could not have been displeased with his place of birth, as these were Rotterdam's golden days. Between 1685 and 1730 the city was foremost in the Netherlands in terms of literature and culture. Rotterdam was internationally oriented, due to the port and commerce, and even had English speakers amongst its population.

Between 1680 and 1685, Bernard was a pupil at the Latin school. Thereafter, aged sixteen, he went to study in Leiden and on 19 March 1689, graduated with a degree in philosophy. His topic belonged to the field of the philosophy of science, in particular the question of whether animals were capable of thought. This study was probably intended as a basis for the study of medicine. Whether Bernard found employment after his graduation is unknown – probably not. In 1690 he was back in the city of his birth, and during that year became actively involved in political clashes. Within this context he produced his first important text, which was directed at a local bailiff and dealt with the subject of good governance in a civil community. The bailiff and his party seem to have had the support of the stadtholder from the House of Orange, William III, while the Mandevilles were possibly sympathetic towards the party opposed to the stadtholder. There were also further divisions within the different Rotterdam parties, which indicate

---

[4] Jonathan Israel provides an excellent description of the manner in which the Enlightenment was just beginning to take root in the Netherlands during Mandeville's lifetime in his *Radical Enlightenment*; about Mandeville: pp. 623-627. A very lucid account of Mandeville's position can be found in Kerkhof, *De mens is een angstig dier*.

religious disagreement, as the bailiff was repeatedly called orthodox. Whatever the case, what is of interest is that the young Mandeville appealed to a
broader public and made use of a satirical pamphlet.

The battle was concluded in favour of the orthodox Orangist party.
Mandeville senior was banned from the city, and subsequently established
himself as a physician in Amsterdam. In Rotterdam, free thought was restricted, and as a result Pierre Bayle (1647-1706), who during these years
was by far the most important proponent of the Enlightenment, lost his chair
at the Athenaeum Illustre. Bayle served as an inspiration to Mandeville, as
is evident from the latter's comments on his *Fable*, and also in his later
work. Rudolf Dekker has remarked that his Rotterdam period must have
taught Mandeville that the greatest scoundrel always comes off best and that
corruption is rewarded.[5]

It is unclear whether Bernard lived in Amsterdam after this episode. He
did return to Leiden, where he graduated once again on 30 March 1691, this
time in the discipline of medicine. After his second graduation, Mandeville
disappears from view. One can guess that he travelled through Europe for a
few years in order to round off his education, before he resurfaced in his
second world, England.

Mandeville in London

Mandeville established himself as a physician in London, probably in
1693,[6] and was married on 1 February 1699. He sought his salvation in
England, possibly not only because the country appealed to him but also because he was unable to obtain the necessary patronage back home. The
crossing could have had an even simpler reason: it is possible that he knew
all kinds of people in London. A tradition of lively interaction existed between the Dutch Republic and England, and many Dutch people lived in
London. Their numbers increased even more after Stadtholder William III,
in the wake of the Dutch invasion of 1688, became king of the British Isles
in 1689, which bound the two States together into something like a marriage
of convenience.

As far as it is known, Mandeville's first text in English was printed in
1703, and was entitled *The Pamphleteers. A Satyr*. This text can be interpreted as partially inspired by Dutch indignation at English conservatism.
After the death of the 'Dutch' king William III in 1702, the Tories (conservatives) regarded the time as ripe to reinstate the old Catholic monarchy.

---

[5] Dekker, 'Schijnheilig atheïst', p. 16.

[6] In that year he obtained a passport and appeared in the annals of the Medical
College: Jansen, *'Het leven'*, pp. 240, 302.

They tried to slander and discredit William, the foreigner who enjoyed the support of the constitutionalist party (the Whigs), as much as possible. William's fellow countrymen naturally also received a strong dose of the same, and Mandeville became involved in the discussion, as Daniel Defoe (1659/61-1731) had also done earlier, in 1701. Defoe ridiculed his suddenly hyper-British compatriots in his satire, *The True-Born Englishman*, which defended William while making fun of the famed typical British identity.

On the basis of some of Mandeville's other texts, as well as recent archival finds, one can gather that after many years in London, Mandeville had not completely rejected his language and his culture. His financial affairs were managed by Dutch friends in London, and he wrote occasional poems in Dutch for these friends. The poems contained numerous references to the prosperity of the British Commonwealth and in this way he succeeded in drawing links between the political and public dimensions and his own trivial daily realities. The tone of these burlesque poems had much in common with that of his fable, with the rawness of life being overwhelmingly present in all of his texts. He had a cheerful, or at any rate ironical, approach to reality. In poems about his ragged clothes and shoes and other daily matters, Mandeville proclaimed that the individual's and the State's basic needs form the basis of everything. For him, clothing was often a metaphor for the artificial gloss and glamour with which people clothe themselves in an attempt to hide the lack of genuine depth or content behind this finery. This was also to be the message of the *Fable*, which finds public morality to be merely an article of clothing and that any rational person should only encourage morality if it is to the benefit of public affairs. Such a person should, however, be aware that morality is nothing more than an embellishment, bait, comfort and a system for rewarding the dreams of the faithful. For Mandeville, morality and religion (which are identical to a certain point) were social utilities without genuine, absolute basis.

There is little to be said of Mandeville's later life. We only know of certain places in London where he lived, and that he continued to practise as a physician, specialising in treating the psychosomatic ailments that were prevalent amongst intellectuals and the upper classes.[7] He died relatively well off on 21 January 1733, supposedly due to influenza.

---

[7] Mandeville's friends came from these circles. Among them, apart from the above-mentioned Dutch, were the Lord Chancellor, the Earl of Macclesfield (1666-1732), the famous essayist Joseph Addison (1672-1719) and Hans Sloane (1660-1753), personal physician to the British royal family and member of the Royal Society. It would have been people such as these, according to Benjamin Franklin's account (1706-1790), among whom Bernard could be found in a London tavern, where he led a 'club', 'of which he was the soul, being a most facetious, entertaining companion'. Cited in Kaye ed., *The Fable of the Bees*, vol. 1, p. xxix.

Bees and hive

Firstly a few remarks are required concerning the basic image or theme of the *Fable*: the bees and their hive. The image is probably as old as the art of storytelling and literature itself, even if it is not used very often in fables. As a rule, the emphasis is on the example provided by the bees' diligence. The story is, in fact, a commonplace, providing an assurance that work will be rewarded. Every authority and religious denomination is satisfied with such a morality. Those who work and hope for honey, even if only in the hereafter, will not be troublesome.

In the Bible, bees were nothing more than troublesome stinging beasts.[8] The writers of antiquity, however, were very interested in them. They did not know much about the bees' anatomy, but they knew of the different functions they performed in the hive. According to them, bees were diligent, brave, chaste, harmonious and tidy. Even more importantly, it was thought that they formed a State with laws. They were also thought to possess ingenuity and a feeling for art.[9] Mandeville utilised this entire complex of imagery.

Thus, a well-read contemporary would have known what the bee represented, and this information could also be found in the popular emblem books of the day, in which the meaning and hidden wisdom behind thousands of thematic symbols was explained. Along with the depiction of a beehive one would have been given a description of the ability of bees to turn what was bitter into sweet, or how useful it would be for a learned person to study bees, as this would provide a better understanding of society. A large number of symbols and their meanings were collected into a single, appealing textbook which every writer or painter at the turn of the seventeenth century would have had on his shelf: the *Iconologia* (1593) by Cesare Ripa (1560-1625). Mandeville doubtlessly would have been familiar with this work. Ripa gave an account of all the characteristics that had been ascribed to bees since classical times. In the light of this, a fable about a hive that flourished not because of its bees' cooperation, but because of their individual selfishness, would have been rather shocking. That there would have been such a reaction can be taken for granted when studying Mandeville.

Perhaps we should first remove the sting from another possibility. The writers of antiquity referred to bees and wasps interchangeably. Even in studies of Mandeville's times, it seems that what might have been called

---

[8] At least in the Dutch Authorised version. See *Deut.*1:44, *Ps.* 118:12.
[9] For more on this view in the classics, see *Der kleine Pauly. Lexicon der Antike (...)* *Band* 1, cols. 898-899.

bees at the time are not what we would consider to be bees today. I became rather concerned with the issue after reading the 1597 edition of the most authoritative and most often reprinted book on bees in the Republic, by Theodorus Clutius (1546-1598). In 1705, yet another edition appeared in Amsterdam, under the title *Van de bijen, haar wonderlijke oorspronk, natuer, eygenschap, krachtighe, onghehoorde seltsame werken* (About the bees, their curious origin, nature, quality, powerful, unheard of rare works). The similarities between bees and human beings are explicitly indicated:

> Waar uyt men bemercken kan de Koninklycke regeering en Polityen, die sy on-der malkanderen strengelijck en wel vast onderhouden die seer na de mensche-lijcke Polityen en regeeringe met haren verstande gelijck zijn.[10]

> [From which one will notice that the Royal government and Polities, which they maintain among themselves strictly and consistently, bear striking simi-larities to the human Polities and governments which are their counterparts.]

To Clutius, wasps were also a type of bee, as were hornets and bumblebees. Furthermore, he chose to label the most important activity of bees as 'loot-ing'. One sometimes has the feeling that bees achieved good results from an inherently bad, selfish action. Mandeville would have read the text very thoroughly, partly because it contained a number of recipes for remedies that required the produce of bees. He was a doctor, after all. In a Dutch edi-tion of Ripa's work, it is said that the work of a particular type of bee, the bumblebee, deserves the label of 'thievery'.[11]

This vision of bees brings us closer to Mandeville's observation that all the diligent goings-on of people and bees, in essence involve greed, in fact thievery, to put it even more plainly. If Mandeville's contemporaries also saw bees in this light due to the bee literature of the day, they would have understood him better than one might have assumed. They would have very rapidly grasped his basic bee metaphor (greed makes good), just like his ad-vice not to burden thieves, whether winged or on foot, with moral princi-ples. That would, after all, reduce the benefits of their methods.

---

[10] Quote from the Dedication to the States of Holland, in the preliminary matter of *About the bees*.

[11] See Miedema, *Beeldespraeck*, p. 58. Similar judgements on the gluttonous behaviour of bumblebees: *Woordenboek der Nederlandsche taal*, vol. 6, cols. 890-891. That there were different types of bees, both good and bad, was also assumed in the *Byencorf der H. Roomsche kercke* (1569), by Philips van Marnix van St. Al-degonde (1540-1598).

Background: cultural circumstances

In the last decades of the seventeenth century, the process of secularisation was accelerated. Absolutism was eroded and a civil society came into being. These developments were most advanced in the Republic, with England following and later catching up. Mandeville came from a commonwealth where the citizenry had for some time managed its own affairs. He was from a city where people such as Bayle, Locke, Furly and others had liked to live. After William III's crossing in 1688 and the Bill of Rights (1689), a similar situation arose in England. New moral and political commonplaces became necessary in Britain, although older powers with older maxims were still at work.

In this climate, in which civil society's power was on the rise, the citizens began to realise that the world, as understood in a recently developed empirical sense, was controlled by the laws of nature and not by continuous divine intervention. Questions about human nature and the society shaped by humankind arose. What was needed for a successful secular society? Was it possible to become better people, with better ethics and a better society? Or was it impossible to tamper with the laws of nature? What were they anyway? A contemporary of Mandeville's, Shaftesbury (1671-1713), came to the conclusion that people were inherently altruistic and virtuous, but that something was obviously amiss. Not everyone agreed with him, although Francis Hutcheson (1694-1746) also thought that human beings possessed an innate moral sense. What they all agreed on, however, was that the new thinkers no longer wanted to discuss doctrines which were not based on worldly realities.

Nonetheless, a particular form of metaphysics was traditionally more or less mandatory. The understanding of where humankind came from, its purpose and the basis of morality had been influenced by the Church, the institution that knew all about such matters, perhaps not based on knowledge of the natural sciences but on the grounds of supernatural knowledge. Knowledge as it had been established in the biblical revelation, was interpreted by the Church – in the contemporary British case, the Anglican Church – which was still fully intertwined with the political system. The Church had the right to determine what was good and just. The separation of Church and State was still far in the future, and the notion that the Enlightenment was dominant during these years is completely inaccurate.

When Mandeville published comments along with his *Fable* to clarify his ideas, his publication was brought before a court. The details are not relevant at this point, but what is important in understanding his *Fable* is that he had to arrange his text in such a manner that his brainchild would not be smothered in its cradle. It was foreseeable that Mandeville's opinion would be understood in an oversimplified way and that people would not accept his claim that vice had a meaningful role in society and that morality formed a part of vice. The metaphysical-religious interest groups preferred to suggest that he was condoning evil and as such propagating vice.

Therefore, it is important to consider an extract from a later text in which Mandeville defended his *Fable* against such an oversimplification by Bishop Berkeley (1685-1753). In *A Letter to Dion* (1732), Mandeville writes:

> When I assert, that Vices are inseparable from great and potent Societies, and that it is impossible, that their Wealth and Grandeur should subsist without; I do not say, that the particular Members of them, who are guilty of any, should not be continually reproved, or not punish'd for them when they grow into Crimes.[12]

In the *Fable*, Mandeville kept his own thoughts to himself: the story had to be convincing as a story. There is no account of a dispute concerning the *Fable*, but in the accompanying text, he provided an explanation. Simultaneously, he created a defence mechanism and tried to safeguard himself from possible attacks by those who believed in biblical revelation.

Revelation and virtue

As he said himself, Mandeville wrote for insiders and not for a broad public (see his *Remark T*).[13] This type of intended reader would have grasped the explanation of his point of departure in his first commentary and what 'the origins of moral virtue' had in store. What were the driving forces of natural humanity? Were there principles which one should uphold? Mandeville's answer was that humanity's driving force is self-interest, and this should be given the form and appearance of virtue. In this sense, virtue was to be considered as the utilisation of self-interest in a form that is useful for and usable by society. Thus, egoism should be regarded as being beneficial to society.

Since the very beginning, according to Mandeville, lawmakers and religious leaders had had the task, by means of flattery, reward and the like, of convincing people that moral behaviour was valuable in itself, that it was honourable to strive to behave in such a way, and that it brought reward. It was made clear to the ordinary person that the imposition of regulations produced good results. People believed that there had to be something in it.

---

[12] Mandeville, *A Letter to Dion*, p. 4.
[13] Kaye ed., *The Fable of the Bees*, vol. 1, pp. 225-238.

Through the course of history, a whole conceptual framework was developed around the notions of vice and virtue. However, for Mandeville, vice in itself was not bad; it was, after all, merely a response to natural urges. Vice only became bad, and by that Mandeville means useless, when it did not contribute to life in the hive:[14] 'The moral virtues are the political offspring which flattery begot upon pride'.[15]

For Mandeville, reaching the highest levels in the arts or in science was only due to the desire to excel. Education was simply the awakening of that very ambition. Furthermore, chastity was only a matter of using the right word, because every woman has thoughts and fantasies that she will not reveal to others – but she blushes only when she suspects that someone knows about them. In addition, excessive chastity only stimulates prostitution. The intelligent person recognises that which is hidden behind all the shiny moral truths.

Mandeville also claims that it is precisely self-interest that enables a State to flourish, and that morality is merely selfishness that has been channelled along a productive route. Nevertheless, criminality and bad behaviour should continue to be condemned because they are detrimental to the well-being of all. However, striving for morality, purely for morality's own sake, upsets this precarious balance. In such a case, morality threatens the beneficial results brought about by the channelling of selfishness and the hive can no longer function. Thus, ethics is utilitarian.[16] We could suggest that this was mere cynicism, but anyone who reads Mandeville's work carefully will recognise that he tries to provide society with the best possible second-hand clothing, rather than strip it bare. Virtue *must* be.

In the 1714 edition, Mandeville concluded his very brief introduction by stressing the following:

> And here I must desire the Reader once for all to take notice, that when I say Men, I mean neither *Jews* nor *Christians*; but meer Man, in the State of Nature and Ignorance of the true Deity.[17]

In other sections, Mandeville also stated that he was merely writing about humanity in its natural state. Thus, he was writing about those on whom judgement should be passed based on our common sense rather than the

---

[14] In his commentary, Mandeville gave countless examples of behaviour that seemed ethically pure and justifiable from the outside but that in the last instance were nothing more than selfish.

[15] Kaye ed., *The Fable of the Bees*, vol. 1, p. 51.

[16] I do not deal with Mandeville's debt to Spinoza and Englishmen such as Thomas Hobbes (1588-1679) and David Hume (1711-1776).

[17] Kaye ed., *The Fable of the Bees*, vol. 1, p. 40.

revelation. With 'neither *Jews* nor *Christians*', Mandeville addressed people who were familiar with the revelation, while other faiths were not yet relevant.

In the quotation above, Mandeville is deftly defending his fable, his description of humankind and society, from attacks from the ranks of theologians and the faithful. He does not attack or deny biblical revelation. He simply turns it into an abstraction. A religious person would at most be able to remark that Mandeville's research is an expedition into a vacuum: after all, in the revelation, humanity's purpose is stated more clearly.[18]

Humanity and world

What is Mandeville's basic intuition? His answer begins as follows:

> Laws and Government are to the Political Bodies of Civil Societies, what the Vital Spirits and Life itself are to the Natural Bodies of Animated Creatures; and as those that study the Anatomy of Dead Carcases may see, that the chief Organs and nicest Springs more immediately required to continue the Motion of our Machine, are not hard Bones, strong Muscles and Nerves, nor the smooth white Skin that so beautifully covers them, but small trifling Films and little Pipes (...); so they that examine into the Nature of Man, abstract from Art and Education, may observe, that what renders him a Sociable Animal, consists not in (...) Graces of a fair Outside; but that his vilest and most hateful Qualities are the most necessary Accomplishments to fit him for the (...) most flourishing Societies.[19]

Here we have the clinical, unattached gaze of someone looking for rules and regularity, for laws that govern the seemingly chaotic whole. It is the gaze of a physician, who analyses the mechanics of bodily functions. This is an example of what is called the mechanisation of a world-view. The author establishes that abstract concepts such as 'virtuousness' or 'morality' do not

---

[18] At the end of his treatise on the origins of moral virtue, Mandeville reaches out to those who believe in biblical revelation, writing in the last paragraph, that if someone finds his views 'injurious to Christianity', such a person could also consider that Godly Wisdom also guides someone's path towards 'worldly happiness'. Who knows, perhaps this Wisdom could influence such a person to be ready to receive 'the true Religion' at a later stage. – In Commentary R, Mandeville gives a veiled indication that God's commandments clash with the morality of society: 'Religion is based on humility, honour is based on pride. How should we reconcile these two beliefs? That is a question we should best leave to folk who are wiser than I am' (Kaye ed., *The Fable of the Bees*, vol. 1, p. 222).
[19] Kaye ed., *The Fable of the Bees*, vol. 1, pp. 3-4.

determine the functions of the body of society. That is only the exterior, the window-dressing. In reality, it is the dirty, ordinary, inherent matters that keep the organism alive. Our surgeon will soon suggest (as you already know) that self-interest, which appears in many forms, is the engine of health and prosperity.

In Mandeville's vision, there is no room for a God who occasionally intervenes in history, and he has as little interest in the physiotheological world-view popular in his day. In this deistic view, an outsider, a God-Creator, was considered to have created and allotted a place to everything and everyone (even evil). Everything thus has a function as a part of the whole, or as Alexander Pope (1688-1744) put it: 'Whatever is, is right'.[20] Mandeville was not looking for an Archimedean point outside reality which would provide an adequate explanation of the inevitability of existence in its entirety. He only asked the empirical question of what the impulses that governed everyday society seemed to be. That was enough for him. As a doctor he examined the disease of society. What exactly were human passions? What, for example, was the use of compassion, in his opinion the weakest of all passions? After all, compassion had only limited and occasional good results. When and why would one do good deeds? Were they not good precisely because society would be damaged if they were not done? As always, his conclusion was that virtue was the ability to control basic passions.

Society

Society consists exclusively of selfish 'scoundrels', Mandeville says. Everyone is intent on self-preservation and bent on realising their own desires. That urge is present in all human beings in their primitive state and the more civilised they become, the more desires they have. One who is known as eager or hard-working is only virtuous by name, for that which is called virtue, always makes use of vice. Vice is therefore called usefulness. Mandeville continues, claiming that the virtue of a salesman comes from the gains of another's vice; of the latter's need for luxury and the urge to squander. Hedonism and luxuriousness, he claims, boost economic activity, while sloths digest that which others first had to produce. Finally, thievery and corruption bring fresh money into circulation and necessitate new investment (perhaps even with the money that some miser had collected from that which had been squandered by others).

According to Mandeville, a government needs to find a balance between waste and investment. It is necessary to keep the poor in their posi-

---

[20] In his *Essay on Man* (1732-1734).

tion as it ensures a supply of cheap labour and that the hive as a whole will be abundant. The poor themselves will benefit as there will be enough work available. The authorities thus benefit from extravagance and luxury, and from vice. Trade in itself is important, but a nation not only has a desire to trade, it also wants to be powerful. Thus, for Mandeville, it has a need for vice! It was a misconception to think that the Dutch were rich because they led such sober lives. For Mandeville, they knew exactly how to extract money from vice (with respect to the Dutch it is clear from Mandeville's *Fable* that he knew the economic practices of his native country very well). Mandeville gives a colourful account of the annual return of the East Indies fleet to Amsterdam. The ships' crews spent lots of money on liquor and prostitution in the designated districts. These practices were usually condemned, but the city knew how to profit from them.

In short, for Mandeville, a government ought to know all about people's motives and how fear, ambition and greed should be utilised. All the thieves, quacks, soothsayers and extortionists (in more refined terms: attorneys, physicians, priests and politicians) should be made subservient to the hive, and these occupations would be given the appropriate parcel of virtues and ideals. According to Mandeville, for those who practise these occupations, these ideals often have the appearance of being real and it is the State's task to make everyone believe in them.

However, the idea is not that everyone should simply put moral ideals into practice and draw conclusions from supposedly real, existing virtues. Humans beings might then suddenly feel no more need for all the abundant luxuries, and at some point industry would become superfluous, new buildings would not be built, and commerce would collapse. If people believe that they can live off peanuts and that a hollow tree-stump provides adequate accommodation, as Mandeville suggests at the end of the *Fable*, the country could no longer be maintained and other hives would seize power.

Mandeville's vision of the State is doubtlessly rather oversimplified. He seems to have had a mercantilist conviction that it was not labour, knowledge or anything else that determine a country's true wealth but rather the amount of money that individuals and the government had at their disposal.[21] At a time when it was still unclear what the role of the State was, his idea of an organism in which vices can form a virtuous whole was quite creative. The solution fitted the needs of the pragmatists among the increasingly powerful English citizenry. Through the *Fable*, the citizens could gain a better understanding of the importance of the public sphere of which they formed an important part. They were provided with commonplaces about

---

[21] Compare Kaye ed., *The Fable of the Bees*, vol. 1, p. 109, note 1.

human nature, virtue and vice. With these, they could create their own 'theology'.

Mandeville argued that his hive was in good condition when there was no tyranny, but also when there was no 'wild Democracy'. In his Commentaries he wrote of a 'limited monarchy'. For him, apparently, this seemed beneficial. There is leadership, but not without control. This accords with his idea that those who are rational ought to provide leadership in society, and that the religious should be restricted with regards to their exclusivist ideas about the definition of virtue and wholesomeness.

It is not surprising that some have regarded Mandeville's ideas as a precursor to economic liberalism because his social sphere was not governed by metaphysics or religion but by the will of all those who had worked their way up through the system. The true founder of economic thought, Adam Smith (1713-1790), was clearly an admirer of Mandeville,[22] and in the reasoning of those who came later, 'vice' as described by Mandeville, was not vice at all, but rather involved normal, positive pursuits.

Form and genre

Literature has of course always been one of the best ways to express the way we see our place in society. Our insight is communicated as convincingly as possible through stories, characters and themes. In this way, 'commonplaces' within culture are given form and become discernable to a wider audience.

During times when cultural paradigms are changing or developing alongside each other, as was the case in Mandeville's day, we see changes in literature. During this time, the novel came into existence, portraying daily lives and ideals. The magazine arose, with its unexpected ability to discuss the world and society. There were many other forms: prolegomena of wisdom, which gave insights into human passions and behaviour (Gracián, La Rochefoucauld); didactic poems about nature; oriental tales and imaginary voyages which often investigated the possibilities of human society and the assumptions on which it should be based.

Was Mandeville a man of letters? It is possible that he regarded himself first and foremost as a doctor. Perhaps he also considered himself to be a 'scholar', which was the contemporary term for an intellectual. In Mandeville's time, a scholar, or intellectual, was almost automatically also a 'writer', who would almost always take part in debates about society through independent publications or through contributions to the many kinds of magazines. Alternatively, one could choose to publish in a more

---

[22] Compare *ibidem*, p. cxxiv and the following.

consciously literary form. Regardless of the form, all literature during this time had an acknowledged purpose: to be useful and instructive, as opposed to being the individual expressions of personal emotion.[23]

Mandeville chose poetry in the form of a fable,[24] rather than a tract, a play or a novel. Why did he find this particular genre appropriate to demonstrate his new vision of society? One answer could be that he used an 'old fashioned' form of literature intentionally, both in order to convince and to appear as innocent as possible to his readers. This form, which assumes genuine wisdom, offers advantages when the message is that the human race consists of wolves disguised as bees. The fable, a genre which has been known since antiquity, automatically creates trust. People expect something that could be read to their children. It may be a story about the harshness of life but ultimately they, and we, will gain some wisdom. In Mandeville's case, however, there is no sweet wisdom to be found. The reader, under the impression that honey will be found in this hive, appears to have flown into a hornet's nest. There is no grace of God, and no real justice. The message, or what seems to be the proposed commonplace that belongs to the new hive-thinking is: limit the damage. It seems that a good manager should have insight into the real motives driving the hive's inhabitants, and convince the workers that fewer moral rules will be to their own benefit. Who knows, perhaps there could even be some progress in the hive. The latter seems to me to be the implication of Mandeville's message, even if he did not state it explicitly. Thus, he offers new wisdom in an old form. The form probably helped the reader to cross the threshold.

The fact that the fable was written in verse and not in prose also helped it appear more convincing. Poetry was, according to the classical poets, supposed to convey general truths. Alternatively, prose dealt with individual affairs or historical characters, and therefore belonged to new genres such as the novel (for this reason, until late into the eighteenth century, it was regarded as dangerous literature by supporters of the Old Truth). Mandeville's most famous contemporary, the Londoner Alexander Pope, also chose to use poetry when raising matters pertaining to the general world-view, with didactic poems such as his *Essay on Man*.

---

[23] See in general, Highet, *The Classical Tradition*.

[24] During these years, Mandeville regarded this genre as the appropriate form for proclaiming his insights into the characters of individuals and humanity. In 1703, his *Some Fables, after the Easie and Familiar Method of Monsieur de la Fontaine* appeared. In 1704, an expanded reprint followed, with the addition of two of his own fables, entitled *Aesop Dress'd, or a Collection of Fables*. This edition contained a total of 39 fables.

Mock-epic poem

Mandeville's *Fable* appears to be related to a completely different literary
genre, the epic poem (epos), which, along with tragedy, was the most important genre in 'classical' literature. During the Enlightenment, one still
found many epic poems in which the well-known heroes from antiquity and
the Bible were gradually given contemporary traits, allowing ordinary citizens to recognise themselves in them. Around 1700, people were especially
charmed by a modern version of the epos: the mock-epic poem. This form
of burlesque epos poked fun at the moral varnish and aristocratic virtues of
antiquity. The well-known rise and fall of the heroes and their society was
ridiculed and made fun of. Here one sees a true inversion of the trusted values. Such a mock-epic poem was also useful to a more modern society.
Thus, the above-mentioned Pope could show his loathing of the new crav-
ing for opulence and fashion in his mock-epic poem *The Rape of the Lock*
(1712), while the money-grubbing habits of publishers and hacks was the
subject of *Dunciad* (1728).[25]

Mandeville clearly liked this genre. Shortly before the *Fable*, in 1704,
he published *Typhon or the Wars Between the Gods and Giants. A Burlesque Poem in Imitation of the Comical Mons. Scarron.*[26] This epos, which
drew on mythology, dealt with the battle of the gods against the giants. It is
an epic poem – but also a travesty. Both Scarron (1610-1666) and Mandeville handled the battle in a burlesque manner. The gods are depicted as
having nothing worthy of honour. Their language is coarse and racy, they
belch and groan, and act from inferior motives. They are insolent and hardly
any better than their opponents, who are themselves no better than uncivi-
lised brutes. Everything is trivial, nothing is elevated, and there is nothing to
be learned from these characters, who show no trace of detectible morality.
On the contrary, all values are turned upside down.

It seems that Mandeville's adaptation of Scarron was no coincidence.
He was well informed about the literary tradition of the mock-epic poem in

---

[25] For the characteristics of the Dutch mock-epic, see Hanou, *Nijmeegse mutsen*. In
the Dutch Republic, for example, *Eneas in zyn Zondagspak* (1715) by Pieter Lan-
gendijk (1683-1745) was well known. He owed much to the example set by the
popular Amsterdam physician-poet, Willem Godschalk van Focquenbroch (1640-
1670), who also created such an Aeneas. The latter also published a *Typhon Of de
Reusen* battle, in 1665. His work is discussed briefly below.
[26] The French poet, Paul Scarron, wrote his *Typhon ou la Gigantomachie* in 1643. It
had a somewhat surprising effect on his readers, who were well educated about the
deadly serious values and figures of antiquity. Scarron continued his victory march
with the creation of another mock-epic poem, *Virgile travesti* (1648-1659). In this
poem he rewrote the Aeneid in a comical manner.

his native country, and he knew of the Dutchman Focquenbroch's *Typhon*, making mention of it in the dedication to his own *Typhon*. Focquenbroch had included his *Typhon* in the first part of a volume of burlesque verses: *Thalia, of Geurige* (facetious) *Zang-Goddin* (1665). The volume is dedicated to 'Miss Sarah, Little Guenon of Madam C.S.', a guenon being a little monkey. In the pages following his dedication, Focquenbroch plays all kinds of literary tricks, suggesting, for example, that such a little monkey could make good use of his book's pages when going about its business – but we digress. What is clear is that Mandeville had read his copy of Focquenbroch very closely.[27]

In literature this type of comic inversion, in which high becomes low, and important becomes trivial, is called *burlesque*. The concept also appears in the subtitle of Mandeville's *Typhon*. At this time, all kinds of satires were used in the service of new ideas, taking aim at outdated concepts and dated forms of government. However, satire did not form a separate genre with its own set of rules. Rather, it was an ingredient in dozens of literary dishes. The concept as such is not of much use when trying to understand the form and contents of the *Fable*.

At the time of writing his *Fable*, it seems that Mandeville was familiar with the satirical mock-epic poem. Elsewhere, it is evident that he was well versed in the differences between the various types of literary texts. This is important, because in one of his remarks relating to the *Fable*, it seems that he took some trouble to make it clear to his contemporaries that his fable was not merely a burlesque or a mock-epic poem. It gives us some indication as to his contemporaries' interpretation of the *Fable*.

In his preface, which he added in 1714, eight years after the first publication of the *Fable*, Mandeville firstly remarks that it would be misconstruing him to think that he was attempting to make a plea for vice (and rightly so, because he only made observations about the manner in which virtue and vice have developed into a function of society). Thereafter, he writes about the form of his fable. A misunderstanding about the form, and the accompanying expectations, could prevent, so he thought, his analysis of society from being taken seriously. As far as he was concerned, it did not matter what people wanted to call his rhyming lines:

> I am in reality puzzled what Name to give them; for they are neither Heroic nor Pastoral, Satyr, Burlesque nor Heroi-comick; to be a Tale they want Probabil-

---

[27] Mandeville mockingly dedicated his epos to his readers/Maecenases in London, as 'serenissime' (the form of address to the highest office bearers) 'society of fools'.

ity, and the whole is rather too long for a Fable. (...) The Reader shall be welcome to call them what he pleases.[28]

Thus, he implicitly makes clear that his fable (it was, after all, a fable according to the booklet) was not simply a burlesque, or a mock-epic poem, of which people did not have to take the deliberations or moral seriously. Some readers did indeed read the *Fable* in such a manner. Reacting according to their expectations, they recognised an inversion of values, but only as part of a literary game. However, Mandeville, who was familiar with the game, must have known this beforehand, when he created a tale in which the boozing, corrupt and debauched heroes (the bees) behave completely atypically and selfishly, just like the gods and the giants in *Typhon*.

One may suspect, as already hinted above, that Mandeville, seemingly using a burlesque genre, needed a literary self-defence mechanism. In this way, he could keep the readers who were also supporters of the Old Truth off his back. The new, harsh truth about society could, after all, be taken as a joke, in accordance with the chosen literary genre, making a witch-hunt unnecessary. It could be argued that the *Fable* was not a serious analysis of society at all, that the hive of old remained and that morality stood fast on its absolute foundations.

Mandeville, however, added to his remark on the genre of his fable in a later edition, stating explicitly that it was absurd to want to eradicate all evil in society. Such an attempt was counterproductive, and he claims that this was what he was trying to say with his fable. Thus, the idea of a purely burlesque mock-epic poem should be banished from the reader's mind.[29]

Conclusion

With Mandeville, the hive becomes a new image of the new society, suggesting a new commonplace. The first reading leaves some room for ambiguity, but thus only makes the horrible truth hit even harder. The bees, so often brave in the literary and philosophical past, but apparently so vicious in fact – seem to bring ruin to their society, precisely when they respond to

---

[28] Text according to Kaye ed., *The Fable of the Bees*, vol. 1, p. 5. The mention of the possibility of the *Fable* being a pastoral, seems out of place. However, there may have been some readers who associated bees with the Arcadian or rural genre. The remark on 'Tale' and 'Probability' refers to the belief that literature should appear to portray true history. In the case of a historical tale, probability is a prerequisite.

[29] In his additional Explanatory Commentaries in 1714 (see Kaye ed., *The Fable of the Bees*, vol. 1, pp. 39-251), Mandeville is even clearer: his lesson/moral (vice has its use) must be taken seriously.

the call of the good. We find that the practice of religion or culture for its own sake only leads to misery!

On this basis, it seems that Mandeville used his preference for and experience with the burlesque and mock-epic, perhaps intuitively, with the help of the industrious bees, to explain the essence of bee-ing human. He knew the power of the literary shock-effect, and he wanted his fable to have an unexpected outcome. The bees' dream that elevated, moral honey is hazardous to life in *every* type of hive, and this is Mandeville's shock effect. He argues that good and evil are not absolute values, and – from an empirical world-view – are not guaranteed by a personal, transcendental God. In Mandeville's time this idea had only recently begun to gain gradual acceptance in society.[30]

In his *Fable,* Mandeville calmly observed that the many ailments of society did not result in an undesirable state of health. An unavoidable, even happy occurrence is that the spiritual quacks propagate virtue and morals, convincing the patient (society) that all that is similar is worthwhile and full of purpose, resting on a moral foundation. It is adequate that the patient believes that moral norms do exist. However, for Mandeville, one should never allow idealists so much power that they are able to convince the patient that virtue should be practised always and everywhere. The fragile structure of society would not be strong enough to withstand it.

---

[30] I know of only one example of a text where appearance and reality are intertwined in a manner which may be comparable and where, in the course of reading, one discovers a terrible truth behind the good intentions. In 1729, Jonathan Swift published *A Modest Proposal For Preventing The Children of Poor People in Ireland From Being A Burden to Their Parents or Country, and For Making Them Beneficial to The Public.* In a very serious tone, Swift proposes the following: England is unable to adequately provide a basic foodstuff, that being meat. The nation is weakening. In Ireland, on the other hand, there is more than enough meat. But there is a poor population, with far too many children. The solution is simple: buy the Irish children, ship them to England and have them processed into meat. In both countries, all are satisfied. – The emotions aroused by Swift's publication, served Swift's purpose to the full. The British public became aware of the miserable state of the Irish, who were ruled and oppressed by the British.

1. Title pages from both mentioned editions of Bernard Mandeville's fable of the bees.

NATURALIZING THE COMMONPLACE

NEW READINGS OF TASSO DURING THE LONG EIGHTEENTH CENTURY (SÉVIGNÉ, ROUSSEAU)

Alicia C. Montoya

The eighteenth century or self-styled Age of Criticism would, at first sight, not seem the most congenial breeding ground for commonplaces, or, as Ann Moss described them, 'opinions commonly accepted as valid (...) deployed primarily as tools for argument in discourse designed to promote and reinforce culturally sanctioned modes of thought'.[1] The eighteenth century, after all, at least in its most polemical, avant-garde manifestation as the Age of Light, based its own self-definition on its systematic critique of authority. A key element in this critique was the willingness of thinkers and writers to turn their back on tradition and knowledge grounded in traditional commonplaces. Ann Moss, whose own history of the commonplace book does not extend beyond the late seventeenth century, provides a compelling analysis of the decline of commonplaces during this period, which she links to several factors.[2] These included the rise of vernacular literature and literary sociability, and the diminishing gatekeeper function of Latin in regulating access to the professions. But most importantly, the Cartesian revolution of the mid-seventeenth century meant that, increasingly, knowledge acquired through observation of the natural world and personal experience was valued more highly than knowledge based on traditional authority, i.e. the authorities whose words and thoughts were the very stuff of commonplace books. As Descartes wrote in the preface to his *Discours de la méthode*, there was no need to 'chercher plus d'autre science, que celle qui se pourrait trouver en moi-même, ou bien dans *le grand livre du monde*' (look for any other science, than that which could be found in myself, or in *the great book of the world*).[3] By provocatively invoking a well-known commonplace, that of the book of the world, Cartesian modernity thus hijacked the notion of textual authority that originally underpinned the commonplace, in order to legitimize its own claims.

---

[1] Moss, 'Power and Persuasion', 1.
[2] *Eadem, Printed Commonplace-Books.*
[3] Descartes, *Discours de la méthode*, p. 9 (my emphasis). All translations are my own.

The argument I will make is not therefore that commonplaces survived in their most traditional sense, at least within elite intellectual culture, during the Age of Criticism. My contention is, rather, that what we *do* find during this period, among certain authors, are a series of citational practices that are strongly reminiscent of humanist commonplacing, but whose ultimate meaning is somewhat more ambiguous. These pseudo-commonplaces, unlike their humanist precursors, are drawn not from classical literature but from modern texts, thereby transferring commonplace modes of reading from Latin texts to vernacular fiction. In addition, they depart from tradition by suggesting a questioning of authority as much as a legitimation. In these new commonplaces, finally, the textuality of the natural world – the book of the world – and the textuality of the commonplace book mingle in an original way, producing a new view of the connections between the two. In the following pages, I will explore this phenomenon by focusing on two texts produced respectively at the beginning and toward the end of the French Enlightenment:[4] Marie de Rabutin-Chantal, Countess of Sévigné's letters to her daughter Françoise de Grignan in Provence, written during the 1670s through the 1690s (but first published only in 1725), and Jean-Jacques Rousseau's epistolary novel *Julie, ou la Nouvelle Héloïse*, which was published in 1761. Although I have not been able to establish whether the use they make of commonplaces is also to be found in other eighteenth-century texts, these texts do clearly constitute two important steps in changing attitudes toward nature and textuality during the long eighteenth century. As such, they merit special attention in the light of the supposed eclipse of commonplace thinking during the Age of Criticism.

Commonplaces, natural style and epistolarity in Sévigné and Rousseau

Despite the fact that these two authors composed their works in a completely different cultural context and historical period, they share a number of attributes that may explain the particular use they made of commonplaces. Both of them were in a sense outsiders, coming to literature not through the traditional, Latin-based *cursus*, but as autodidacts – Madame de Sévigné because she was a woman, and Rousseau because of his mediocre social provenance. Their literary education, consequently, was essentially grounded in salon culture, which claimed to reject the learned, pedantic style associated with commonplacing in favour of a more natural, spontane-

---

[4] I adopt here Jonathan Israel's new dating of the Enlightenment, which places its beginning – not completely uncontroversially – in the late seventeenth century, and its effective conclusion by the mid-eighteenth century. See Israel, *Enlightenment Contested*.

ous style. Their 'classical' language was not Latin, which they read only with difficulty, but rather, Italian, and it is to Italian authors and literary models that they consistently turned in their own works. Yet at the same time, because of their very status as autodidacts, commonplaces would also have held a particular attraction for them, i.e. as an easy way to gain knowledge of the mechanics of literary composition. Commonplace thinking actually played an ambiguous role within salon culture, which has as yet to be fully explored. Despite his criticism of the commonplace book, 'qui sentoit trop son Colége' (which smelled too much of the classroom),[5] a salon luminary such as Dominique Bouhours still drew on commonplaces in his best-selling *Manière de bien penser dans les ouvrages d'esprit* (1687). Another important figure for nascent salon culture, Nicolas Perrot d'Ablancourt, produced new commonplace books even while explicitly condemning the genre.

A second defining attribute Sévigné and Rousseau share is their idealization of nature. In Sévigné's case, nature is advocated in the realm of literary style. Rejecting 'ce style de cinq sols' (this five-*sols* style) (I, 187, 258)[6] associated with the epistolary manuals or *secrétaires* of her day,[7] she self-consciously refers to her own 'style négligé' (neglected style) (I, 355, 398, etc.) or 'style naturel' (natural style) (I, 428). Yet, as several scholars have pointed out, the ideal of 'style négligé' or 'naturel' did not in any way preclude the use of commonplaces. This is unintentionally demonstrated by one of Sévigné's correspondents, Jean Corbinelli, who provides a schoolroom example of artificial, highly rhetorical style even while outlining the characteristics of the so-called natural style:

> De plus, il faut quelquefois n'être rien de tout cela, mais simplement un galant homme, qui parle sans trop d'ordre ni de règle, et qui ne laisse pas de charmer par sa négligence, qui ne pousse jamais trop avant son esprit, qui supprime souvent mille belles choses qui lui viennent en foule sur son sujet, parce qu'il ne veut point paraître bel esprit: *Interdum [urbani] parcentis viribus, atque / Extenuantis eas consulto*[8]. (I, 510)

---

[5] Cited in Moss, *Printed Commonplace-Books*, p. 261.

[6] All volume and page numbers refer to the three-volume Pléiade edition of Sévigné's letters, edited by Roger Duchêne.

[7] Because such manuals of epistolary rhetoric were supposedly sold for five *sols*, or a pittance. (There were twenty *sols* or *sous* to one *livre*. In Madame de Sévigné's days, one livre per day was considered an adequate subsistence wage.)

[8] 'The man of the world who spares his strength and deliberately weakens it' (Horace, *Satires* I.10.13-14)

[Furthermore, sometimes one should be nothing of all that, but simply a man of elegance, who speaks without too much order or rule, and who cannot avoid charming by his negligence, who never displays his wit too much, who frequently suppresses a thousand clever remarks that occur to him on the subject, because he does not want to appear a wit: *Interdum [urbani] parcentis viribus, atque / Extenuantis eas consulto.*]

As the citation of Horace demonstrates, Corbinelli himself couldn't resist showing off his schoolroom learning, even when it contradicted his ostensible message. More importantly, in his definition of what constitutes natural style, he equated it with 'galanterie', the defining quality of the 'galant homme', or the aristocratic literary dilettante who made his home in the literary salons of the period. Madame de Sévigné's adoption of 'style négligé' can be explained in large part by the fact that this aristocratic ideal was also fully compatible with the construction of a female authorial persona. An essential component in this ideal of 'spontaneous' or 'natural' style was, indeed, the denial of any intent to publish the works thus produced. Epistolarity itself was redefined not as a textual or rhetorical genre, but as natural, spontaneous conversation written down. As Madame de Sévigné rhetorically asked her daughter, contrasting her letters to her to more conventional letters, 'croyez-vous que je ne prenne moins de plaisir que vous à notre conversation [i.e. their epistolary exchanges]? Je me repose des autres lettres quand je vous écris' (do you think I take any less pleasure than you do in our coversation ? I take a rest from other letters when I write to you) (III, 393). Thus, Sévigné's letters could come to represent one of the most fully developed examples of 'literature without literature' (because never intended for publication) or even 'texts without texts' (letter texts as recorded conversation).[9] To her eighteenth century readers, it was precisely the letters' purportedly non-textual nature that served as a guarantee of the authenticity of the emotions they expressed, thereby ultimately conferring an ethical value to her stylistic ideal.

Whereas the natural for Sévigné was to be sought primarily in the domain of literary style, for Rousseau the concept of nature was a more straightforwardly moral one – although for Rousseau as for Sévigné, the stylistic and the moral are never completely divorced from one another. This is perhaps most clear in his *Essai sur l'origine des langues*, his extended meditation on the inability of language and writing to express authentic experience. In this work, Rousseau explains how language started

---

[9] On the 'galant' notions of 'literature without literature' and letters as written conversation, see among others Châtelain, 'La fréquentation des livres', pp. 9-47.

out as pure expression, i.e. music, and progressively fell from this original
state of grace:

> Voilà comment le chant devint par degrés un art entiérement séparé de la parole
> dont il tire son origine, comment les harmoniques des sons firent oublier les in-
> fléxions de la voix, et comment enfin, bornée à l'effet purement phisique du
> concours des vibrations, la musique se trouva privée des effets moraux qu'elle
> avoit produits quand elle étoit doublement la voix de la nature.[10]

> [This is how song by degrees became an art entirely separate from the spoken
> word from which it derives its origin, how the harmony of the sounds made
> men forget the inflections of the voice and how finally, restricted to the purely
> physical effect of the concourse of vibrations, music found itself deprived of
> the moral effects that it had produced when it was doubly the voice of nature.]

Nature is here defined not only as a state of pristine morality, but just as
importantly, it has a voice and language that can be heard if one but listens
attentively. Condemning 'la manie des livres' and book learning – 'rien
n'est plus trompeur que les livres' –, Rousseau returns to Descartes's metaphor of the book of the (natural) world, and gives it an explicitly moral,
even theological meaning:

> J'ai donc refermé tous les livres. Il en est un seul ouvert à tous les yeux, c'est
> celui de la nature. C'est dans ce grand et sublime livre que j'apprends à servir
> et adorer son divin auteur. Nul n'est excusable de n'y pas lire, parce qu'il parle
> à tous les hommes une langue intelligible à tous les esprits.[11]

> [I have therefore closed all books. There is one book only that is open to all
> eyes, the book of nature. It is in this great and sublime book that I learn to serve
> and adore its divine author. No one can be excused from reading in it, because
> it speaks to all men a language intelligible to all.]

While Sévigné does not go so far as to attribute an independent 'voice'
to nature, as does Rousseau, she does clearly share in his idealization of nature (in her case, natural style) above man-made art. A third attribute Sévigné and Rousseau share, finally, is their choice of genre: both wrote epistolary works, Sévigné her real letters to her daughter, Rousseau the fictional
letters between two lovers that make up his *Nouvelle Héloïse*. Now despite
Sévigné's redefinition of letters as written conversation, letters were in fact

---

[10] Rousseau, *Essai sur l'origine des langues*, p. 142.
[11] *Idem, Emile ou de l'éducation*, p. 401.

one of the genres par excellence that made use of commonplaces. In her
own day, this was reflected by the existence of an entire subgenre of manuals of epistolary rhetoric drawing on the medieval *ars dictaminis*, and providing readers with readymade lists of epistolary commonplaces. During the
course of the seventeenth and eighteenth centuries, the commonplace-book
letter came to be more exclusively identified with another literary subgenre:
the love letter, as exemplified by the classic model furnished by the medieval nun Héloïse, whose name Rousseau invoked in the programmatic second half of his novel's title:[12]

> The commonplace-book formula is here incorporated into French-language
> manuals of epistolary rhetoric, which, besides the model phrases (now hardly
> quotations), arranged under heads which point both to abstract concepts and to
> stratagems for argument, also include model love letters, sometimes arranged in
> a narrative sequence, like an embryonic novel. Letter-writing was the most
> 'elementary' form of composition. Significantly, these rather ramshackle col-
> lections are directed to a female readership literate in the vernacular, as well as
> to men.[13]

Interestingly, Moss suggests here that the vernacularization of the commonplace-book was accompanied by a feminization of the genre. This point indeed appears borne out by Madame de Sévigné's epistolary practice. Even
before she had begun writing her letters, women had increasingly been considered – on little empirical evidence – to be the most accomplished letter-
writers. At the beginning of the eighteenth century, the publication of her
correspondence was hailed as providing proof to this long-held assumption.
Not surprisingly, it was henceforth Sévigné's letters, more often than any
others, that were excerpted and incorporated into commonplace manuals, or
reproduced more extensively in manuals of epistolary rhetoric.[14]

These three attributes shared by Sévigné and Rousseau – their outsider
status, which implied an ambivalent attitude toward commonplace learning;
their moral-aesthetic ideal of nature; and their choice of the epistolary genre
– together create a fundamental tension in their work. This is the tension
between convention and spontaneity, between the genre conventions of the
letter, with its traditional use of commonplaces on one hand, and the ideal

---

[12] And whose epistolary model was followed by several authors of popular narrative
fiction in the seventeenth and eighteenth centuries. See Charrier, *Héloïse dans
l'histoire.*

[13] Moss, *Printed Commonplace-Books,* p. 263.

[14] On women's reputed epistolary preeminence, see Longino Farrell, *Performing
Motherhood,* pp. 28-56. On Sévigné's eighteenth-century reception, see Nies, *Les
lettres de Madame de Sévigné.*

of a 'natural', non-pedantic style on the other. It is my thesis that this tension is mediated by a fourth attribute they share. This is their pronounced affinity with a particular text – Torquato Tasso's Renaissance epic *Gerusalemme Liberata* – which they read in a manner both highly reminiscent of humanist commonplacing, and highly original. In their epistolary works, indeed, Sévigné and Rousseau cite Tasso's epic more frequently than almost any other literary text. In Sévigné's letters, if one excludes the Bible and contemporary authors,[15] the work most often referenced is the *Gerusalemme*, to which she alludes 38 times, according to the index in the Pléiade edition of her correspondence. Characteristically, she cites works in French and in Italian, but – with a very few rare exceptions – never in Latin. In Rousseau's oeuvre, similarly, Tasso is a recurring reference, and Rousseau's admiration for, indeed lifelong identification with Tasso has been well documented.[16] In *La Nouvelle Héloïse*, as in Sévigné's letters, Latin citations are notably absent, replaced by a range of citations from various Italian authors. Among these, the authors most often cited are his contemporary Pietro Metastasio, and, foremost among the vernacular 'classics', Tasso, both of whom he cites ten times.[17]

Commonplacing Tasso and the Querelle des Anciens et Modernes

Madame de Sévigné and Rousseau were, of course, not the first to use Tasso's *Gerusalemme* as a source of commonplaces. Starting in the sixteenth century, a tradition had grown up whereby some humanist critics, often with a polemical intent, had proclaimed certain contemporary works of chivalric fiction to be in fact 'modern classics'. These works included the French *Amadis* cycle and, more importantly, the Renaissance medievalist epics of Ariosto and Tasso. An important element in proclaiming these works vernacular classics was their elevation to the status of works that, like the Latin-language classics of antiquity, were suitable for commonplacing. In Italy, as Daniel Javitch has shown, Ariosto was adopted with gusto by

---

[15] Whom she cited, for example, on the occasion of the publication of one of their works or the performance of one of their plays. The contemporary works she most frequently cites are Pierre Nicole's *Essais de morale* (cited 89 times) and Jean de La Fontaine's *Fables* (cited 66 times).

[16] Benedetto, 'Jean-Jacques Rousseau tassofilo', pp. 217-238; Starobinski, 'L'imitation du Tasse', pp. 265-297; Domenech, 'Saint-Preux et Julie', pp. 119-147; Hammann, 'La vie de Jean-Jacques Rousseau', pp. 859-883; *eadem*, 'Rousseau citant le Tasse', pp. 511-528.

[17] My number is higher than Domenech's, who lists only six references, because I include all allusions, not only direct quotations. Domenech, 'Saint-Preux et Julie', p. 119.

compilers of *florilegia* such as the one appended to the 1542 Giolito edition of the poem, containing '"Descritiioni, (...) proverbi, sentenze, & altre cose di memoria", intended to serve readers who quickly wanted to extract from the poem ornaments, beautiful descriptions, or pithy moral sayings with which to enrich their own rhetorical efforts'.[18] Later anthologies of *Imprese* provided readers with collections of pithy sayings and phrases extracted from Ariosto, Tasso, and other vernacular authors. In France itself, similar practices developed. Referring to the hugely popular *Amadis de Gaule*, Etienne Pasquier, in the *Recherches de la France*, praised it as a 'roman dans lequel vous pouvez cueillir toutes les belles fleurs de nostre langue Françoise' (a novel in which you can gather all the fine flowers of our French language).[19] By using the commonplace simile of flower gathering, Pasquier was consciously inscribing this modern work into the tradition of medieval *florilegia* and their French successors, the sixteenth-century *Marguerites* and *Fleurs de bien dire*. By the end of the seventeenth century, the status of certain Renaissance epics as vernacular classics was so firmly established that the self-proclaimed arbiter of French classicist taste, Nicolas Boileau-Despréaux, felt the need to condemn his contemporaries' appreciation of Tasso by claiming it befit only a fop:

Tous les jours à la cour un sot de qualité
Peut juger de travers avec impunité;
A Malherbe, à Racan, préférer Théophile,
Et le clinquant du Tasse à tout l'or de Virgile.[20]

[Every day at court a fop of quality
Is allowed to misjudge with impunity;
To Malherbe, to Racan prefer Théophile,
And the glitter of Tasso to all the gold of Virgil.]

Following the example set by Boileau's criticism of Tasso's 'clinquant', Dominique Bouhours, in his influential *Manière de bien penser*, mocked one of his characters, Philante, for likewise also preferring Tasso to Homer and Virgil:

Pour Philanthe, tout ce qui est fleuri, tout ce qui brille, le charme. Les Grecs & les Romains ne valent pas à son gré les Espagnols & les Italiens. Il admire

---

[18] Javitch, *Proclaiming a Classic*, p. 35.
[19] Cited in Rothstein, *Reading in the Renaissance*, p. 38.
[20] Boileau, Satire IX, in: *idem, Satires, Epîtres, Art poétique*, p.111.

entr'autres Lope de Vegue & le Tasse; & il est si entêté de la Gierusalemne [sic] liberata qu'il la préfere sans façon à l'Iliade & à l'Enéide.[21]

[As for Philante, all that is flowery, all the glitters, charms him. The Greeks and the Romans in his opinion are not equal to the Spanish and the Italian. He admires among others Lope de Vega and Tasso; and he is so taken with the *Gerusalemme liberata* that he prefers it offhand to the *Iliad* and the *Aeneid*.]

Tasso is here characterized, in an assessment that itself had become a commonplace by this time, as both flowery ('fleuri') and glittering ('qui brille'). These qualities were supposedly the opposite of the more sober, restrained classicist ideal. Significantly, however, Bouhours's own frequent use of citations from the *Gerusalemme* in his other works, most notably the *Entretiens d'Ariste et d'Eugène*, provides ample evidence as to the enduring, everyday currency of citations from Tasso in contemporary salon culture.

Yet if the practice of commonplacing Tasso was well established by the seventeenth century, there is also evidence suggesting that, toward the end of the century, Tasso acquired a new meaning for readers. In opposing Tasso to Homer, Philante is in fact assuming a polemical standpoint in the foremost literary quarrel of the day, the Querelle des Anciens et des Modernes.[22] As younger and less-established authors sought to position themselves against the great names of French classicism, they increasingly turned to non-classical authors, including Tasso, in search of poetic inspiration. During the newly kindled Querelle, the Modern camp argued against the Ancients that modern, vernacular literature had finally succeeded in equalling the great works of classical antiquity, and could creditably be used as a literary model by new authors. The comparison that Boileau and Bouhours had drawn between Tasso and Homer and Virgil itself became a topos of critical discourse.[23] Philippe Quinault, a member of the Modern camp and the only dramatic author whose commercial success equalled the classicist Racine's,[24] drove the point home by basing his later 'tragédies lyriques' or operas, *Amadis de Gaule* (1684), *Roland* (1685) and *Armide et Renaud* (1686), not on classical sources but on Renaissance epics. To this aesthetic provocation, Nicolas Boileau, now the leader of the Ancient camp,

---

[21] Bouhours, *La Manière de bien penser*, p. 2.

[22] For an overview of the role Tasso played in the French Querelle, see Simpson, *Le Tasse et la littérature*, pp. 112-117, 136-142.

[23] For another example of its use, by one of Tasso's most prominent defenders, see De Méré, *Les Oeuvres*, vol. 2, p. 76.

[24] Although they were of course not exact contemporaries. For a comparison of Racine and Quinault and a discussion of the latter's *Armide*, see Norman, *Touched by the Graces*.

replied by condemning not only the genre of opera (which, having no classical antecedents, he considered unworthy of inclusion in the literary canon), but also by again taking aim at Tasso. Significantly, the argument for or against Tasso's 'glitter' ('clinquant') was couched in terms that referred to commonplace thinking. Criticizing Quinault's *Armide et Renaud*, for example, Boileau referred mockingly to 'tous ces *lieux communs* de morale lubrique, / Que Lulli réchauffa des sons de sa musique' (all those *commonplaces* of lewd morality, / Which Lully warmed up with the sounds of his music).[25] In doing so, he gave a moral dimension to his condemnation. Tasso was guilty of practising easy rhetoric, producing false glitter or 'clinquant' rather than literature that rang true. Even more seriously, this false glitter could entice readers away from the path of true light (read: Christian virtue). In his tenth *Satire*, Boileau described the corruption of a young, convent-educated girl, led astray by Quinault's Tasso-inspired opera:

> Mais de quels mouvements dans son cœur excités
> Sentira-t-elle alors tous ses sens agités?
> Je ne te répons pas, qu'au retour moins timide,
> Digne écoliere enfin d'Angélique et d'Armide,
> Elle n'aille à l'instant pleine de ces doux sons,
> Avec quelque Médor pratiquer ces leçons.[26]

> [But by what movements excited in her heart
> Will she now feel all her senses agitated?
> I cannot guarantee you that, less timid upon her return,
> Worthy pupil finally of Angelica and Armida,
> She will not immediately, filled by these sweet sounds,
> Go practice her lessons with some Médor.]

By evoking, alongside Ariosto's Angelica, the pagan temptress Armida, who had figured so prominently in Tasso's *Gerusalemme*, Boileau irrevocably associated Tasso with the arts of seduction, in a contest that hinged on the notion of authority itself. Indeed, while the Moderns cited Tasso as a means to question the authority of classical antiquity, the Ancients replied by buttressing the authority of Greece and Rome, with unabashed anachronism, with the authority of Christianity and Christian morality. The irony that Tasso, a Christian (Counter-Reformation) author, should be looked upon as 'less Christian' than the pagan Horace and Virgil, was in turn linked to the fact that the magical events and creatures described in his

---

[25] Boileau, Satire X, in: *idem, Satires, Epîtres, Art poétique*, p. 127 (my emphasis).
[26] *Ibidem.*

works were increasingly deemed irreconcilable with the purer forms of Christianity advocated toward the end of the French seventeenth century, especially during the so-called 'Querelle du merveilleux'. Most importantly, as the Modern use of Tasso demonstrates, commonplacing him did not necessarily imply blind acceptance of tradition, but quite the contrary, thus opening up new literary possibilities for later, eighteenth-century authors.

Madame de Sévigné's and Rousseau's citational practices

If we turn again now to Madame de Sévigné's and Rousseau's citations of Tasso, it appears that they too, in keeping with the increasing prominence given to the role of seduction in contemporary discussions of Tasso's merits, frequently give their citations a strong affective content. Although Sévigné, whose Tasso citations are more numerous than Rousseau's, refers to him in a greater variety of contexts,[27] the reference often serves to establish an emotional complicity with her absent daughter. In one letter, she imagines her daughter joining her in the act of reading the *Gerusalemme*:

> Nous lisons toujours Le Tasse avec plaisir. Je suis assurée que vous le souffririez, si vous étiez en tiers; il y a bien de la différence entre lire un livre toute seule, ou avec des gens qui entendent et relèvent les beaux endroits et qui, par là, réveillent l'attention. (I, 296)

> [We continue to read Tasso with pleasure. I am sure that you would suffer him, if you were with us; there is a great difference between reading a book all alone, or with people who understand and pick out the finest passages and who, by these means, awaken our attention.]

The ideal reading situation described here is that of reading with a loved one and, while reading, actively noting the 'beaux endroits' or possible commonplaces. Reading, throughout Sévigné's correspondence, becomes a means to create a bond with her absent daughter, and is an important element in her motherly rewriting of the genre of the love-letter. In this erotization of the activity of commonplacing, the reading of Tasso evokes the absent other, and the *Gerusalemme* itself becomes the sign of an absence. Tasso is invoked elsewhere, too, in the mother's elegiac meditations on the daughter's absence. The setting for these citations is typically the wooded park of Sévigné's estate in Brittany, Les Rochers, whose seclusion recalls the traditional classical and medieval *locus amoenus*. Sévigné describes

---

[27] Often when describing the events – quarrels, marriages, deaths, rise and fall in favour – that marked the lives of her aristocratic circle.

how she takes long walks through the park's alleys, in which she has had a labyrinth built:

> Pour mon labyrinthe, il est net; il y a des tapis verts, et les palissades sont à hauteur d'appui. C'est un aimable lieu, mais, hélas! ma chère enfant, il n'y a guère d'apparence que je vous y voie jamais.
> *Di memoria nudrirsi, più che di speme.*[28]
> C'est bien ma vraie devise. Nos sentences ont été trouvées jolies. Ne comprenez-vous point bien qu'il n'y a ni jour, ni heure, ni moment, que je ne pense à vous, que je n'en parle quand je puis, et qu'il n'y a rien qui ne m'en fasse souvenir? (I, 307)

> As for my labyrinth, it is flawless; it has green carpets, and the hedgerows are elbow-high. It is an agreeable site, but, alas, my dear child, it hardly appears that I will ever see you in it.
> *Di memoria nudrirsi, più che di speme.*
> That is truly my real device. Our *sententiae* have been found pleasant. Do you not really understand that there is no day, no hour, no moment that I do not think of you, that I do not speak of you when I can, and that there is nothing that does not remind me of you?

The verse cited recalls a verse in the sixth book of *Gerusalemme Liberata* (VI, 60), which Sévigné cites from memory. According to her modern editor Roger Duchêne, it is likely she culled it from one of the many popular collections of *Imprese* then in circulation in France, suggesting that despite her criticism of commonplace books, she may have relied on them more than she cared to admit. In describing how, like Herminia longing for Tancredo, she 'is nourished more by memory than by hope', Sévigné touches here on a crucial aspect of her use of Tasso, i.e. his association with memory. Tasso, for her, is linked to the memory of times past, and in citing him she expresses a sense of longing or nostalgia. In the most immediate sense, as for Rousseau, this role may of course be linked to the fact that Tasso had been her girlhood reading, and may thus have become indelibly associated with the memory of childhood insouciance.

But there is more to the citations of Tasso than merely the remembrance of past, youthful pleasures. In Rousseau, too, the citations of *Gerusalemme Liberata* are associated with love and desire. At the beginning of *La Nouvelle Héloïse*, the protagonist Saint-Preux strategically invokes

---

[28] This is an imprecise citation of a verse in Tasso, *Nudrisce nel sen l'occulto foco / Di memoria via più che di speranza* (VI, LX) (In her heart she tends the hidden fire / more with memory than with hope.)

Tasso in the letters of seduction he addresses to his young pupil Julie. The erotic connotations become clear when Saint-Preux, describing his own lustful gaze, cites Tasso's description of Armida appearing before the Crusaders (IV, 31):

> Ne soyez pas surprise de me trouver si savant sur des mystères que vous cachez si bien (...) L'œil avide et téméraire s'insinue impunément sous les fleurs d'un bouquet; il erre sous la chenille et la gaze, et fait sentir à la main la résistance élastique qu'elle n'oserait éprouver.
>
> *Parte appar delle mamme acerbe e crude,*
> *Parte altrui ne ricopre invida vesta;*
> *Invida, ma s'agli occhi il varco chiude,*
> *L'amoroso pensier gia non arresta.*[29] (I, 23; I, p. 128-129)[30]

[Do not be surprised to find me so knowledgeable about mysteries that you hide so well (...) The avid and temerary eye insinuates itself with impunity under the flowers of a bouquet; it errs beneath the chenille and gauze, and makes the hand feel the elastic resistance that it would not dare put to the test.

> *Parte appar delle mamme acerbe e crude,*
> *Parte altrui ne ricopre invida vesta;*
> *Invida, ma s'agli occhi il varco chiude,*
> *L'amoroso pensier gia non arresta*]

While Saint-Preux is attracted to Julie precisely because of her modesty – hence the allusion to the veil she wears, which will later in the book become a real veil during her marriage ceremony to Monsieur de Wolmar – Saint-Preux himself also uses a veil of sorts in hiding behind Tasso's verses to seduce his charge. As in Sévigné's letters, Tasso's Italian thus acquires the role of a lover's secret language. The 'artifice' of Tasso, which even his most ardent French admirers condemned in this particular description of Armida,[31] is used to express Saint-Preux's true feelings.

Saint-Preux, however, is not the only character in *La Nouvelle Héloïse* to express feelings he will not talk about openly by resorting to Tasso. Julie too, understanding the weight Tasso carries with her lover, rebukes him

---

[29] Her firm and harsh breasts can be seen / a jealous dress vainly covers the greatest part / envious, but if it covers them from the eye / It does not cover them from amorous desire (IV, 31).

[30] References are to Rousseau's original book and letter number, followed by volume and page numbers in Henri Coulet's two-volume edition of *La Nouvelle Héloïse*.

[31] For example De Méré, *Les Oeuvres*, vol. 1, p. 251.

when he prepares to fight a duel on her behalf by citing some other Tasso verses at him:

> Le fanfaron, le poltron veut à toute force passer pour brave;
>> *Ma verace valor, ben che negletto*
>> *È di se stesso a se freggio assai chiaro.*[32]
> Celui qui feint d'envisager la mort sans effroi, ment. Tout homme craint de mourir; c'est la grande loi des êtres sensibles, sans laquelle toute espèce mortelle serait bientôt détruite. (I, 57; I, p. 208)

> The braggart, the coward wants by any means to appear brave;
>> *Ma verace valor, ben che negletto*
>> *È di se stesso a se freggio assai chiaro.*
> He who pretends to look upon death without fear, lies. Every man is afraid of dying; it is the great law of sensitive beings, without which every mortal species would soon be destroyed.

By reminding him of the contrast Tasso had drawn between the arrogance of the infidels Argante and Alete on one hand, and the true virtue and bravery of Goffredo on the other, Julie can avoid insulting Saint-Preux by calling him a 'fanfaron' to his face. At the same time, she uses the maxim drawn from Tasso as a pretext to launch into a long sermon of her own in which she exhorts Saint-Preux to follow the path of true virtue. Significantly, in what I believe may be an intentional reference to her namesake, the historical Héloïse, Julie ends her sermon with the rhetorical question:

> Tu m'as honorée quelquefois du tendre nom d'épouse: peut-être en ce moment dois-je porter celui de mère. Veux-tu me laisser veuve avant qu'un nœud Sacré nous unisse? (I, 57; I, p. 213)

> You have sometimes honoured me with the tender name of spouse: perhaps at this moment I should bear that of mother. Do you want to leave me widowed before a Sacred bond unites us?

I would posit that the similarity between Julie's onomastic question and the single most frequently quoted passage from the real Héloïse's letters is more than accidental:

---

[32] But real valor, although neglected / takes its worth from itself (II, 60).

Le nom & la qualité d'épouse, je l'avoüe, ont quelque chose de plus saint & de plus solide que le nom de maîtresse: cependant celui-ci m'étoit infinement plus cher & plus doux que l'autre, parce que je vous faisois un plus grand sacrifice.

Et si uxoris nomen sanctius ac validius videtur, dulcius mihi semper extitit amicæ vocabulum; aut, si non indigneris, concubinæ vel scorti.[33]

[The name and quality of spouse, I admit, has something holier and more solid than the name of mistress: however I cherish the latter infinitely more than the former, because I made you a greater sacrifice in bearing it.]

The citation allows Julie, like Saint-Preux citing Tasso, to suggest that which she cannot put openly into words: her fear that, in associating freely with Saint-Preux as she has been doing, she has – against her better instincts – allowed herself to become his mistress or, as several eighteenth-century adaptations of Héloïse's epistle put it less kindly, his 'whore' ('putaine'). Thus, in her reply to his Tasso citation, and in her own strategic redeployment of another Tasso citation, Julie finally reveals how high the stakes really are in this seemingly innocent game of commonplacing.

Nature versus artifice, or how to read Tasso

As Saint-Preux's strategic use of Tasso and Julie's coded reply suggest, there is something problematic in Sévigné's and Rousseau's use of verses from Tasso to describe their own amorous longing. This is, quite simply put, the contradiction between virtue and true feeling on one hand and artifice, or the 'clinquant', the false glitter Boileau had condemned in the Italian poet, on the other. As during the Querelle des Anciens et des Modernes, this is an ethical problem as much as a stylistic one. In other words, how do Sévigné and Rousseau reconcile their use of commonplace-book citations with the ideal of a natural style? How can ready-made commonplaces be used to describe or express true sentiment? And perhaps just as importantly, given the strong religious subtext both of Sévigné's correspondence and Rousseau's *Nouvelle Héloïse*, how can commonplaces of seduction be reconciled with the practice of Christian virtue? Both Sévigné and Rousseau present this is as a moral problematic of reading. Thus, Sévigné draws a contrast between morally elevating reading on one hand, and Tasso on the other. Most often, an opposition is suggested between Tasso's *Gerusa-*

---

[33] [Gervaise, ed.], *Les veritables lettres*, vol. 1, p. 26. This was the most complete French-language translation of Héloïse's letters, and the only one to include the Latin original, that was available in Rousseau's day.

lemme Liberata, described as a mere 'bagatelle divertissante' and the more serious moralistic-theological works of Pierre Nicole, described as 'bonnes lettres' (I, 285).[34] Rousseau, similarly, has Saint-Preux create an implied opposition between two kinds of reading when he enumerates the books he has left not the virtuous Julie, but her 'ordinary' cousin Claire:

> J'ai laissé par égard pour votre inséparable cousine quelques livres de petite lit-
> térature que je n'aurais pas laissés pour vous. Hors le Pétrarque, le Tasse, le
> Métastase, et les maîtres du théâtre français je n'y mêle ni poètes ni livres
> d'amour (...) Qu'apprendrions-nous de l'amour dans ces livres? Ah, Julie notre
> cœur nous en dit plus qu'eux, et le langage imité des livres est bien froid pour
> quiconque est passionné lui-même! (I, 105).

> [I have left, out of consideration for your inseparable cousin, some little books
> of literature that I would not have left for you. Besides Petrarch, Tasso, Metas-
> tasio, and the masters of French theatre, I have included neither poets nor love
> stories (...) What could we learn of love from these books? Ah, Julie, our heart
> tells us more about it than they do, and the imitated language of books is truly
> cold for whoever is passionate himself!]

Sévigné and Rousseau suggest various solutions to this problem of the 'coldness' ('froid') and inauthenticity of 'imitated language' ('langage imité') or writing. One solution is to 'detextualise' Tasso's text, so to speak, i.e. to treat his *Gerusalemme* not as a fixed, artificial text but rather as living language. Sévigné does this primarily through her practice of citing Tasso imprecisely, ostensibly from her own memory rather than in direct consulta-tion of the text. This of course is reminiscent of oral, living tradition rather than schoolroom learning, and fits well with her own self-conscious con-struction of an authorial persona as untrained, 'natural' stylist. Rousseau, on the other hand, detextualises Tasso by associating him with music. Echoing his comments in his *Essai sur l'origine des langues* on the inherent musical-ity of the Italian language, he has Julie learn singing by reading Tasso:

> J'attribue la facilité avec laquelle j'ai pris le goût de cette musique à celui que
> mon frère m'avait donné pour la poésie italienne, et que j'ai si bien entretenu
> avec toi que je sens aisément la cadence des vers, et qu'au dire de Regianino
> [her instructor], j'en prends assez bien l'accent. Je commence chaque leçon par
> lire quelques octaves du Tasse, ou quelque scène du Métastase: ensuite il me

---

[34] On Sévigné's reading of Nicole, see Cartmill, 'Madame de Sévigné, lectrice', pp. 351-359.

fait dire et accompagner du récitatif, et je crois continuer de parler ou de lire, ce qui sûrement ne m'arrivait pas dans le récitatif français. (I, 194)

[I attribute the ease with which I have acquired a taste for this music to that which my brother had given me for Italian poetry, and that I have kept up so well with you that I easily feel the cadence of the verses, and that according to Reginiano, I have acquired the accent fairly well. I begin each lesson by reading several octaves of Tasso, or a scene from Metastasio: afterwards he makes me sing and accompany some recitative passages, and I feel as if I am continuing to speak or read, which would surely not have been the case if I had been singing a French recitative.]

In these instances, Tasso is presented not as immobile text but, rather, as performance, hence resolving somewhat the tension between the ideal of nature and the perceived artificiality of the written text. The association with music is especially noteworthy since, as we have seen, Rousseau had also intimated in his *Essai sur l'origine des langues* that music was originally a universal, more 'natural' language. Because it was a direct expression of experience, music, unlike writing, did not rely for its meaning on arbitrarily established convention. In the *Essai*, significantly, Rousseau draws a telling comparison between the epics of Homer, which, he holds, were never written down by their author, and the singing of verses from Tasso's *Gerusalemme* by modern-day Venetian gondoliers.[35] The commonplace comparison between Tasso and Homer, which had figured prominently in the Querelle's treatment of the Italian poet, is now given an additional meaning by this reference to music and the human voice.[36] If writing, in the *Essai*, is the ultimate sign of absence, then it is only through song or speech that this solitude can be broken, however momentarily:

(...) sitôt que des signes vocaux frapent vôtre oreille, ils vous annoncent un être semblable à vous, ils sont, pour ainsi dire, les organes de l'ame, et s'ils vous peignent aussi la solitude ils vous disent que vous n'y étes pas seul. Les oiseaux sifflent, l'homme seul chante, et l'on ne peut entendre ni chant ni simphonie sans se dire à l'instant; un autre être sensible est ici.[37]

---

[35] The comparison also appears in the entry on 'Barcarolles' in Rousseau's *Dictionnaire de musique*, vol. 5, p. 651.

[36] Significantly, by drawing his commonplaces back into the realm of speech and musical expression, Rousseau implicitly recalls the importance originally assigned to rhetoric, or persuasive speech, in discussions of commonplacing.

[37] Rousseau, *Essai sur l'origine des langues*, p. 132.

[(...) as soon as vocal signs strike the ear, they announce a being similar to yourself; they are, so to speak, the organs of the soul, and if they thus describe solitude, they also tell you that you are not alone in it. Birds whistle, man alone sings, and one cannot hear either song or symphony without immediately telling oneself: there is another sensitive being here.]

For Rousseau as for Sévigné, the attempt to render text as spoken language or song – epistolarity as transcribed conversation in Sévigné, Tasso as music in Rousseau – appears part of a deeper preoccupation with textuality as the expression of an absence, a non-concordance of expression with that which is expressed. As Jacques Derrida writes about Rousseau's *Essai sur l'origine des langues*, which he considers a key text in the development of grammatology or a modern problematic of textuality, 'la condamnation de l'écriture déchue et finie prendra une autre forme, celle dont nous vivons encore: c'est la non-présence à soi qui sera dénoncée' (the condemnation of failed and finished writing will assume another form, the one in which we still live today : it is the non-presence to oneself that will be denounced).[38]

Inscribing Tasso in nature

But there is also another way in which Sévigné and Rousseau attempt to address the problem of using the artificial textuality of Tasso, as condensed in a series of more or less well-known commonplaces, to express pure sentiment or 'nature'. Both their works, in fact, contain descriptions of the literal inscription of verses from Tasso in a natural setting, in such a way as to make them, as it were, become part of nature. Madame de Sévigné describes how, walking through the woods at Les Rochers, her random thoughts lead her to inscribe on the tree trunks a verse from Tasso, which she may well have found in Bouhours's *Entretiens*:[39]

> J'étais hier dans une petite allée, à main gauche du mail, très obscure; je la trouvai belle. Je fis écrire sur un arbre:
> *E di mezzo l'horrore esce il diletto.*[40] (I, 364)

> [Yesterday I was in a little alley, to the left of the mall, that was very dark; I found it beautiful. I ordered to be written on a tree:

---

[38] Derrida, *De la grammotologie*, p. 29.
[39] The verse is cited in the first entretien, 'La mer', p. 7.
[40] This is an approximate citation of two verses of Tasso, *Bello in sì bella vista anco è l'orrore, / e di mezzo la tema esce il diletto* (XX, XXX) (Amid the beauty even horror / is beautiful, and with fear comes pleasure).

E di mezzo l'horrore esce il diletto.]

The meaning of the verse, which remains opaque in the context of this particular letter, becomes clearer when the reader turns back to a previous letter in which Sévigné had quoted the same verse. Written several months earlier, it referred to her daughter's trip to Marseille, where she had been struck in the city's port by the sight of companies of condemned galley convicts embarking on their ships (I, 250). Thus, the verse from Tasso is again used as a secret lover's language referring, ultimately, to Provence and to the missing daughter. But perhaps more strikingly, like an earlier reader whose work she admired, Montaigne, Sévigné records her private readings in a highly personal commonplace book of her own making. Just as Montaigne had engraved his commonplaces on the beams of his tower study-room, Sévigné engraves her commonplaces in her own place of seclusion, the woods of her country estate. While scenes depicting the inscription of verses in trees or stone had already figured in the works of Tasso and Ariosto themselves, what is noteworthy here is the emphasis put on the fact that the setting is now a natural one rather than a man-made one. The commonplace survives in a recognizable form, but is integrated into a new context, whereby it is the book of nature that is valued as a source of authority and knowledge rather than the man-made books produced by previous ages. Tasso speaks now not from the pages of a book, but from the reconstituted book of nature. One could indeed even imagine the tree trunks slowly growing and Tasso's verses physically expanding along with them, thus making his verses very literally come alive. Something of this sense of the pantheistic presence of nature is actually expressed elsewhere by Sévigné when she describes another forest, in which she had made long walks in her youth and which thereby provides an echo to her 'own', inscribed forest at Les Rochers. In this description, however, she is witness to a scene of devastation, for her girlhood forest has been cut down for profit:

> Toutes ces dryades affligées que je vis hier, tous ces vieux sylvains qui ne savent plus où se retirer, tous ces anciens corbeaux établis depuis deux cents ans dans l'horreur de ces bois, ces chouettes qui, dans cette obscurité, annonçaient par leurs funestes cris les malheurs de tous les hommes, tout cela me fit hier des plaintes qui me touchèrent sensiblement le cœur. Et que sait-on même si plusieurs de ces vieux chênes n'ont point parlé, comme celui où était Clorinde? Ce lieu était un *luogo d'incanto*, s'il en fut jamais. (II, 950)

[All those afflicted dryads I saw yesterday, all those old forest divinities who no longer know where to retreat, all these ancient crows established for two hundred years in the darkness of these woods, these owls that, in this obscurity,

announced with their funereal cries the misfortunes of men, all these creatures
addressed plaints to me yesterday that perceptibly touched my heart. And how
do we even know whether several of those old oaks did not speak, like the one
where Clorinda was? This place was a *luogo d'incanto*, if ever there was one.]

Not only did Sévigné make Tasso's verses come alive by inscribing them
on a tree trunk. Here, the reverse effect is obtained when a dying and rav-
aged forest is made to come alive again through the memory of another
verse in the *Gerusalemme*. Through the reference to the dryads of classical
mythology and, more importantly, to a modern 'classic' text, nature is made
to speak and acquire a voice of its own. Nature is given a new, sentimental
value, but only after it has been made to resemble a text.

Rousseau's *Nouvelle Héloïse*, too, includes a key scene in which verses
from Tasso are inscribed in a natural setting. The protagonist Saint-Preux,
returning from his voyages to find his beloved Julie married to another man,
leads her to a secluded clearing by the lake of their former love-making,
where he recalls his past feelings for her:

> Quand nous eûmes atteint ce réduit et que je l'eus quelque temps contemplé:
> quoi! dis-je à Julie en la regardant avec un œil humide, votre cœur ne vous dit-
> il rien ici, et ne sentez-vous point quelque émotion secrète à l'aspect d'un lieu
> si plein de vous? Alors sans attendre sa réponse, je la conduisis vers le rocher et
> lui montrai son chiffre gravé dans mille endroits, et plusieurs vers du Pétrarque
> et du Tasse relatifs à la situation où j'étais en les traçant. (IV, 17; II, p. 140)

> [When we had reached this retreat and I had gazed upon it for some time: what!
> I said to Julie looking at her with humid eyes, does your heart not say anything
> to you here, and do you not feel some secret emotion at the aspect of a place so
> full of your presence? Then without waiting for her reply, I took her to the rock
> and showed her her initials carved in a thousand places, and several verses from
> Petrarch and Tasso relative to the situation in which I had been when I had
> carved them.]

In Rousseau as in Sévigné, the inscription in nature of verses from Tasso
takes as its setting a classic *locus amoenus*, a secluded realm dedicated to
love and closed off from everyday preoccupations. Both share a heightened
awareness of the fact that Tasso denotes an absence but, significantly, they
cannot express this other than by textual means, i.e. by re-inscribing his
verses in a new setting. It appears that even the language of nature is an
'imitated language', taking textuality as its model. The metaphor Rousseau
uses elsewhere is not only that of nature speaking but indeed writing, and
this text, i.e. the book of nature, becomes the basis of his moral philosophy:

'la loi naturelle (...) est encore gravée dans le cœur de l'homme en carac-
téres inéfacables' (natural law ... is still engraved in the hearts of men in in-
effaceable characters).[41] Thus, although he explicitly rejects the inauthenticity of text, which he perceives, in opposition to sung language, as mere
commonplace or convention, Rousseau is unwilling or unable to think outside of the cognitive framework it provides.[42]

But Rousseau adds still another twist to the inscription scene. In the key
episode recounted in *La Nouvelle Héloïse*, the verses from Tasso are inscribed not on a tree trunk, but on a rock. While the inscription in nature
suggests a naturalisation of Tasso, the inscription in stone also evokes another practice: the inscription of an epitaph on a tombstone. It is indeed at
this point in the narrative that Saint-Preux begins to accept that he will
never again be able to possess Julie, and in this sense the inscription of
Tasso serves as an epitaph for his love. Thus, while at first the clearing had
suggested a traditional *locus amoenus*, it actually announces a second, more
real *locus amoenus*, which Saint-Preux will be allowed to enter only after
having effectively buried his old love for Julie. This is the secluded garden
Julie refers to as her Elysée, which she has created with the moral and material support of her new husband. By turning his back on his previous love,
Saint-Preux gains knowledge of true love, as exemplified by the conjugal
and filial harmony that reigns within the Wolmar family and is reflected in
the Elysée. The verses from Tasso have now come to illustrate the falseness
of Saint-Preux's former, sensual love, which, so the second part of the novel
instructs us, was in fact nothing more than false glitter or 'clinquant'. The
memory of Tasso is opposed to the true light of his present, disinterested
and purely spiritual love for Julie.[43] *La Nouvelle Héloïse* comes very close,
finally, to being a tale of Christian redemption, with Julie finding her true
self, as the nun or Héloïse of the book's second title, after she has taken the
veil during her marriage ceremony to Wolmar.

The inscription of verses from Tasso in a natural setting therefore turns
out to have an ambiguous function in the epistolary works of Madame de
Sévigné and Rousseau. It is tempting, indeed, to view the tombstone function of the final Tasso verses mentioned in *La Nouvelle Héloïse* as an epitaph for commonplace reading itself, whose artificiality is ultimately unable
to convey true sentiment. Thus, it is perhaps no coincidence that in the
works of both authors the citations of Tasso progressively become less fre-

---

[41] Rousseau, *Écrits sur l'abbé de Saint-Pierre*, p. 602.
[42] This is, of course, the starting point for Derrida's discussion of Rousseau's *Essai
sur l'origine des langues*.
[43] Christine Hammann has thus rightly pointed out that, despite his enduring admiration for Tasso, Rousseau was also deeply aware of the artifice of his writing. Hammann, 'Rousseau citant le Tasse'.

quent. In *La Nouvelle Héloïse*, the scene by the lake is the last episode in which Tasso is referenced. In Sévigné's correspondence, too, the citations from Tasso decrease steadily, without however disappearing completely. Just as Rousseau's heroine has found her true identity as the Héloïse of the book's second title, and consequently no longer needs the artifice of Tasso, Sévigné too increasingly finds her own, truly personal style, which is indeed more 'natural' than the commonplace-filled epistolary style she had adopted at the beginning of her career as a writer.

Conclusion

Sévigné's and Rousseau's use of commonplaces drawn from Tasso's *Gerusalemme Liberata* suggests that commonplace reading did not entirely disappear in the eighteenth century, but was instead integrated into new cognitive frameworks. Because personal observation of the natural world was increasingly perceived to be a more reliable source of authority than reliance on received wisdom, the only way authors could credibly preserve commonplaces was by inscribing them into a natural setting and, in this sense, 'detextualizing' them. The commonplace book was thus replaced by the book of the world, and the voice of conventional authority by the voice of nature. This ideal of a 'literature without literature' or 'text without text' was certainly not new: one finds it already in the seventeenth-century aristocratic ideal of 'style négligé'. What does however seem unique to the eighteenth century is authors' heightened consciousness of language as a fundamental absence or 'non-présence à soi', to recall Derrida's phrase. Sévigné's ever-receding stream of letters, interrupted only by her own death, are ample testimony to the power of written language not to speak a presence, but an eternally renewed and relived absence. Rousseau's forceful critique of the written word and false book learning is just as revealing of his disillusionment with writing's power to express presence. In later life, as he sought to live out his own precepts, he personally embodied this critique by casting off the books he owned – yet significantly, during the last months of his life, as he consciously neared death, there remained a single volume he was unable to part with: Tasso's *Gerusalemme Liberata*. [44] This is, perhaps, the most eloquent testimonial of all to his century's ultimately ambivalent attitude toward the textual modes of thought exemplified by the commonplace.

---

[44] As Pierre Prévost wrote sixteen months before his death, 'Je vois quelquefois le concitoyen J.J. toujours plein de chaleur et d'imagination, fort occupé de sa musique, ne lisant plus que le Tasse'. Rousseau, *Correspondance complète*, vol. 39, p. 256.

THE TOPOLOGY OF CHANCE MEETINGS IN
THE EARLY MODERN EUROPEAN NOVEL

Carsten Meiner

In this article I would like to analyse the role of the *carriage* in a series of
European literary texts. I will first analyse the thematic implications that the
carriage seems to engender and then, on the basis of these analyses, propose
a new way of conceiving of their topological status. More precisely, I will
analyse some important passages from a series of works which together
demonstrate that the role of the carriage is to de-rationalise movement. I
will then undertake a conceptual investigation of the de-rationalisation of
movement operated by the carriage, in order to demonstrate that the repetition of this de-rationalisation in a large number of literary works constitutes
a positive exploration of a generalised cultural contingency.

There has been a somewhat confusing combination of radical and subversive discourse and an eagerness to rehabilitate old-fashioned theoretical
concepts such as rhetoric or stylistics in literary criticism over the last two
decades, and it must be conceded that the theory of commonplaces in literature has been paid almost no attention by either side. *Topology* was the
name given to the study of literary commonplaces by German philologist
Ernst Robert Curtius in his magisterial study *Europäische Literatur und
lateinisches Mittelalter* of 1948. However, although it is clear that Curtius
modernises ancient rhetorical topology, it is less clear what he actually
means by 'topos', as is evident from the debates following the publication
of the book.[1]

One problem seems to be that Curtius explicitly means to conceive of
topology as a historical science: the topoi are not just a universal means of
persuasion as was the case in classical Greek and Roman topology, but are
also inscribed in the mental historicity of a specific period. An important
quotation from Curtius' work demonstrates this point:

> To poetic topics belongs the beauty of nature in the widest sense – hence the
> ideal landscape with its typical equipment. So do dreamlands and dream ages:
> Elysium (with eternal spring without meteorological disturbances), the Earthly
> Paradise, the Golden Age. So do the active principles in life: love, friendship,

---

[1] Baeumer, 'Vorwort'; Obermayer, 'Zum Toposbegriff'.

transience. All these themes concern basic relations of existence and hence are
timeless – some more, some less. Less: friendship, love. They reflect the se-
quence of psychological periods. But in all poetical topoi the style of expression is historically determined. Now there are also topoi that are wanting
throughout Antiquity down to the Augustan age. They appear at the beginning
of late Antiquity and then are suddenly everywhere (…). They have a twofold
interest. First, as regards literary biology, we can observe in them the genesis of
new topoi. Thus our knowledge of the genetics of the formal elements of literature is widened. Secondly, these topoi are indications of a changed psychological state; indications which are comprehensible in no other way. Thus our understanding of the psychological history of the West is deepened, and we
approach spheres that the psychology of C. G. Jung has explored (…). But
whereas antique topics is part of a didascalium, and hence is systematic and
normative, let us try to establish the basis for a historical topics.[2]

The complexity of Curtius' conception of a topos is revealed in this passage. He explicitly aims to establish a historical topology which will identify how, during the early medieval period, the topoi of rhetoric and poetics
are entangled and how this mutation constitutes the point of departure of the
historicity of topology. More precisely, in Curtius' view the stylistic features function as indications (*Anzeichen*) of the evolution of the human
spirit. This affirmation, however, which reveals Curtius' debt to German
Geistesgeschichte, from Dilthey to Cassirer, also assigns an ambiguous
status to the topoi. On the one hand, they are nothing less than signs of the
evolution of the soul of occidental civilisation – in the sense Toynbee as-
cribes to this term – while, on the other hand, they are 'universal'. The topoi
are tied to 'the primitive conditions of existence' and are thus 'timeless'.
Thus, the question arises of whether or not the topoi are universal or historical signs of the evolution of human spirit. Do they denote the ageless conditions of human existence or are they historical forms?

   One way of grasping this apparently paradoxical definition of the topoi
is to have recourse to another definition: '[t]opoi, that is, fixed clichés or
schemas of thought and expression'.[3] One could interpret the idea of the topos as an intermediary form between existential themes and stylistic features. Here we should keep in mind that Curtius stressed 'the active principles'. A topos can, according to the context, be conceived of as an
existential theme or as a form, a metaphor, a cliché, or, briefly put, as a stylistic feature. For Curtius, the topoi are both 'schema of expression' and

---

[2] Curtius, *European Literature*, pp. 82-82.
[3] Curtius, 'Beiträge zur Topik der mittellateinischen Literatur', p. 1. The German
original reads: 'Topoi, d. h. feste Clichées oder Denk- und Ausdrucksschemata'.

'schema of thought'. The topoi can be placed at different levels within this topological space and it is this conceptual flexibility that Curtius hints at in the above using the formulation 'some more, some less'. Considered from this point of view the status of the topoi differs according to their content, for example, the poetical topos 'invocation of nature', the rhetorical topos 'affected modesty', or the metaphorical topos 'human spirit is like a boat'. Each of them can be placed in the topological space constituted by the 'existential theme' and 'historical form'. In this sense, each topos can be said to contain degrees of both, and it can also be said that concrete mediations operate between the two. That is the reason why Curtius can propose the imprecise definition of the topoi (as it seems, at least on the face of it) as 'fixed clichés', 'schemas of thought', as well as 'schemas of expression'. Thus, topology is, according to Curtius, to be conceived of as a heuristic science whose goal is to identify the entanglement of stylistic features and existential themes in a given topos.

However convincing and rejuvenating this definition may be, one dimension of the conventionality of a given topos seems to be missing. The topoi that Curtius is dealing with all possess historical traits but these are only taken into account as stylistic traits. However, around the seventeenth century, a range of topoi seem to enter European literature whose historicity does not show itself in stylistic features and whose content are not necessarily universal existential themes. The seventeenth century integrates and represents real, material places such as the inn, the road and the castle; the eighteenth century integrates and conventionalises the salon, the coffeehouse, the convent or the church; the nineteenth century integrates topoi such as the restaurant, the theatre, the boulevard, the clerk's office and the train; while the twentieth century could be said to be more oriented towards places such as the airport, the hotel, the factory or the beach. When Curtius talks about topology as a heuristic science this should be taken as an invitation to develop the very notion of literary place.[4] As opposed to the classical topoi these new places do not gain meaning as existential themes and they do not differentiate themselves historically through their stylistic specificity. These new inventions, technologies, media and institutions are real places whose materiality or phenomenology, whose value or prestige, symbolic power and connotations lead to new literary places. Even if these places are new, they naturally deserve the designation 'topoi' in the sense of commonplaces – the fact that they are immediately recognisable as such, warrants their topological status.

---

[4] Curtius, 'Topik als Heuristik', pp. 197-199.

The functions of the literary carriage

While the descriptions of feelings, thoughts and conversations are numerous in the novel of the seventeenth and eighteenth centuries, there are fewer descriptions of real objects and things, especially in the French tradition. However, one of the objects which is present in these novels is the horse-drawn carriage. While these are ubiquitous they are rarely described as real objects, instead having the functional role of making something else work or happen. When attempting to provide a description of the literary carriage from a functional point of view, that is, when asking what becomes operational through the carriage, it becomes evident that it integrates not only an extremely wide range of functions, but also functions that actually exclude one another. It is a stable and closed space which nevertheless moves. It is an object which leaves the spaces of the city and the law, and in doing so becomes vulnerable and liable to attack, while at the same time the carriage is a means of escape and protection. The carriage is also a space that allows new ways of perceiving the exterior world – a means of discovery and of getting in touch with reality. However, it also, inversely, allows for the possibility of being nowhere – of lowering the blinds and shutting out the world. Of course, the enclosure of this space also makes it possible for a human being to make contact, not with the exterior world but, on the contrary, through meditation, with the inner world or, through a dreamlike state, the imagination. The carriage is at the same time a place of solitude and of public meetings. The carriage also has various narrative and symbolic functions, ranging from being a simple linguistic shifter between two scenes to being the very decorum of the action, as is the case, for example, in Guy de Maupassant's *Boule de suif* of 1880.

Again, contrary to transportation, one of the most recurrent functions of the carriage in literature is that of *stopping* the literary action: it is a convention for the carriage to break down because of the frailty of its construction, for it to become bogged in the mud on a country road or caught in traffic in the city, or even to be driven off into a field by a drunken driver. Being more than a means of transportation, the literary carriage is artificial. Rather than the movement of the carriage being interesting, it is the possibility of movement being disturbed or halted and, as it were, de-rationalised, that matters. Consequently, the real literary interest of the carriage is that it first of all implies functions other than that of transporting people between two fixed points and, more to the point, that its strategic objective is precisely not to transport people as planned but, as mentioned above, to de-rationalise their movements. Actually, it is not impossible for the literary existence of the carriage to be synonymous not only with a de-rationalisation of movement but also with the literary invention of a modern notion of chance. Regardless of its transportation of people, the carriage introduces what was not necessarily foreseeable at the point of departure and the carriage consequently has a fundamental heuristic function in the representation of movement.

Themes such as love, death, dialogue and sociability, from Cervantes to Goethe, are no longer presented as necessary but as fundamentally arbitrary or contingent. Literature is one of the very few discourses that has a positive or affirmative way of formulating and exploring this contingency, precisely because literature has recourse to the carriage as a material and tangible mediator of chance. Therefore, one could suggest that the carriage subordinates these themes (love, death, sociability) to the category of chance in a very general way. The semantic function of the carriage is consequently to integrate the accidental and fortuitous aspect of these themes, for example, the accidental aspect of the relationship between man and woman.

A last preliminary remark: having put forward the idea that one of the most recurrent functions of the carriage in literature is that of breaking down or being caught in traffic or on a muddy country road, that is, of halting movement, it might be objected that, as such, the carriage simply continues a long tradition of literary accidents, starting with Homer and Virgil and continuing to the no less classic and extremely voluminous seventeenth-century novels, which were often ten to twelve volumes in length, for example, the works of Scudéry and La Calprenède. The difference between classical and early modern literature is, however, easy to identify. The heroes in Homer and Virgil are hindered by a transcendental event which controls and judges their fate, with the accidental shipwrecks being an effect of godly will. Contrary to this tradition, early modern literary accidents are not dictated by such transcendental forces.

The literary carriage from Furetière to Diderot

If we take a passage from *Le Roman bourgeois* by Antoine Furetière from 1666, it will become clear that the accidents created by the carriage begin to liberate themselves from transcendental events. No such events seem to govern the whereabouts of chance:

> Il songea, comme il était assez discret, à chercher quelqu'un qui le pût introduire chez elle; en tout cas, il se résolvait de se servir du jeu qui est le grand passe-partout pour avoir entrée dans de telles compagnies; il n'eut besoin de l'une ni de l'autre, car dès le lendemain, passant en carrosse dans la rue de Lucrèce, il la vit de loin sur le pas de sa porte. L'impatience qu'elle avait de voir que personne n'était encore venu l'y avait portée, et dès qu'elle entendit le bruit d'un carrosse, elle tourna la tête de ce côté-là, pensant que c'était quelqu'un qui

venait chez elle. Le marquis se mit à la portière pour la saluer et tâcher à nouer conversation. Voici une malheureuse occasion qui lui fut favorable: un petit valet de maquignon poussait à toute bride un cheval qu'il piquait avec un éperon rouillé, attaché à son soulier gauche; et comme la rue était étroite et le ruisseau large, il couvrit de boue le carrosse, le marquis et la demoiselle (…). Il descendit tout crotté qu'il était, pour consoler Lucrèce et lui dit en l'abordant: 'Mademoiselle, j'ai été puni de ma témérité de vous avoir voulu voir de trop près; mais je ne suis pas si fâché de me voir en cet état que je le suis de vous voir partager avec moi ce vilain présent.[5]

[As the marquis was quiet shy, he tried to find a way to be introduced to her. He eventually decided to participate in the games of card organised at Lucrèce's house, but that proved not to be necessary because when he drove down her road in his carriage on the following day he saw her standing in front of the entrance. It was the impatience that she felt from not having received any visitors yet which had brought her out there and when she heard the sound of the carriage she turned around and thought that there was finally a visitor. The marquis placed himself in the window to greet her and try to start a conversation, but that was when he had a stroke of bad luck, which, however, would prove to be a blessing in disguise. A horse tradesman drove his horse forward with a rusty spur attached to his left boot; and as the road was narrow and the gutter large he covered both the carriage, the marquis and the young girl with mud (…). The marquis, all muddy, got out to excuse himself and said: 'I've been punished for having wanted to see you at close range; but I'm not as upset by being in this state as by seeing you sharing it with me.][6]

In this passage the carriage is closely connected to chance. Two people from two distinct social groups are attempting to make contact. The nobleman and 'la bourgeoise', Lucrèce, both want to engage but do not know how, and as the narrator explicitly mentions the accident is fortuitous. Their contact is only possible at the price of having their social differences accidentally muddied. As a consequence, two distinct and hierarchically organised social classes are brought to the same level. However, even if the accident is the narrative touchstone of the passage it is not liberated from external determinations. The meeting is not really accidental, firstly because the marquis intended to go to Lucrèce's house and secondly because the narrator explicitly anticipates the accident. Furthermore, the marquis takes advantage of the situation with such natural rhetorical skill that no accident

---

[5] Furetière, *Le Roman bourgeois*, p. 103.
[6] Translations without a reference are my own.

seems to have occurred. The accident is not really accidental but already tainted with both conventional traits and social power.

If we continue into the eighteenth century, the liberation of the carriage from external determinations continues. In fact chance starts to become the literary factor which subverts the very ideological and social structures that regulate the individual's place in society. Taking an example from Marivaux's *Le Paysan parvenu* from 1734, the principal character, Jacob, a young man from the country, is moving up the social ladder. Just before the events in the passage quoted below, Jacob was charged with a murder he did not commit and was taken to prison and subsequently acquitted of the crime. In this passage Jacob is leaving prison in the fancy carriage of Mme de Ferval, a friend, and in the company of Mlle Habert, whom he is going to marry:

> Nous approchions de la maison de Mlle Habert, où Mme de Ferval voulait nous mener, quand nous rencontrâmes, à la porte d'une église, la sœur aînée de ma future et M. Doucin, qui causaient ensemble, et qui semblaient parler d'action. Un carrosse, qui retarda la course du nôtre, leur donna tout le temps de nous apercevoir. Quand j'y songe, je ris encore du prodigieux étonnement où ils restèrent tous deux en nous voyant. Nous les pétrifiâmes (...) il y a des choses qui terrassent, et pour surcroît de chagrin c'est que nous ne pouvions leur apparaître dans un instant qui leur rendît notre apparition plus humiliante et plus douloureuse. Le hasard y joignait des accidents faits exprès pour les désoler ; c'était triompher d'eux d'une manière superbe, et qui aurait été insolente si nous l'avions méditée ; et c'est, ne vous déplaise, qu'au moment qu'ils nous aperçurent, nous éclations de rire... de quelque chose de plaisant que j'avais dit.[7]

> [We approached Mlle Habert's house where Mme de Ferval wanted to take us when, in front of a church, we met my future wife's sister and M. Doucin, who were talking together and seemed upset. A carriage which slowed down the course of ours gave them all the time needed to see us. When I think about it, I laugh at the prodigious astonishment that seized both of them when they saw us. We petrified them (...) and on top of that we couldn't have come into their sight at a more humiliating and painful moment for them because Chance added incidents that seemed created exclusively to annoy them; it was a superb way of triumphing, which would have been dishonourable had we prepared it, because in the very moment they saw us we started laughing at something funny I had just said.]

---

[7] Marivaux, *Le Paysan parvenu*, p. 160.

By chance, Jacob is seen riding in the elegant carriage by his Parisian enemies. However, even if the role of chance is made quite explicit by the narrator, compared to the passage in Furetière the accident is more spontaneous
and subtle. All that is needed is a slight and neutrally described slowing of
the vehicle to make the carriage a filter through which chance manifests itself. Compared to the narrator in Furetière, who not only knew precisely
that the accident was going to happen but also what it meant, it is only after
the incident that Jacob understands its full implications (the novel being a
first-person account written by Jacob long after the events took place).
What is interesting in this novel is that every time Jacob takes another step
up the social ladder it happens as a result of some more or less neutral accident in a carriage. On the basis of such a repetition of chance as the structuring principle of the events, it might be claimed that the carriage functions
to normalise or naturalise such events, in the sense that they are no longer
warnings from above, either as a punishment or a test, but are autonomous,
occurring purely by chance. At the beginning of the eighteenth century, the
accident becomes *naturally* accidental and the carriage is a privileged instrument in the representation of natural chance, with the various incidents
recognisable to the reader as problems of everyday life and as such useful in
the literary naturalisation of chance.[8]

However, it is not necessary to move many decades into the eighteenth
century to realise that the naturalisation of chance using the carriage has become a convention and at the same time a problem. This is because if an
accident is not recognised as such, but as a literary convention, its integrity
has of course been compromised. This is precisely the kind of logic that
seems to underlie one of the most famous scenes in modern European literature – where Werther meets Lotte in Goethe's *Die Leiden des jungen Werther* from 1771.

> Ich schrieb dir neulich, wie ich den Amtmann S. habe kennen lernen, und wie
> er mich gebeten habe, ihn bald in seiner Einsiedelei oder vielmehr seinem klei-
> nen Königreiche zu besuchen. Ich vernachlässigte das, und wäre vielleicht nie
> hingekommen, hätte mir der Zufall nicht den Schatz entdeckt, der in der stillen
> Gegend verborgen liegt. Unsere jungen Leute hatten einen Ball auf dem Lande
> angestellt, zu dem ich mich denn auch willig finden ließ. Ich bot einem hiesi-
> gen guten, schönen, übrigens unbedeutenden Mädchen die Hand, und es wurde

---

[8] Julian Munby: 'Il me semble que nous avons affaire ici à un phénomène technique
très intéressant, comparable, peut-être, au développement du navire à trois mâts: un
objet standard reconnaissable, identique partout en Europe, et utilisé par les rois,
l'aristocratie et la bourgeoisie. Nous ne savons pas pour autant d'où il provenait ou
plus précisément comment il s'était développé (…)', 'Les Origines du coche', p. 81.

ausgemacht, daß ich eine Kutsche nehmen, mit meiner Tänzerin und ihrer Base nach dem Orte der Lustbarkeit hinausfahren und auf dem Wege Charlotten S. mitnehmen sollte. 'Sie werden ein schönes Frauenzimmer kennenlernen', sagte meine Gesellschafterin, da wir durch den weiten, ausgehauenen Wald nach dem Jagdhause fuhren. 'Nehmen Sie sich in acht', versetzte die Base, 'daß Sie sich nicht verlieben!' 'Wieso?' sagte ich. 'Sie ist schon vergeben,' antwortete jene, 'an einen sehr braven Mann, der weggereist ist, seine Sachen in Ordnung zu bringen, weil sein Vater gestorben ist, und sich um eine ansehnliche Versor-gung zu bewerben'. Die Nachricht war mir ziemlich gleichgültig. Die Sonne war noch eine Viertelstunde vom Gebirge, als wir vor dem Hoftore anfuhren. Es war sehr schwül, und die Frauenzimmer äußerten ihre Besorgnis wegen ei-nes Gewitters, das sich in weißgrauen, dumpfichten Wölkchen rings am Hori-zonte zusammenzuziehen schien. Ich täuschte ihre Furcht mit anmaßlicher Wetterkunde, ob mir gleich selbst zu ahnen anfing, unsere Lustbarkeit werde einen Stoß leiden. Ich war ausgestiegen, und eine Magd, die ans Tor kam, bat uns, einen Augenblick zu verziehen, Mamsell Lottchen würde gleich kommen. Ich ging durch den Hof nach dem wohlgebauten Hause, und da ich die vorlie-genden Treppen hinaufgestiegen war und in die Tür trat, fiel mir das reizendste Schauspiel in die Augen, das ich je gesehen habe.[9]

[I mentioned to you the other day that I had become acquainted with S——, the district judge, and that he had invited me to go and visit him in his retirement, or rather in his little kingdom. But I neglected going, and perhaps should never have gone, if chance had not discovered to me the treasure which lay concealed in that retired spot. Some of our young people had proposed giving a ball in the country, at which I consented to be present. I offered my hand for the evening to a pretty and agreeable, but rather commonplace, sort of girl from the imme-diate neighbourhood; and it was agreed that I should engage a carriage, and call upon Charlotte, with my partner and her aunt, to convey them to the ball. My companion informed me, as we drove along through the park to the hunting-lodge, that I should make the acquaintance of a very charming young lady. 'Take care,' added the aunt, 'that you do not lose your heart.' 'Why?' said I. 'Because she is already engaged to a very worthy man,' she replied, 'who is gone to settle his affairs upon the death of his father, and will succeed to a very considerable inheritance.' This information possessed no interest for me. When we arrived at the gate, the sun was setting behind the tops of the mountains. The atmosphere was heavy; and the ladies expressed their fears of an approach-ing storm, as masses of low black clouds were gathering in the horizon. I re-lieved their anxieties by pretending to be weather-wise, although I myself had some apprehensions lest our pleasure should be interrupted. I alighted; and a

---

[9] Goethe, *Die Leiden des jungen Werther*, pp. 20-21.

maid came to the door, and requested us to wait a moment for her mistress. I walked across the court to a well-built house, and, ascending the flight of steps in front, opened the door, and saw before me the most charming spectacle I had ever witnessed.][10]

In this passage one feels how the early romanticism of Goethe opposes itself to the carriage as an accidental meeting place. On the one hand the meeting cannot take place in the now conventional carriage, while on the other hand the carriage seems, if not required, at least useful in the construction of a surprise meeting. The meeting is announced in the carriage by women who Werther, always privileging unmediated and authentic relationships, finds uninteresting. Werther then leaves these women and the conventional carriage to see Lotte in her natural element, on the threshold of the house, cutting slices of bread for her sisters and brothers. Lotte and Werther could very well have met at the cottage where the ball is taking place, but they do not and hence the carriage still holds an important function as an instrument for producing unpredicted events. What has changed is the fact that the literary representation must limit the presence of the carriage because it is capable of contaminating the authenticity of the meeting. The same structure can be observed later in the novel, when Werther is returning to his hometown in a carriage. He actually stops the carriage before he reaches the town because he wants to walk into town, the cultural conventionality of the carriage hindering him from experiencing an authentic feeling of homecoming.

The naturalisation of chance through the mediation of the carriage has come to an end with Werther, although without disappearing. The same paradox can be observed in Rousseau. Like Goethe, Rousseau insists on the authenticity of natural man and he is naturally sceptical towards the carriage, which is considered a sign of a depraved urban culture. In *La Nouvelle Héloïse* and *Emile* we find several attacks on the culture of carriages, and in the second promenade of the *Rêveries du promeneur solitaire* (1776-1778), we find a particularly radical image of the carriage, with Rousseau recounting the story of how he was almost hit by a carriage at Ménilmontant and was only saved by a dog that knocked him over, preventing him from being hit by the machine of death:

J'étais sur les six heures à la descente de Ménilmontant presque vis-à-vis du Galant Jardinier, quand des personnes qui marchaient devant moi s'étant tout à coup brusquement écartées je vis fondre sur moi un gros chien danois qui, s'élançant à toutes jambes devant un carrosse, n'eut pas même le temps de

---

[10] *Idem, The Sorrows of Young Werther*, pp. 20-21.

retenir sa course ou de se détourner quand il m'aperçut. Je jugeai que le seul moyen que j'avais d'éviter d'être jeté par terre était de faire un grand saut si juste que le chien passât sous moi tandis que je serais en l'air. Cette idée plus prompte que l'éclair et que je n'eus le temps ni de raisonner ni d'exécuter fut la dernière avant mon accident. Je ne sentis ni le coup ni la chute, ni rien de ce qui s'ensuivit jusqu'au moment où je revins à moi. [11]

[I was on the road down from Ménilmontant almost opposite the Galant Jardinier at about six o'clock when some people walking ahead of me suddenly swerved aside and I saw a huge Great Dane rushing down upon me. Racing before a carriage, the dog had no time to check its pace or to turn aside when it noticed me. I judged that the only means I had to avoid being knocked to the ground was to make a great leap, so well-timed that the dog would pass under me while I was still in the air. This idea, quicker than a flash and which I had the time neither to think through nor carry out, was my last before my accident. I did not feel the blow, nor the fall, nor anything of what followed until the moment I came to.][12]

Here the carriage is a kind of death machine, which we also know from Nicolas Boileau and Louis-Sébastien Mercier. Goethe had limited the role of the carriage to a minimum in *Werther*. To retain the contact between nature and himself, Werther prefers to walk, keeping his distance from the carriage, which is now deemed too conventional and a threat to his authenticity.[13] However, this scepticism does not eliminate the carriage, it redefines its value. Rousseau actually pursues this redefinition, and the elegance of the passage in his work stems from the fact that the carriage changes from being a death machine to becoming a birth machine, the passage continuing:

L'état auquel je me trouvai dans cet instant est trop singulier pour n'en pas faire ici la description. La nuit s'avançait. J'aperçus le ciel, quelques étoiles, et un peu de verdure. Cette première sensation fut un moment délicieux. Je ne me sentais encore que par-là. Je naissais dans cet instant à la vie, et il me semblait que je remplissais de ma légère existence tous les objets que j'apercevais. Tout entier au moment présent je ne me souvenais de rien ; je n'avais nulle notion distincte de mon individu, pas la moindre idée de ce qui venait de m'arriver ; je ne savais ni qui j'étais ni où j'étais ; je ne sentais ni mal, ni crainte, ni inquiétude. Je voyais couler mon sang comme j'aurais vu couler un ruisseau, sans

---

[11] Rousseau, *Les Rêveries du promeneur solitaire*, pp. 47-48.
[12] *Idem, The Reveries of the Solitary Walker*, p. 15.
[13] Cf. Seeber, 'Von den Wordsworths zu De Quincey', pp. 7-32.

songer seulement que ce sang m'appartînt en aucune sorte. Je sentais dans tout mon être un calme ravissant, auquel chaque fois que je me le rappelle, je ne trouve rien de comparable dans toute l'activité des plaisirs connus.[14]

[The state in which I found myself in that instant is too unusual not to give a description of here. Night was coming on. I perceived the sky, some stars, and a little greenery. The first sensation was a delicious moment. I still had no feeling of myself except as being 'over there'. I was born into life at that instant, and it seemed to me that I filled all the objects I perceived with my frail existence. Entirely absorbed in the present moment, I remembered nothing; I had no distinct notion of my person nor the least idea of what had just happened to me; I knew neither who I was nor where I was; I felt neither injury, fear, nor worry. I watched a brook flow, without even suspecting that this blood belonged to me in any way. I felt a rapturous calm in my whole being; and each time I remember it, I find nothing comparable to it in all the activity of known pleasures.][15]

The accident gives birth to a new man. It cleanses him, erases his memory and his individuality, as well as his sense of place and time, it alleviates and lightens his very being, which unites itself with the objects surrounding him. This state of grace resembles a birth and its pre-reflexive peace, and this change from death to birth is logically followed by the first steps into his new existence as 'promeneur'. Rousseau is actually urged by the people who witnessed the accident to take a carriage home, but he concludes that the 'promenade' is a much better way to keep warm than sitting in a cold vehicle. He thus proceeds without taking the uncomfortable and cold carriage and avoids the traffic. The modus operandi of early romantic subjectivity was precisely the promenade, a choice which sidelines the carriage from subjective experience. The only *raison d'être* of the carriage is that of designating what this subjectivity must avoid to remain authentic. The carriage is in decline as a means of representing chance in an authentic way; it is, so to speak, losing its accidental virtue having been revealed as a primary force in the rhetoric of chance.

Despite the violence of the accident, it evokes in Rousseau the sensation of being reborn, as he says 'I didn't know who I was'. Just as occurs in *Werther*, the carriage still functions as a negative but apparently necessary element in the construction of early romantic sensibility, which appears to be dependent on accidental events as a means of convincing itself of its authenticity.

---

[14] Rousseau, *Les Rêveries du promeneur solitaire*, pp. 48-49.
[15] *Idem*, *The Reveries of the Solitary Walker*, p. 16.

A last example comes from Diderot's novel *La Religieuse* written in 1780 and finally published in its entirety in 1796. The main character, Suzanne, who was forced to become a nun, is trying to escape from her convent with the help of a monk who has shown unselfish and compassionate interest in her and her miserable situation:

Ma fuite est projetée. Je me rends dans le jardin entre onze heures et minuit. On me jette des cordes, je les attache autour de moi, elles se cassent et je tombe; j'ai les jambes dépouillées et une violente contusion aux reins. Une seconde, une troisième tentative m'élève au haut du mur: je descends. Quelle est ma surprise! Au lieu d'une chaise de poste dans laquelle j'espérais être reçue, je trouve un mauvais carrosse public. Me voilà sur le chemin de Paris avec un jeune bénédictin; je ne tardai pas à m'apercevoir au ton indécent qu'il prenait et aux libertés qu'il se permettait qu'on ne tenait avec moi aucune des conditions que j'avais stipulées. Alors je regrettais ma cellule et je sentis toute l'horreur de ma situation. C'est ici que je peindrai ma scène dans le fiacre. Quelle scène! Quel homme! je crie; le cocher vient à mon secours, rixe violente entre le fiacre et le moine. J'arrive à Paris. La voiture arrête dans une petite rue, à une porte étroite qui s'ouvrait dans une allée obscure et malpropre.[16]

[The plan of my flight was arranged. I repaired to the garden between eleven and twelve at night. Ropes were thrown over the wall, which I fixed round me; they broke, and I fell to the ground. The skin of my legs was torn, and I received a violent contusion on the back. After a second and a third attempt, I reached the top of the wall. I descended; but how great was my surprise, when, instead of a post-chaise, in which I hoped to be received, I found a wretched public coach! I was now upon the road to Paris, with a young Benedictine. I very soon perceived, by the indecent tone which he assumed, and the liberties which he indulged, that none of the conditions which had been stipulated with me, would be observed. At this moment I regretted my cell and felt the horror of my situation. Here I will paint the scene which took place in the coach. What a dreadful scene! What a profligate man! I cried out; the coachman came to my assistance; a violent brawl ensued between the coachman and the monk. I arrived at Paris. The carriage stopped in a little street, at a little narrow door, which opened into an obscure dirty alley.][17]

In what is probably one of the best carriage scenes in the eighteenth century, it is again the place where unforeseen and fortuitous events take place. Suzanne was supposed finally to leave her 'prison' and her unhappy life,

---

[16] Diderot, *La Religieuse*, pp. 281-282.
[17] *Idem, The Nun*, pp. 157-158.

but is exposed to a premeditated rape. In that way the carriage is the place where freedom surprisingly turns into its opposite, that of dominatory physical power and rape. However, that is not all, something which, by the way, seems to be the rule with Diderot: the attentive reader will not only hear the terror and alarm in Suzanne's screams but also a certain amount of pleasure in her words: 'Quelle scène, quel homme, je crie!'. The reader witnesses first a movement from the 'topos of escape' to the 'topos of rape', but secondly this assault ends up in a thematic condensation where rape and pleasure become difficult to distinguish.

Once again the carriage is the place for the integration of the unforeseen, of the accidental, of chance: not because the escape from the convent becomes rape but because their is a hint of pleasure. In that way the carriage in Diderot still seems to be a commonplace, a conventional resource for the constitution of new relationships between the principal character and the world which the novel tries to open up for her. However, the carriage as a conventional commonplace is also given a twist: the semantic density of the scene eclipses its conventional aspect in that the evidence of the chance register is muted by the rich semantic implications of the scene. The semantic densification exceeds the conventional aspect of the scene. Chance is everywhere and nowhere, a fact which of course is characteristic of Diderot's dialectical conception of determinism and freedom.

Reflections on the theory of topology

As mentioned above, the real literary gain in focusing on the carriage is that it involves functions other than that of transportation. The literary existence of the carriage is synonymous with a de-rationalisation or de-instrumentalisation of movement. This is true insofar as the quoted passages all connect the carriage with the powers of chance, regardless of the function of transportation. Actually the category of chance is the category *par excellence* which contradicts and negates rational movement and, on the basis of the historical outline, the carriage can be said to have had a heuristic if not logical function in the constitution of the new and the unexpected in the literary universes critically created in early modern and modern literature. In the rhetoric of the early modern European novel the carriage has the role, not of being a 'reality effect' but of being a 'chance effect' or an 'accident effect'.

There are of course many possible objections or questions that come to mind when confronted with this interpretation. One of the objections is that the carriage is not the only way of integrating chance into literature, as accidental meetings take place elsewhere and in other ways. In response, however, the carriage is not a necessary means of integrating chance into literature, it is simply an important means, and probably the most important. To use a chiasmus, one could say that the function of the carriage is as decisive as it is relative.

This leads to another question linked intimately to the reflections on the topology of Curtius at the beginning of this article: What theoretical concept is suited to identify what is occurring in these scenes? The notion of topos seems well chosen, with the carriage being a conventional *place* in literature. One attempt at developing Curtius' topology can be discerned clearly in the declaration of the Société de l'Analyse Topique du Roman avant 1800 (SATOR), which works on topological issues:

> Le topos narratif donne une information narrative, au sens fort du mot 'information': il rend compte d'un événement diégétique ou narratologique. Il faut, dans la phrase exprimant le topos, un prédicat qui soit une action ou une information narratives, par exemple 'dans un *locus amoenus*, une jeune fille vient rêver à celui qu'elle aime' ou 'des amis font un festin dans un *locus amoenus*' ou encore 'deux vieillards vivent heureux dans un *locus amoenus*'. Le terme '*locus amoenus*' seul (présenté comme topos par Curtius) n'est pas un topos narratif pour SATOR, car il ne raconte rien, mais une catégorie topique qui rassemblera tous les topoi contenant ce terme. Le topos résume un événement: ce qui arrive dans la diégèse. A condition que ce narré soit d'une récurrence intertextuelle reconnue.[18]

[The narrative topos provides narrative information in the strong sense of the word 'information': it establishes a diegetic or narratological event. In the sentence expressing the topos, a predicate is needed, i.e. a narrative action or narrative piece of information, for example, 'a young girl dreams of her beloved in a *locus amoenus*' or 'friends have a feast in a *locus amoenus*' or 'an old couple live happily in a *locus amoenus*'. The term '*locus amoenus*' in itself (presented as a topos by Curtius) is not, according to SATOR, a true narrative topos, since it tells us nothing. Rather, it is a topological category which will serve to gather together all the topoi containing this term. The topos sums up an event: what happens in the diegesis, on condition that this element of narrative information is an acknowledged intertextual recurrence.]

The analyses of the carriages fit this description of a topos quite well: carriages carry information and present themselves as events which are repeated within the history of literary discourse. However, one problem remains: the distinction between the topos as a narrative event and the topos as a category. The latter is not a literary reality but an abstract conceptual

---

[18] See the website http://alor.univ-montp3.fr/SATOR/, Programma scientifique.

framework gathering together the different events. What is problematic in this definition is the causal relationship between these two. The carriages fulfil the conditions of being events and of being recurrent but they are in no way part of a topological category as were the events in the *locus amoenus*. The *locus amoenus* category has an a priori meaning which semantically determines the events taking place: the examples given by SATOR actually demonstrate this point very clearly: 'dans un *locus amoenus*, une jeune fille vient rêver à celui qu'elle aime' or 'des amis font un festin dans un *locus amoenus*' or 'deux vieillards vivent heureux dans un *locus amoenus*'. The category determines in advance what events can take place concretely: elements such as dreaming, feasting, happiness and friendship determine in advance and categorically what kind of event is allowed inside the topos and what value it will have. Hatred, murder or anguish would simply not fulfil the a priori criteria of inclusion into the category of the *locus amoenus*.

Conclusion

In relation to the carriage scenes analysed above, no a priori meaning seems to determine their functionality, with the only recurrent semantic function being that of integrating chance. However, chance is probably the only category which does not have an a priori meaning and that is why it is reasonable to talk about a new kind of topology based on an a posteriori semantics.

This leads to a final objection concerning the notion of theme. The theme of chance seems to fit the topos, that is, the carriage, extremely well, however, perhaps that kinship conceals other themes which are just as important. In other words, does the topos, that is, the carriage, not also integrate themes other than chance, for example, those of love, death or social prestige? The first response is that it proves the multifunctionality of the carriage as a topos. The carriage condenses many different themes within the same scene. However, if it is possible to write the literary history of chance with the carriage as its catalyst, it seems less evident that the literary history of love, sociability or death can be written through the medium of the carriage. Such histories would at any rate be incomplete, whereas the history of literary chance does not possess, at least in my opinion, a better medium than that of the carriage.

Consequently it would be possible and perhaps necessary to invent a thematic hierarchy for the carriage, having as its fundamental theme the category of chance, which then determines the relationship that human beings have to love, public conversation and death, themes which consequently become fundamentally arbitrary. From this perspective, the carriage, considered as the means of introducing chance into literature, participates in a general version of the modern world according to which humanity has lost what Georg Lukacs called its 'transcendental topography', the world presenting itself to human beings as fundamentally arbitrary. If human beings have no interior map indicating to them how to navigate emotionally, religiously and socially in a contingent world, the carriage is an almost perfect instrument to express that very de-rationalisation of movement. In that modern world only two categories seem to remain – those of movement and existential uncertainty – and if it seems obvious that it is exactly these two categories that the history of modern literature explores, it seems less accepted that this very exploration would not have been possible without its ever-deviating carriages.

COMMON SENSE, COMMON PLACE? *BON SENS* AND THE *ENCYCLOPÉDIE*

Rebecca Ford

In 1637, René Descartes opened his *Discours de la méthode* (*Discourse on Method*) with the claim that 'Le bon sens est la chose du monde la mieux partagée' (Common sense is the most widely shared commodity in the world); some 140 years later, in 1772, the baron d'Holbach, one of the leading *philosophes* of his day, anonymously published a work entitled *Le Bon-Sens; ou, Idées naturelles opposées aux idées surnaturelles* (*Common Sense: or, Natural Ideas Opposed to Supernatural Ideas*). The Enlightenment, the 'age of reason', may thus be seen to be neatly book-ended not by reason but by common sense – on the one hand by Descartes, hailed by many *philosophes* as a founding-father of the Enlightenment, and on the other by d'Holbach, one of the Enlightenment's most radical *philosophes*. Yet while the notion of 'reason' as a fundamental Enlightenment value has been amply examined,[1] what of 'bon sens', 'common sense'? Was it as commonplace in the Enlightenment as its positioning in Descartes' and d'Holbach's work suggests? Is it to be understood as simply synonymous with reason, or does it have its own epistemological and functional identity? And if it may be understood as a commonplace idea, to what uses might this 'commonplace' status lend it? To answer such questions in the context of the Enlightenment as a whole would be a huge undertaking – this article will thus concentrate on the uses and analysis of the term 'bon sens' in one of the Enlightenment's central works, the *Encyclopédie*.[2] After some consideration of the connections between the encyclopaedic and commonplace traditions, I will go on to examine the use of 'bon sens' as a commonplace term and its relationship to reason and philosophy, to morality and to social concerns.

The encyclopaedic and commonplace traditions

In its 28 volumes (17 of text and 11 of plates), published between 1751 and 1772, the *Encyclopédie* sought to bring together all of human knowledge

---

[1] See, for example, Brewer, 'Constructing Philosophers', pp. 21-36.
[2] Diderot and d'Alembert, eds, *Encyclopédie* (version from 1749-1772).

through an altruistic collaboration between its many contributors, who
ranged from anonymous specialists on obscure arts to some of the most famous thinkers of the age: Voltaire, Jean-Jacques Rousseau, the baron Paul-
Henri Thiry d'Holbach and, of course, its editors Denis Diderot and Jean Le
Rond d'Alembert.[3] The *Encyclopédie* is a useful site for an investigation of
Enlightenment commonplaces not only because of its position at the heart
of the French Enlightenment, but also because of its dual relationship towards, on the one hand, the tradition of the commonplace book, and on the
other, the notion of 'commonplace' in its more modern sense, that of 'a
common or ordinary topic; an opinion or statement generally accepted or
taken for granted; a stock theme or subject of remark, an every-day saying'.[4] The question of the relationship between commonplace books and
eighteenth-century encyclopaedias has been examined by Richard Yeo in
the context of Ephraim Chambers' *Cyclopaedia* (1728).[5] Yeo concludes that
while there may seem to be some initial similarity between the commonplace and encyclopaedia traditions (the desire to create a compendium of
knowledge, with material arranged under discrete headings in an organisation which has an element of the spatial and thematic), and that this similarity was certainly exploited in the marketing of later editions of the *Cyclopaedia*, such a surface similarity is countered by the essential difference in
motivation and in the perception of the knowledge contained within an encyclopaedia's pages.[6] For Yeo, commonplace books were essentially documents for private study, whereas the *Cyclopaedia* was conceived as a text to
perform a public service, and this lies at the heart of the essential distinction
between the two traditions: 'the *Cyclopaedia* was (...) intended as a spur to
innovation and the acquisition of new empirical knowledge. In contrast, the
aim of commonplace books was imitation of, and improvisation on, a stable
body of authoritative ideas and motifs'.[7] The ambiguity Yeo uncovers con-

---

[3] The central works on the *Encyclopédie* remain those of Proust, *L'"Encyclopédie"*
and *Diderot et l'"Encyclopédie"*, and of Lough, *The "Encyclopédie"*. One of the
foremost recent studies of the *Encyclopédie* project is the volume of essays entitled
Using the "Encyclopédie": Ways of Knowing, Ways of Reading, ed. by Brewer and
Hayes.
[4] *Oxford English Dictionary*.
[5] Chambers' *Cyclopaedia, or an Universal Dictionary of the Arts and Sciences*, first
published in 1728, was the source for the initial *Encyclopédie* project, which was
conceived in its early stages as a fairly direct translation into French of the English
Cyclopaedia. By the time Diderot and d'Alembert had established themselves as
editors, however, the *Encyclopédie* project had far outgrown this initial idea. For
more information on the *Cyclopaedia*, see Bradshaw, 'Ephraim Chambers'
Cyclopaedia', pp. 123-40, and. Yeo, 'Reading Encyclopaedias', pp. 24-49.
[6] Yeo, 'Ephraim Chambers', pp. 157-175.
[7] *Ibidem*, p. 173.

cerning the *Cyclopaedia* and the commonplace tradition is also to be found in the *Encyclopédie*'s own pages. The *Encyclopédie*'s article on commonplace books, 'Recueil' (Collection), is an almost word-for-word translation of that found in the *Cyclopaedia*, and it notes that 'Les *recueils* sont d'une grande utilité, ce sont des especes de magasins où l'on dépose les meilleurs & les plus beaux endroits des auteurs afin de les avoir toujours prêts pour s'en servir';[8] moreover, in his article 'Encyclopédie', often seen as the manifesto for the *Encyclopédie* project as a whole, Diderot seems to present the *Encyclopédie* as the ultimate commonplace book:

> Si l'on anticipe sur les siecles à venir, & qu'on se représente la face de la Littérature, (...) on la trouvera partagée derechef en deux classes d'hommes. Les uns liront peu & s'abandonneront à des recherches qui seront nouvelles ou qu'ils prendront pour telles, (car si nous ignorons déjà une partie de ce qui est contenu dans tant de volumes publiés en toutes sortes de langues, nous saurons bien moins encore ce que renfermeront ces volumes augmentés d'un nombre d'autres cent fois, mille fois plus grand); les autres, manouvriers incapables de rien produire, s'occuperont à feuilleter jour & nuit ces volumes, & à en séparer ce qu'ils jugeront digne d'être recueilli & conservé. Cette prédiction ne commence-t-elle pas à s'accomplir? & plusieurs de nos littérateurs ne sont-ils pas déjà employés à réduire tous nos grands livres à de petits où l'on trouve encore beaucoup de superflu? Supposons maintenant leurs analyses bien faites, & distribuées sous la forme alphabetique en un nombre de volumes ordonnés par des hommes intelligens, & l'on aura les matériaux d'une *Encyclopédie*.[9]

> [If we consider the face of literature in the centuries to come, (...) we will see it divided between two groups of men. The first group will read little and devote themselves to new research, or research which they perceive to be so (because if we are now unaware of some of the material in all the volumes published in all languages, we will know even less of that in those of the future, a hundred times more numerous and a thousand times larger); the other group, simple workers, incapable of producing anything themselves, will busy themselves by leafing day and night through these same volumes, extracting everything they deem to be collected and conserved. Has this prediction not already begun to be fulfilled? and are not several current writers engaged in reducing all our large works into smaller ones, although in which there is still much that is superflu-

---

[8] 'Receuil' ('Collection'), (no author), *Encyclopédie*, vol. 8, p. 868. Chambers' original runs as follows: '*Common-places* are things of infinite service: they are a kind of Promptuaries or Storehouses, wherein to reposit the choicest and most valuable Parts of Authors, to be ready at hand when wanted.' Chambers, *Cyclopaedia*, vol. 1, p. 276.

[9] Diderot, 'Encyclopédie', p. 643.

ous? Let us suppose their analyses well done, and arranged in alphabetical form in volumes edited by intelligent men, and we will have the material for an Encyclopaedia.]

Yet turning to the *Encyclopédie*'s article on the use of commonplaces themselves – this time not adopted from Chambers but an original contribution by Louis de Jaucourt – we find quite a different assessment of them. De Jaucourt focuses his article on the use of commonplaces in oratory, and while he notes that such practices were encouraged by Demosthenes and Cicero, he questions their validity. Men who have a genuine talent for oratory, he argues, have no need for a storehouse of the words of others; and those who do call on such a resource are no more than 'esprits médiocres qui faisoient (...) une espece de trafic de l'éloquence' (mediocre minds who undertook merely to traffic eloquence) – the use of commonplaces in rhetoric is thus at best superfluous, and at worst a superficial veil seeking to cover a lack of real argument and meaning.[10]

How, then, to account for the seeming disagreement between Diderot and de Jaucourt on the value of commonplacing? Of course, and most obviously, we are dealing with the opinions of two different writers, and the *Encyclopédie* text offers many other examples of different articles offering different opinions on the same matter. However, this is not necessarily the case here: the articles of Diderot and de Jaucourt may be seen rather to embody the two faces of the *Encyclopédie*'s dual aim. In its content, the *Encyclopédie* seeks to encompass the entirety of human knowledge, and in such an undertaking incorporating the best work of others is at times a practical necessity; but for the *Encyclopédie*'s ultimate goal to be accomplished, that of changing the very way people think ('changer la façon commune de penser'), the real work has to be done by the reader. Rather than simply absorbing the knowledge of others, the *Encyclopédie*'s readers must learn to use their reason to compare, critique and combine what they find in its articles in order to form their own understanding of the world and the human experience.

It may be said, then, that it is not merely commonplacing, but the interrogation of such commonplacing that lies at the heart of the *Encyclopédie* project; and it is here that the more modern interpretation of the term enters our discussion. For the *Encyclopédie* aimed to present to its readers not just the best and the rarest of human achievement, but the mundane, the everyday, the 'commonplace' – and it was from the questioning and understanding of such lowly or seemingly self-evident aspects of human knowledge that true independent knowledge was to grow. As the quotation from

---

[10] De Jaucourt, 'Lieux-communs' ('Common-places'), *Encyclopédie*, vol. 9, p. 499.

Horace on the work's title page runs: '*Tantùm series juncturaque pollet, Tantùm de medio sumptis accedit honoris!*' (What grace may be added to commonplace matters by the power of order and connection!)[11] It is against this background, then, that I will now turn to examining the nature of the Enlightenment commonplace of 'common sense'.

Common sense and reason in the Encyclopédie

Despite the pre-eminence given to the concept of common sense by Descartes and d'Holbach, the term itself seems at first sight to have fallen out of favour with the Encyclopedists. Although there are in fact two articles dedicated to 'bon sens' in the *Encyclopédie* – Diderot's 'Bon-sens', and de Jaucourt's more aesthetically-focused 'Sens (le bon), Gout (le bon)' (Sense [good], Taste [good]), the term *bon sens* itself appears in only 197 of the *Encyclopédie*'s 72,000 articles – a relatively small number in comparison to the use of the term 'raison', which appears in several thousand *Encyclopédie* articles.[12] However, the spread of articles in which 'bon sens' occurs and the range of authors who employ it suggest that it nevertheless has a valuable role as a commonplace term in *Encyclopédie* discourse. Of the 24 Encyclopedists who make use of 'bon sens' in their articles, those who employ the term the most are Louis de Jaucourt, Diderot, d'Alembert and the abbé Edmé François Mallet. Other authors include the chemist Gabriel François Venel, Diderot's amanuensis Jacques André Naigeon and the professor of mathematics and military affairs Guillaume Le Blond; but the majority of other references come from the *Encylopédie*'s men of letters – César Chesneau Dumarsais, Jean-François Marmontel, Friedrich Melchior Grimm, Jacques Philippe Augustin Douchet, Nicolas Beauzée, and Voltaire,[13] suggesting that *bon sens* is a term used more frequently in literary and philosophical circles than in the 'new' areas of knowledge promoted by the *Encyclopédie* project – areas ranging from the new sciences such as chemistry and mineralogy to the wealth of practical arts and manufacturing procedures perceived by previous encyclopaedia compilers as unworthy of attention. Such a conclusion may be supported and further refined by a con-

---

[11] Cited in Furbank, *Diderot*, p. 83.

[12] Statistics gathered from the online edition of the *Encyclopédie* produced by ATLIF (Analyse et Traitement Informatique de la Langue Française) in collaboration with ARTFL (The Project for American and French Research on the Treasury of the French Language) at the University of Chicago (http://portail.atilf.fr/encyclopedie).

[13] Biographical details of *Encyclopédie* authors, as well as accounts of their involvement with the project, may be found in Kafker and Kafker, *The Encyclopedists as Individuals*.

sideration of the types of articles in which this term occurs and the classification given to each article in order to place it on the *Encyclopédie*'s schematic presentation of knowledge, the 'Système figuré des connoissances humaines'. Once again, while references to 'bon sens' may be found in articles relating to law, games and leisure, magic and music, the greatest number of uses of the term come in articles classified as philosophy, religion, morality and grammar, as well as 'belles-lettres' and medecine. In contrast, the much-vaunted presentation of the arts and sciences in the *Encyclopédie* contains remarkably few references to 'bon sens' – the term is found in only ten articles on the practical arts and in nine on the entire spectrum of the sciences. And while it is well known that the title and classification of an article are not necessarily completely reliable indicators of the content of the article itself, an examination of the contexts in which 'bon sens' is used does not materially change these initial conclusions – references to 'bon sens' in the context of religious belief and theological controversy become slightly more common, but philosophy and its history, medicine, literature and morality remain the key concerns of authors referring to man's common sense as an authority for their argument or a basis for the attack on a different point of view.

I would not wish to suggest, however, that common sense is sharply delineated from reason in the *Encyclopédie* – indeed, perhaps it is the nature of a commonplace term that as its meaning is widely and tacitly accepted rather than explicitly defined, there is a certain blurring of boundaries with other, related terms. It is true that in several *Encyclopédie* articles 'bon sens' is used as a synonymous term for raison – in 'Connoissance' (Knowledge), for example, the author contrasts 'les visions d'un enthousiaste' (the visions of an enthusiast) with 'les raisonnemens d'un homme de bon sens' (the reasoning of a man of good sense).[14] This sharing of a semantic field is doubled with the similar deployment of *bon sens* and *raison* in *Encyclopédie* discourse on key philosophe themes such as religion, politics, and the nature of human experience, and using common *Encyclopédie* strategies. One frequently-used strategy in the *Encyclopédie*'s treatment of religious issues, for example, was to expose them to a double-edged scrutiny under the light of reason on the one hand and the teachings of Christ on the other. Thus the obtuse doctrine of the Amsdorfiens that good works were not merely irrelevant to, but a positive obstacle to salvation, is criticised as a 'doctrine aussi contraire au bon sens qu'à l'Ecriture' (doctrine as opposed to common sense as it is to Scripture);[15] and in 'Pères de l'Eglise' (Patriarchs) de Jau-

---

[14] 'Connoissance' ('Knowledge'), (unsigned), *Encyclopédie,* vol. 3, p. 895.
[15] Mallet, abbé Edme-François, 'Amsdorfiens' ('Amsdorfians'), *Encyclopédie*, vol. 1, p. 383. The Amsdorfians were a sixteenth-century Protestant sect named after its

court continues his campaign for tolerance with an attack on Saint Augustine using a strikingly similar argument:

> Mais son opinion sur la persécution pour cause de religion, est d'autant plus inexcusable qu'il avoit été d'abord dans des sentimens de douceur & de charité. Il commenca par l'*esprit* & finit par la *chair*. Il osa le premier établir l'intolérance civile, maxime contraire à l'Evangile, à toutes les lumieres du bon sens, à l'équité naturelle, à la charité, à la bonne politique.[16]

> [However, his opinion on persecution in the name of religion is all the more inexcusable given his earlier emphasis on gentleness and charity. He began with the *soul*, and finished with the *flesh*. He was the first to dare to establish the principle of civil intolerance, a principle opposed to Scripture, to all the promptings of common sense, to natural equity, to charity, to good practice.]

Yet while Encyclopedists in the above examples seem to suggest that Biblical teachings and common sense are of equal weight and support the same conclusions, it is clear from Diderot's article 'Raison' where the supreme guarantee of truth lies:

> Il est donc inutile de presser comme articles de foi des propositions contraires à la perception claire que nous avons de la convenance ou de la disconvenance de nos idées. Par conséquent, dans toutes les choses dont nous avons une idée nette & distincte, la *raison* est le vrai juge compétent; & quoique la révélation en s'accordant avec elle puisse confirmer ces décisions, elle ne sauroit pourtant dans de tels cas invalider ses decrets; & par-tout où nous avons une décision claire & évidente de la *raison*, nous ne pouvons être obligés d'y renoncer pour embrasser l'opinion contraire, sous prétexte que c'est une matiere de foi. La raison de cela, c'est que nous sommes hommes avant que d'être chrétiens.[17]

> [It is therefore pointless to insist upon as articles of faith those propositions opposed to the clear perception we have of the fitness or unfitness of our ideas. Consequently, in all matter of which we have a clear and distinct understanding, *reason* is the true competent judge; and although revelation in according with *reason* may confirm its decisions, revelation can never invalidate it; and wherever we have a clear and evident decision based on *reason* we can never be obliged to renounce it in favour of the opposite position on the pretext that is

---

founder, the bishop Nikolaus von Amsdorf.

[16] De Jaucourt, Louis, 'Pères de l'Eglise' (Patriarchs'), *Encyclopédie*, vol. 12, p. 346.

[17] [Diderot], 'Raison' ('Reason'), *Encyclopédie*, vol. 13, p. 774.

it a matter of faith. The reason for this is that we are men before we are Christians.]

It is independent, rational human thought, and not authority (Scriptural or otherwise), which is the source of truth in all human endeavours: 'Qu'importe que d'autres ayent pensé de même, ou autrement que nous, pourvu que nous pensions juste, selon les regles du bon sens, & conformément à la vérité?' states the anonymous author of 'Autorité', (What does it matter whether others have thought the same as us or not, as long as we have reasoned soundly, following the rules of common sense, and in accordance with the truth?) and a concrete example of this is given in Diderot's defence of the painter Chardin's opinion of copies: 'On lui objecta des autorités, il n'en fut point ébranlé; il opposa la raison et le bon sens aux témoignages & aux faits prétendus' (People countered with the arguments of other experts; he was not disturbed by this, but opposed his reason and common sense to accounts and supposed facts).[18]

The contrast between reason and common sense on the one hand, and the accounts and claims of other people on the other, suggests a further element of reason and common sense's shared claim to truth – their basis in personal, lived experience. To some extent this may be seen to stem from the empirical and sensationalist epistemology of John Locke and, in France, Etienne Bonnot de Condillac. According to Locke and Condillac (and in opposition to Descartes' claim that we are born with a number of innate ideas already contained in the mind), at birth our mind is a *tabula rasa* and all our knowledge derives from our sense impressions and the action of our reason upon these impressions. Similarly, if we are 'hommes avant que d'être chrétiens', true knowledge comes from our lived human experience rather than the abstract principles of organised religion. Thus, common sense is frequently linked with experience and the two are offered as a necessary complement to written knowledge, even to that offered by the *Encyclopédie* to its readers. As de Jaucourt states in 'Ouvrage' (Work), 'On doit faire grand cas des *ouvrages* qui nous développent d'une main savante, les principes d'un art ou d'une science; mais c'est au bon sens & à l'expérience à déterminer l'application de ces mêmes principes'.[19] (We should applaud those *works* which expertly demonstrate the principles of an art or a science; but it is up to common sense and experience to establish the application of these same principles.) And such a reliance on the reader's own good sense to complete the work of the text (and to overcome its flaws) is

---

[18] 'Autorité' (Authority'), (unsigned), *Encyclopédie*, I, p. 900; Diderot, 'Copie', *Encyclopédie*, vol. 4, p. 177.

[19] De Jaucourt, 'Ouvrage' ('Work'), *Encyclopédie*, vol. 11, p. 722.

visible even with regard to the *Encyclopédie* text itself, in d'Alembert's discussion of terms not included in this compendium of all human knowledge:

> Il y a des notions qui sont communes à presque tous les hommes, & qu'ils ont dans l'esprit avec plus de clarté qu'elles n'en peuvent recevoir du discours. Il y a aussi des objets si familiers, qu'il seroit ridicule d'en faire des figures. Les Arts en offrent d'autres si composés, qu'on les représenteroit inutilement. Dans les deux premiers cas, nous avons supposé que le lecteur n'étoit pas entierement dénué de bon sens & d'expérience; & dans le dernier, nous renvoyons à l'objet même.[20]

> [Some notions are common to almost all men, and which they hold in their minds with more clarity than they could receive from argument. Some objects are so familiar, that it would be ridiculous to draw diagrams of them. The practical arts use other objects so complex that it would be pointless to draw them. In the two former cases, we have assumed that the reader is not entirely devoid of common sense and experience; and in the latter, we refer him to the object itself.]

The identity of 'bon sens'

While reason and common sense may be similar, however, they are not one and the same. Neither of the articles 'Raison' and 'Bon Sens' define one term as synonymous with the other. Indeed, a certain hierarchical relationship may be observed between *raison, bon sens* and *esprit,* as for example in de Jaucourt's description of one Mlle de Chatillon in 'Portrait' as a woman who 'avoit ordinairement de l'esprit, rarement du bons sens, jamais de la raison' (had normally a lively mind, rarely any common sense, and never any reason), and in Mallet's alignment, in 'Epigramme' of 'les discours d'un homme de bon sens' (the arguments of a man of common sense) with 'un enfant qui a de l'esprit' (a child with a lively mind).[21] This seemingly lower status accorded to common sense may also be seen from the context of d'Holbach's work of 1772, *Bon Sens* being essentially a shortened, simplified version of the earlier *Système de la nature* (1770). The distinction drawn by Mallet above recurs in numerous other *Encyclopédie* articles: while reason may lead one to 'philosophie', common sense functions as the basic capacity by which man is made man. When lost, he is little

---

[20] D'Alembert, 'Discours Préliminaire' ('Preliminary Discourse'), *Encyclopédie*, vol. 1, p. xl.
[21] De Jaucourt, 'Portrait', *Encyclopédie*, vol. 13, p. 155; Mallet, 'Epigramme', *Encyclopédie*, vol. 5, p. 793.

more than a machine – 'Otez à l'homme le *bon-sens*, & vous le réduirez à la qualité d'automate ou d'enfant' (Take away a man's common sense and you make him in essence an automaton or an infant), states Diderot in 'Bon sens', or enters the liminal zone of the mad, the drunk and the monstrous.[22] Similarly, when a man falls into a coma, his recovery is marked by the transition from a purely mechanically-functioning state to the point at which he recovers the use of his *bon sens*.[23] Such somewhat anecdotal accounts are supported, moreover, by several articles dealing with jurisprudence and ecclesiastical law: a recurrent condition for the revocation of vows and for the invalidity of wills, for example, is the absence of the novice's or testate's common sense.[24] What emerges from all these accounts is that common sense is an absolute quality: it may be possessed, used, or lost, but it cannot be abused or perverted.

It is this essential quality of common sense which distinguishes it from reason and philosophy. For the Encyclopedists, common sense functions as the measure by which to judge the philosophies of the past and the good or bad use of reason. Indeed, such an interpretation is supported by the 1762 *Dictionnaire de l'Académie française*'s entry on reason: 'Raison se prend aussi quelquefois pour Le bon sens, le droit usage de la raison'.[25] ('Reason is also sometimes understood as common sense, the right use of reason'). Diderot's criticism of the dialectics of Eclecticism, for example, claims that 'ce sont des idées aristotéliques si quintessenciées & si rafinées, que le bon sens s'en est évaporé, & qu'on se trouve à tout moment sur les confins du verbiage' (these aristotelian ideas are so refined that all common sense has

---

[22] 'Les hommes qui ont plus d'imagination que de bon-sens, sont esclaves de milles fantaisies' ('Men who have more imagination than common sense are enslaved to a thousand fantasies'), 'Fantaisie' (Fantasy'), (unsigned), *Encyclopédie*, vol. 6, p. 403; 'un homme yvre (...) descendit dans un fleuve pour se laver; il fut si vivement saisi par la fraicheur subite de l'eau, qu'il rentra tout-de-suite dans son bon sens' (a drunk man got into a river to was himself; he was so shocked by the sudden chill of the water, that he was at once restored to common sense), Jean-Joseph Menuret de Chambaud, 'Yvresse' ('Drunkenness'), *Encyclopédie*, vol. 17, p.683; 'après qu'ils ont passé la nuit dans cet état [de lycanthropie], ils retournent au point du jour chez eux, & reprennent leur bon sens' (after having spend the night in this state [of lycanthropy], they returned at daybreak to their homes and their good sense'), 'Lycanthropie' ('Lycanthropy'), (unsigned), *Encyclopédie*, vol. 9, p. 772.

[23] Diderot, 'Assoupissement' ('Drowsiness'), *Encyclopédie*, vol. 1, p. 773.

[24] De Jaucourt, 'Inofficiosité' ('Void'), *Encyclopédie*, vol. 8, p. 772; 'Invalide' ('Invalid'), [unsigned], *Encyclopédie*, vol. 8, pp. 846-47; Antoine-Gaspard Boucher d'Argis, 'Profession en religion' ('Religious vow'), *Encyclopédie*, vol. 13, p. 426; *idem*, 'Reclamation' ('Objection'), *Encyclopédie*, vol. 13, p. 855; *idem*, 'Testament' ('Will'), *Encyclopédie*, vol. 16, p. 190.

[25] *Dictionnaire de l'Académie française* , p. 528.

evaporated from them, and one is constantly lost in verbiage), and he goes on to widen this criticism out to a general conclusion that 'au reste, on est presque sûr d'en venir-là toutes les fois qu'on ne mettra aucune sobriété dans l'argumentation, & qu'on la poussera jusqu'où elle peut aller' (in any case, one is almost certain to reach this point when there is no sobriety in argumentation, and when the argument is pushed as far as it may go).[26] Similarly, the author of 'Hippocratisme' notes in praise of Hippocrates, that

> ce qui est très-remarquable, ni ses raisonnemens, ni ses observations, ni ses remedes n'ont pas la moindre teinture de cette superstition philosophique qui régnoit de son tems: son bon sens la lui fit mépriser, & lui fit sentir la nécessité d'ôter l'exercice de l'art de guérir des mains de ceux qui n'étoient que philosophes; à quoi il travailla de tout son pouvoir & avec succès: ce qui a fait dire qu'il avoit séparé la Medecine de la Philosophie, dont en effet il ne retint que ce qui pouvoit être d'une utilité réelle; c'est-à-dire qu'il joignit avec sagesse le raisonnement à l'expérience, en prenant toûjours celle-ci pour principe; ce qu'aucun médecin n'avoit fait avant lui.[27]

> [What is remarkable is that neither his reasoning, nor his observations, nor his remedies, are in the least tainted by that philosophical superstition which reigned at the time; his common sense led him to mistrust it, and made him feel the necessity of removing the art of healing from the hands of those who were merely philosophers; this is what he worked at with all his might and with some success; and therefore it was said that he had separated Medicine from Philosophy, from which he only retained that which had a real utility; that is to say, he wisely joined reason to experience, always taking the latter as his guiding principle, which no other physician had done before him.]

In contrast to the convoluted reasoning and superstitious philosophies mentioned above, common sense is shown to be at the origin of the revolution in philosophy brought about by Descartes:

> Le nouveau philosophe posant pour principe fondamental qu'on ne devoit admettre aucun terme auquel ne répondît une notion claire ou qui ne fût résoluble par sa définition en idées simples & claires, cet arrêt, émané du bon sens, proscrivit tous les termes ontologiques alors usités.[28]

---

[26] Diderot, 'Eclectisme' ('Eclecticism'), *Encyclopédie*, vol. 5, p. 285.

[27] 'Hippocratisme' ('Hippocraticism'), (unsigned), *Encyclopédie*, vol. 8, p. 211.

[28] 'Ontologie' ('Ontology'), (unsigned), *Encyclopédie*, vol. 11, p. 486.

[The new philosopher taking as his fundamental principle that one should not
accept any term to which did not correspond a clear notion, or which was not to
be resolved into clear and simple ideas, this edict, based in common sense, pro-
scribed all the ontological terms then in use.]

'Bon sens' is not used merely to judge the philosophies of the past,
however; rather, it can be used to delineate 'proper' Enlightenment philosophy from that which has lost its grounding in empirical reality, or, indeed, to distinguish the true *philosophe* from other claimants to the title.
Diderot's *Lettre sur les aveugles* of 1748 (elements of which were later
quoted by d'Alembert in his article 'Aveugle', [Blind]) takes as its starting-
point the experiment by René-Antoine Ferchault de Réaumur to remove the
cataracts from a patient blind from birth. Effectively barred from this experiment by lack of a personal invitation, and almost certainly piqued by
Réaumur's ungracious insistence on secrecy, Diderot decides to undertake
his own research by visiting a man blind from birth and questioning him
himself, commenting that 'On cherche à restituer la vûe à des aveugles nés;
mais si l'on y regardait de plus près, on trouverait, je crois, qu'il y a bien
autant à profiter pour a philosophie, en questionnant un *aveugle* de bon
sens' (Attempts have been made to restore sight to those blind from birth;
but if we were to look more closely, we would find, I believe, that philosophy has as much to gain by questioning a blind man in possession of common sense).[29] Common sense and lived experience are evidently as valid a
foundation for knowledge as even Enlightenment science. Moreover, if we
return to the issue of the categorization of articles in which 'bon sens' is
mentioned in the *Encyclopédie*, it may seem at first that there is somewhat
of a contradiction in that 'bon sens' – denoting a basic, functional, non-
elevated means of thinking – is, as a term, found predominantly within the
fields of literature, philosophy and religion rather than in the field of the
functional, everyday, practical arts. However, this may in fact be seen as
one further example of the use of common sense as an idea in the regulation
of philosophy and the liberal arts: in the *Encyclopédie*'s intention to rede-
fine what was counted as 'worthy' knowledge and to correct the imbalance
between the highly regarded sciences and liberal arts on the one hand, and
the practical arts on the other, the latter are raised through the language of
their articles to the field of science and 'raison', while 'bon sens' is called
in to root the excesses of philosophical and theological speculation back to
the essentialities of the human condition.

---

[29] Diderot, *Lettre sur les aveugles*, p. 65.

Common sense and its moral attributes

Yet it is not just in the realm of knowledge that common sense plays an important role. As a natural, innate faculty, and following the Enlightenment's concern for a morality grounded in nature and human experience rather than in religious principle, common sense also acts as an arbiter of morality. Numerous articles, in their praise of individuals, list common sense alongside other virtues: similarly, the origin of the Algerian sovereign prince, or *dey*, according to Mallet, was in elected from among the militia of 'un homme de bon sens, de bonnes moeurs, de courage, & d'expérience, afin de les gouverner sous le nom de *dey*' (a man of good sense, good morals, courage, and experience, in order to govern as a *dey*).[30] More specifically, common sense is often called upon as a guard against vices: flattery is described as 'insupportable au bon sens' (unbearable for those of common sense), and common sense, together with reason and an awareness of human weakness and human equality, is said to guard against pride.[31]

One corollary of the emphasis on common sense as a natural, essential capacity, is a tendency to align it with the 'natural' and 'unsophisticated' lower classes in opposition to the over-refined civilities and corrupting 'civilisation' of upper reaches of society. One example of this comes in de Jaucourt's article 'Sobriété':

> Comme ami de Mecene, [Horace] n'osoit pas louer directement la *sobriété* à la cour d'Auguste; mais il en fait l'éloge dans ses écrits d'une maniere plus fine & plus persuasive, que s'il eût traité son sujet en moraliste. Il dit que la *sobriéte* (…) elle procure de grands avantages à l'esprit & au corps. Ces propositions sont d'une vérité sensible; mais le poëte n'a garde de les debiter lui-même. Il les met dans la bouche d'un homme de province, plein de bon sens, qui sans sortir de son caractere, & sans dogmatiser, débite ses réflexions judicieuses, avec une naiveté qui les fait aimer. Je prie le lecteur de l'écouter, (...) 'Mes amis, la *sobriété* n'est point une petite vertu. Ce n'est pas moi qui le dis, c'est Ofellus, c'est un campagnard sans étude, à qui un bon sens naturel tient lieu de toute philosophie & de toute littérature.'[32]

> [As a friend of Maecenas, [Horace] did not dare to praise outright the *sobriety* of the Augustan court; but he does so in a more delicate and persuasive manner in his writings, than if he had treated the subject as a moralist. He says that *so-*

---

[30] Mallet, 'Dey' ('Dey'), *Encyclopédie*, vol. 4, p. 925.
[31] 'Flaterie' ('Flattery'), (unsigned), *Encyclopédie*, vol. 6, p. 844; De Jaucourt, 'Orgeuil' ('Pride'), *Encyclopédie*, vol 11, p. 641.
[32] De Jaucourt, 'Sobriété' ('Sobriety'), *Encyclopédie*, vol. 15, p. 248.

briety (...) procures great advantages for the mind and body. The truth of this is evident; but the poet took care not to state them directly. He put these truths in the mouth of a country man, full of common sense, and who, without departing from his natural character, and without preaching, utters his reflections with an engaging naivety. I ask the reader to listen to his words (...) 'My friends, sobriety is not a minor virtue. But it is not I who tells you this, rather Ofellus, a countryman without refinement, in whom natural common sense takes the place of all philosophy and all literature.']

Here, then, are the various previously-mentioned elements of common sense brought together in a single example: epistemologically, the 'naturel' of common sense is a replacement for taught philosophy; socially, the campagnard's common sense is opposed to the empty intellectual sophistication of the court, and the morality inspired by this common sense is brought into stark contrast with the vices inherent in court life.

How legitimate is it, then, to see a social stratification in the use of 'bon sens' and 'raison'? Certainly, philosophe anxiety about the 'peuple''s actual ability to correctly employ reason and understand the ideas of the philosophes has been well documented by modern Enlightenment scholars,[33] and while de Jaucourt praises the simple, practical lifestyle of the *peuple*, Diderot comments in 'Misere' that 'Le petit peuple est d'une stupidité incroyable' (The lowest classes are incredibly stupid).[34] Is it possible, then, to see reason and philosophy as the province of the educated and comfortable, and common sense as the consolation prize for the 'peuple', enough to distinguish them from animals and automata, and to endow them with a simple virtue, but not enough to threaten the intellectual capacity of the philosophes? I would argue, in fact, that this is not the case. Although it is tempting to join an epistemological hierarchy with a social one, this is not borne out within the *Encyclopédie* text. For while common sense may be aligned with the lower classes, it is certainly not restricted to them, and indeed, it is an essential element in 'Syllogisme's praise of one of France's greatest kings: 'Henri IV a été un des plus grands princes qu'il y ait eu. Il avoit autant de prudence, de bon sens & de justesse d'esprit, qu'il avoit de valeur' (Henri IV was one of France's greatest princes. He had as much prudence, common sense and sound judgement as he had valour).[35]

---

[33] See for example Payne, *The Philosophes and the Peuple*; Koepp, 'Making Money', pp. 99-118.

[34] De Jaucourt, 'Peuple' ('People'), *Encyclopédie*, vol. 12, pp. 475-77 ; [Diderot], 'Misere' ('Misery'), *Encyclopédie*, vol. 10, p. 575.

[35] 'Syllogisme' ('Syllogism'), (unsigned), *Encyclopédie*, vol. 15, p. 723.

Conclusion

What, then, to make of 'bon sens' as a commonplace term? How common-place is common sense? Like many commonplaces, 'bon sens's' seemingly self-evident, widely-recognised meaning has, upon interrogation, revealed a number of unspoken assumptions which underpin its broader understand-ing. And this may be seen to be doubly the case for 'bon sens' – a widely-used term in itself, it also stands for that instinctive yet empirical access to understanding which is opposed by its very nature to lengthy and detailed analysis. Nevertheless, its use in the various contexts discussed in the course of this article has revealed, on the one hand, Enlightenment concerns about some of the period's most fundamental concepts – not only epistemo-logical, but also philosophical, moral and social – and, on the other, its own role as a touchstone of human identity and possibility. Indeed, as an innate human quality, common sense is a constant throughout human history, and even while Encyclopédists at times display concern about the continued and ultimate perfection of humanity, it is common sense which guards against mankind's ultimate fall into superstition and vice: 'Les mêmes folies sem-blent destinées à reparoître de tems en tems sur la scene du monde, mais aussi le bon sens en est le même dans tous les tems' (The same mistakes seem destined to repeat themselves from time to time across the world, but common sense is also the same in all ages).[36] If the *Encyclopédie*'s ultimate goal, and by extension that of the Enlightenment, is to enlighten successive generations '[afin] que nos neveux, devenant plus instruits, deviennent en même tems plus vertueux et plus heureux' (in order that our descendants, in becoming more knowledgeable, become also happier and more virtuous), then common sense, at the origin of knowledge and virtue, is key to the Enlightenment project itself.

---

[36] De Jaucourt, 'Schisme des Grecs' ('Greek Schism'), *Encyclopédie*, vol. 14, p. 767.

THE COMMONPLACE OF THEATRE AS A SCHOOL OF VIRTUE: THE CASE OF VOLTAIRE'S *TANCRÈDE* (1760)

Thomas Wynn

Ann Moss argues that the decline of the commonplace-book at the end of the seventeenth century derives in part from 'a social code of polite behaviour' and 'a consensual aesthetic of good taste which were inimical to its primary qualities of abundance and display'. The book's 'open-ended acceptance of variety and self-contradiction' was 'a potential irritant to a political culture centred on uniformity'.[1] Evidence indicates, however, that in the eighteenth century it is as a result of a very different social code of contestation, liveliness and novelty that such a book's contents degenerate into platitudes. In much the same terms as those used by Moss, Voltaire describes the process by which once authoritative knowledge is rendered banal:

> Vous aurez toujours en France des esprits cultivés et des talents. Mais tout étant devenu lieu commun, tout étant problématique à force d'être discuté, l'extrême abondance et la satiété ayant pris la place de l'indigence où nous étions avant le grand siècle, le dégoût du public succédant à cette ardeur qui nous animait du temps des grands hommes: la multitude des journaux et brochures et des dictionnaires satiriques occupant le loisir de ceux qui pourraient s'instruire dans quelques bons livres utiles, il est fort à craindre que le goût ne reste que chez un petit nombre d'esprits cultivés, et que les arts ne tombent chez la nation.[2]

> [You will always have cultured minds and talents in France. But everything has become commonplace, everything is problematic for having been discussed, extreme abundance and satiation have taken the place of the poverty in which we found ourselves before the *grand siècle*, the public's disgust has taken the place of the ardour which drove us in the time of great men: the multitude of newspapers and brochures and satirical dictionaries now occupy the leisure of those who could educate themselves with some good, useful books; and so it is greatly to be feared that taste remains only amongst a small number of cultured minds, and that the arts collapse in the nation.]

---

[1] Moss, *Printed Commonplace-Books*, pp. 275-276.
[2] Voltaire, the preface to *Les Lois de Minos* (1773), ed. S. Davies, in *The Complete Works of Voltaire*, vol. 73, p. 80.

It is precisely the abundance of voiced opinion and textual material within the public realm – that space of debate and re-evaluation – that prevents an effective consensus as to what constitutes good taste, such as was once evidenced in printed matter. In this age of conversation, familiarity with and exposure to previously canonical texts appear to have contributed to the sapping of the authority of such works, as the academician Antoine-Léonard Thomas signals in 1773:

> Notre siècle est généralement tourné vers l'esprit de discussion; et ce genre d'esprit, occupé sans cesse à comparer des idées, doit nuire un peu à la vivacité des sentiments. D'ailleurs, il faut des choses nouvelles pour ébranler l'imagination; et presque tous les grands tableaux ont été épuisés par les orateurs de tous les siècles. Ce qui eût produit autrefois un grand effet, n'est plus aujourd'hui que lieu commun.[3]

> [Our century is generally turned towards a spirit of discussion; and this kind of spirit, endlessly busy with comparing ideas, must somewhat harm the vivacity of feelings. Besides, new things are needed to shake the imagination; and almost all the great tableaux have been exhausted by orators throughout the centuries. What would have produced a great effect in the past, is now no more than commonplace.]

The eighteenth-century mind thus appears to consider commonplace that which is trivial, banal and unremarkable.[4] According to the *Encyclopédie* a commonplace can prettify or make a given subject more forceful,[5] and while such a figure of speech may yet retain a persuasive power, the addresser and the addressee do not invest it with equal conviction. Letter 125 of Laclos's *Les Liaisons Dangereuses* (1782) provides a good example of this ironic discrepancy, as does Loaisel de Tréogate's novel *Dolbreuse* (1783), in which the hero cynically and successfully recites commonplaces:

> Je la remerciai par ces lieux communs de phrases et de paroles obligeantes que la bouche adresse, en même temps que le cœur et les yeux prodiguent les témoignages du plus profond mépris (…).[6]

---

[3] Thomas, *Essai sur les éloges*, vol. 2, p. 218.
[4] Moss, *Printed Commonplace-Books*, p. 2.
[5] Diderot and d'Alembert, eds, *Encyclopédie, ou Dictionnaire raisonné*, vol. 9, p. 499 (version from 1751-1765).
[6] Loaisel de Tréogate, *Dolbreuse*, vol. 1, p. 1.

[I thanked her with those commonplace phrases and obliging words that the mouth utters, at the same time that the heart and the eyes lavishly express the deepest contempt.]

And in Prévost's *Manon Lescaut* (1731), the heroine is swayed by the money not the banal words contained with the letter sent by her rich lover:

> Outre les lieux communs de tendresse, [la lettre] elle contenait le détail des promesses de mon rival. Il ne bornait point sa dépense.[7]

[Beside the commonplaces of tenderness, the letter detailed the promises of my rival. He did not limit his expenditure.]

Despite its likely rhetorical ineffectiveness, the formulaic commonplace still performs a socially useful function, as evidenced in the novel *Margot la ravaudeuse* (1748):

> Nous nous saluâmes réciproquement, et liâmes conversation par les lieux communs ordinaires des gens qui ont envie de jaser, quoiqu'ils n'aient rien à se dire.[8]

[We greeted each other, and joined in conversation through the ordinary commonplaces of people who want to chat, even though they have nothing to say to each other.]

Commonplaces similarly facilitate social intercourse, albeit briefly, in Mme Riccoboni's *Lettres d'Adélaïde de Dammartin* (1767), when the heroine and the Marquis de Montalais are left troubled and speechless when reunited:

> Les lieux communs viennent à notre aide, s'épuisent, se tarissent; la conversation languit.[9]

[Commonplaces come to our aid, but peter out and dry up; the conversation languishes.]

These examples indicate that in the eighteenth century the commonplace has a conflicted relationship with the public sphere, a realm that debases a

---

[7] Prévost d'Exiles, *Histoire du chevalier*, p. 131.
[8] Fougeret de Montbron, *Margot la ravaudeuse*, p. 9.
[9] Riccoboni, *Lettres d'Adélaïde de Dammartin*, vol. 2, p. 19.

once prized insight, and is nonetheless sustained and eased by the exchange of that same platitude.

This article examines how one particular commonplace hinges on precisely that duality of banality and social cohesion, how it retains or rather attains new relevance, and what the limits are to its effectiveness as a tool intended 'to promote and reinforce culturally sanctioned modes of thought' during a period characterized by debate and contestation.[10] This commonplace is that of the theatre as a school of virtue, a metaphor that positions the playhouse as a secular place of social, moral and increasingly patriotic improvement. Moreover, this commonplace generally assumes the theatre itself to be a *common place*, or the site of communion and shared experiences, and thereby reflects the Cartesian insistence that knowledge is acquired through observation and experience of the material world. This redoubled commonplace will be examined primarily with reference to Voltaire's tragedy *Tancrède*; first publicly staged at the Comédie-Française on 3 September 1760, it was one of the century's greatest theatrical successes, particularly in the provinces, where it was the dramatist's most performed play.[11] This aesthetically experimental work was created at a time when the theatre as an institution was under renewed attack, when the *philosophes*' cause was suffering at the hands of their newly confident opponents, and when French national identity was bruised by England's successes in the Seven Years War. At this difficult time *Tancrède* represents Voltaire's declaration of faith in theatre, and sees him make full and spectacular use of the theatrical apparatus so as to create a didactic and nationalistic work of especial emotional and moral force. Moreover, Voltaire's massive investment in the theatre as a common place of shared experience, signals his commitment to the commonplace that such a space is a school of virtue, particularly of national virtues.

While the theatre audience has been considered a key example in the elaboration of the public realm and of national identity in eighteenth-century France,[12] Benedict Anderson has argued that the nation, born at this time, is a concept partly founded on shared texts, and that the novel and the newspaper 'provided the technical means for "re-presenting" the *kind* of imagined community that is the nation'.[13] Richard Wittman similarly proposes that 'between the end of the seventeenth century and the middle of the eighteenth, literate people experienced their most prestigious social attach-

---

[10] Moss, 'Power and Persuasion', 1.

[11] Fuchs, *La Vie théâtrale*, pp. 140-142.

[12] Ravel, *The Contested Parterre*; Friedland, *Political Actors*; Maslan, *Revolutionary Acts*.

[13] Anderson, *Imagined Communities*, p. 25. Emphasis in original.

ments more and more in relation to despatialized communities of discourse (nation, public), constituted principally by the circulation of printed matter'.[14] *Tancrède*'s performance and reception history illuminates the tensions between what might be termed the '*parterre*-model' and the '*cabinet*-model' of nation formation.[15] The move from the assembled audience within the playhouse to a diffuse community of readers beyond that place has significant implications for a work's moral and political ambitions, given that *Tancrède*'s avowed aim to stage inspirational French characters is predicated on the group effect realized within the theatre. It may thus be argued that a theatrical rather than lectorial experience is privileged, since disparate and despatialized readers are less likely to produce this effect. As Voltaire notes:

Le théâtre instruit mieux que ne fait un gros livre. [16]

[The theatre is a better teacher than a big book.]

'Un sujet si rebattu': examples of the commonplace

Deriving in part from Horace's recommendation that poets should combine 'the giving of pleasure with some useful precepts for life',[17] the commonplace of the theatre as a school of virtue recurs frequently in the early modern period. In the face of ecclesiastical opposition to the theatre,[18] it asserts the institution's credentials as a positive influence on the public, although it could be inverted by the anti-theatrical writers as a school of vice; this is a commonplace with a ritualised character rather than a self-evident veracity. The abbé d'Aubignac, for example, declares in the *Pratique du théâtre* (1657) that one may call the theatre 'l'école du peuple',[19] and in the preface to *Phèdre* (1677) Racine writes that ancient theatre was 'une école où la vertu n'était pas moins enseignée que dans les écoles des philosophes' (a school where virtue was taught no less than in the philosophers' schools).[20] Pierre Nicole, on the contrary, states in the *Traité de la comédie* (1667) that

---

[14] Wittman, *Architecture, Print Culture, and the Public*, p. 92.

[15] There is also the 'coulisses-model', which is more attentive to the realia of distracted and social spectatorship, and for which the play constitutes a minor if not incidental element of the overall playhouse experience.

[16] Voltaire, 'Les Trois manières', in: *Œuvres completes*, vol. 10, p. 30.

[17] Horace, *On the Art of Poetry*, p. 90.

[18] Phillips, *The Theatre and its Critics*.

[19] Aubignac, *La Pratique du théâtre*, p. 8.

[20] Racine, *Œuvres complètes*, p. 765.

theatre is by its very nature a school of vice,[21] a charge that François Caffaro refuted in 1694, arguing that the institution was less the school of vice than that of virtue.[22] Caffaro's *Lettre* prompted Bossuet's *Maximes et réflexions sur la comédie* (also 1694), in which he denies the theatre any pedagogical utility, in part due to the pernicious group effect that takes hold of the audience:

> Il suffit d'avoir observé ce qu'il y a de malignité spéciale dans les assemblées, où comme on veut contenter la multitude, dont la plus grande partie est livrée aux sens, on se propose toujours d'en flatter les inclinations par quelques endroits: tout le théâtre applaudit quand on les trouve; on se fait comme un point d'honneur de sentir ce qui doit toucher, et on croirait troubler la fête, si on n'était enchanté avec toute la compagnie. Ainsi, outre les autres inconvénients des assemblées de plaisir, on s'excite et on s'autorise, pour ainsi dire, les uns les autres par le concours des acclamations et des applaudissements, et l'air même qu'on y respire est plus malin.[23]

> [It is sufficient to have observed that what is especially malignant in these gatherings where, as the intention is to please the multitude, whose greater part is given over to the senses, the intention is always to flatter its inclinations through some parts: the whole theatre applauds when those are found; it is like a point of honour to feel what must be touching, and one would believe oneself to be disrupting the festivities if one were not enchanted along with the whole company. Thus, besides the other drawbacks of gatherings founded on pleasure, people get excited and allow themselves free rein, so to speak, through the combination of acclamations and applause, and the very air that one breathes there is more malignant.]

Bossuet's contention that the group effect, whereby physical proximity stimulates spectators to experience a unified reaction, is necessarily inimical to theatre's pedagogical benefit, is, as we shall see, contrary to the model of spectatorship elaborated by Diderot and Voltaire.

Eighteenth-century writers continue to employ this commonplace, although they rarely interrogate its assumptions, perhaps thereby implying that it is an obligatory banality to include within the argument, even though the Church was now less vocal in its opposition.[24] On 6 August 1726 the ballet *L'homme instruit par le spectacle, ou le Théâtre changé en école de*

---

[21] Nicole, *Traité de la comédie*, pp. 13-111.
[22] Caffaro, *Lettre d'un théologien*, vol. 1, p. 41.
[23] Bossuet, *Maximes et réflexions sur la comédie*, pp. 39-40.
[24] Barras, *The Stage Controversy*, p. 186.

vertu was performed at Louis-le-Grand; the prologue, written by the Jesuit Charles Porée, states that this work aims not to justify theatre against often deserved reproaches, but to show that tragedy, comedy, ballet and opera can be 'instructions aussi utiles qu'agréables' (lessons as useful as they are pleasant);[25] Porée gave a speech on the same subject on 13 March 1733.[26] Luigi Riccoboni states in 1743 that his only aim is to ennoble and render useful an amusement that might one day become 'une école de vertu'.[27] Voltaire returns to this commonplace on several occasions. For example, he writes in the *Lettre à un premier commis* (1733) that he regards tragedy and comedy as lessons of virtue, reason and seemliness, and that Corneille and Molière established schools of magnanimity and civil life respectively.[28] In the *Dissertation sur la tragédie ancienne et moderne* (1748), he describes true tragedy as an 'école de vertu';[29] and in his tale *Le Monde comme il va* (also 1748), the character Babouc mistakes actors for preachers, and is moved to tears by a theatrical performance.[30] According to one contemporary, the debate over the morality of the theatre prompted few new ideas:

> Il y a longtemps, Monsieur, que l'on écrit pour et contre les spectacles, et je doute qu'on puisse rien dire de nouveau sur un sujet si rebattu.[31]

> [People have been writing for a long time, Monsieur, for and against plays, and I doubt that anything new can be said on such a hackneyed subject.]

Nonetheless, the commonplace resurfaces throughout the century in works by, for instance, Fénouillot de Falbaire, Beaumarchais, Cailhava d'Estendoux, and even Sade.[32] These and other French writers insist that their national theatre (both the building and the canon of works) should form a space in which their compatriots might recognize and repeat appro-

---

[25] Porée, *L'homme instruit par le spectacle*, p. 2; for lengthy extracts, see *Mercure de France*, August 1726, pp.1895-1904.

[26] The speech was given in Latin, and is reproduced alongside J. Lockman's English translation, *An Oration in which an Enquiry is made.*

[27] Riccoboni, *De la réformation du théâtre*, p. ix.

[28] Voltaire, *Lettre à un premier commis*, ed. R. Rétat, in *The Complete Works*, vol. 9, p. 321.

[29] Voltaire, 'Dissertation sur la tragédie ancienne et moderne', preface to Sémiramis, ed. R. Niklaus, in: *The Complete Works*, vol. 30A, p. 164.

[30] Voltaire, *Le Monde comme il va*, ed. M. Cardy, in: *The Complete Works*, vol. 30B, p. 50.

[31] *L'Année littéraire*, 15 December 1757, vol. 8, p. 184.

[32] Fenouillot de Falbaire, *L'Honnête Criminel*, p. iii; Beaumarchais, 'Essai sur le genre dramatique sérieux' (1767), in: *Œuvres*, p. 134; Cailhava d'Estendoux, *De l'Art de la comédie*, vol. 1, p. 346; Sade, *Aline et Valcour*, in: *Œuvres*, vol. 1, p. 689.

priate civic virtues; the disparate spectators are united as a single harmonious audience, and a near orthodox ideology is re-legitimized within this assembly.[33]

The theatre as a common place

The move to unite the theatre audience as a single entity forms a thread through the century's architectural reforms and technological developments; spectators are removed from the stage in order to create a single audience on one side of the *rampe*,[34] the *parterre* is seated so that spectators see each other and regulate their syncretised behaviour accordingly,[35] advances in differential lighting covers the audience in the same darkness,[36] and the structure of London theatres is criticised for preventing any connection between the spectators.[37] The effectiveness of theatre's moral education is similarly connected to that institution's characterization as a site of assembly, a link Diderot makes explicit in *De la poésie dramatique* (1758), in which he argues that theatre should be considered alongside all kinds of public instruction.[38] Central to theatre's instructive value is the uniting of disparate spectators into a single whole, and he insists upon the central role that pathos plays in this process:

> Le parterre de la comédie est le seul endroit où les larmes de l'homme vertueux et du méchant soient confondues. Là, le méchant s'irrite contre les injustices qu'il aurait commises; compatit à des maux qu'il aurait occasionnés, et s'indigne contre un homme de son propre caractère. Mais l'impression est reçue; elle demeure en nous, malgré nous; et le méchant sort de son loge, moins disposé à faire le mal, que s'il eût été gourmandé par un orateur sévère et dur.[39]

> [The theatre pit is the only place where the tears of a virtuous man and a wicked man mingle. There, the wicked man becomes angry against the injustices he would have committed, sympathizes with the harm he would have caused, and becomes indignant with a man of his own character. But the impression is made; it stays within us, in spite of ourselves, and the wicked man

---

[33] For a detailed account of this notion in the Revolutionary period, see Frantz, 'Schule, Kirche und Radau', pp. 258-269.

[34] Mittman, *Spectators on the Paris Stage*.

[35] La Harpe, *Éloge de Racine*, p. 54.

[36] Lavoisier, 'Mémoire sur la manière', pp.125-234.

[37] Patte, *Essai sur l'architecture théâtrale*, p. 118.

[38] Diderot, 'De la poésie dramatique', in: *Œuvres esthétiques*, p. 259

[39] *Ibidem*, p. 196.

leaves his box, less disposed to commit bad deeds, than if he had been berated by a severe and harsh orator.]

Theatre is itself intended as a common place, a space where spectators in close physical proximity incite each other to an enthusiastic and unified response to the staged fiction, a process Diderot also describes in his *Lettre à Mme Riccoboni* (1758). Implicitly challenging Bossuet, he insists that this kind of cohesion underpins theatre's claims to be a school of virtue:

> Celui qui ne sent pas augmenter sa sensation par le grand nombre de ceux qui la partagent, a quelque vice secret.[40]

> [He who does not feel his sensation increase due to the large number of those who share it, has some secret vice.]

Similar claims are made the same year in the *Journal encyclopédique*, in which the anonymous writer states 'il faut une école du monde, et le théâtre est cette école', and that this educative purpose is best served by harnessing the group effect:

> Quand le théâtre ne ferait que rassembler les hommes de toutes les conditions, ce serait un grand bien. Mais il les rassemble pour pleurer et même pour rire, c'est un autre bien.[41]

> [Were the theatre to do nothing more than to assemble men of all conditions, it would be a very fine thing. But it assembles them to cry and even to laugh, and that is another fine thing.]

In the *Lettre à M. d'Alembert* (1758) Rousseau directly confronts this commonplace, or in John McManners's franker description, the 'smug assumption of the *philosophes* that the theatre was an educative institution'.[42] He inverts the commonplace several times, condemning theatre as 'une école de vices et de mauvaises mœurs', 'une école de mauvaises mœurs' and as a 'dangereuse école', and describing French tragedies in which women and men perform together as 'autant d'écoles de mauvaises mœurs'.[43] Rousseau's critique is founded on the notion that the theatrical experience engenders not cohesion but isolation within the playhouse: 'L'on croit

---

[40] Diderot, 'Entretiens sur le Fils naturel' (1757), in: *Œuvres esthétiques*, p. 122.
[41] *Journal encyclopédique*, November 1758, first part, p. 60 and p. 57.
[42] McManners, *Church and Society*, vol. 2, p. 329.
[43] Rousseau, *Lettre à M. d'Alembert*, pp.148, 201, and 150.

s'assembler au spectacle, et c'est là que chacun s'isole'.[44] Whereas Bossuet argued that the group effect renders impossible moral improvement in the theatre, Rousseau contends that this isolation of the spectator is inimical to empathy and recognition, and so precludes the morally beneficial group effect, which may be engineered in his *cercles*. This process is compounded by the ruinous financial expenditure that theatre demands, both of the troupe and the (primarily female) spectators, who wish to distinguish themselves through expensive clothes.[45]

As Voltaire observed, ideas wilt and become routine when thoroughly discussed in the public realm. Ideas, arguments and metaphors had become stale by the early 1760s, arguably because of rather than despite Rousseau's intervention in the debate and the ensuing polemic. It is unsurprising to read the same commonplace repeated in, for instance, Mézières's response to Rousseau.[46] As Élie Catherine Fréron writes in 1761, 'cette matière commence à vieillir' (this subject is beginning to age).[47]

Voltaire's investment in the commonplace

Voltaire's dedication of *Tancrède* to Mme de Pompadour nonetheless repeats a number of re-heated platitudes, including the commonplace under investigation:

> De tous les arts que nous cultivons en France, l'art de la tragédie n'est pas celui qui mérite le moins l'attention publique; car il faut avouer que c'est celui dans lequel les Français se sont le plus distingués. C'est, d'ailleurs, au théâtre seul que la nation se rassemble, c'est là que l'esprit et le goût de la jeunesse se forment: les étrangers y viennent apprendre notre langue; nulle mauvaise maxime n'y est tolérée, et nul sentiment estimable n'y est débité sans être applaudi; c'est une école toujours subsistante de poésie et de vertu.[48]

> [Of all the arts that we cultivate in France, the art of tragedy is not that which deserves the least public attention; for it must be recognized that it is the one in which the French have most distinguished themselves. Besides, it is at the theatre alone that the nation gathers, it is here that young people's wit and taste is formed; foreigners come here to learn our language; no wicked maxim is toler-

---

[44] *Ibidem*, p. 134.
[45] *Ibidem*, pp. 172-173, and pp. 197-199.
[46] Mézières, *Critique d'un livre*, pp.79 and 90.
[47] *L'Année littéraire*, 18 May 1761, vol. 3, p. 190.
[48] Voltaire, *Tancrède* (Paris, 1761), p. 7.

ated, and no worthy sentiment is uttered without being applauded; it is a school
of poetry and virtue that continues to survive.]

This declaration is deceptively banal, for a new sense of urgency energizes
these commonplaces of assembly, virtue and education. *Tancrède* sees Voltaire reclaim theatre's moral agency in the face of Rousseau's attacks. His
denial on 5 May 1759 that he was writing a new tragedy after what 'le
grand Jean-Jacques' had written against the theatre is disingenuous,[49] for
Voltaire's thinking about theatre at this period is precisely due to the situation created by the *Lettre à d'Alembert*.[50] Moreover Voltaire uses *Tancrède*
to reassert the status if not the ideas of the embattled *philosophes*. With the
suspension and condemnation of Helvétius's *De l'esprit* in 1758-1759, the
censure and temporary suspension of the *Encyclopédie* on 8 March 1759,
the rash of anti-*philosophe* publications, and the première of Palissot's *Les
Philosophes* on 2 May 1760, the public stock of this faction was threatened,
as Voltaire recognised:

> A-t-on lâché un plat Aristophane contre les Socrates pour accoutumer le public
> à leur voir boire la ciguë sans les plaindre?[51]

> [Has a dull Aristophanes been let loose against a group of Socrates so that the
> public may become accustomed to seeing them drink hemlock without pitying
> them?]

Tancrède forms part of Voltaire's strategy to affirm the literary pre-
eminence of the *philosophes*.[52]

Tancrède is intended above all as a patriotic gesture, as the 'preuve incontestable du goût qui subsiste parmi nous, et preuve de nos ressources
dans les temps les plus difficiles' (incontestable proof of the taste that survives amongst us, and proof of our resources in the most difficult of times).[53] Created during the Seven Years War, the tragedy affirms French
identity and cultural supremacy at a time when England's geo-political as-
cendancy came at the expense of France's 'humiliation'.[54] It may not engage explicitly with the hostilities, but in content and form it promotes a

---

[49] Voltaire, 'Correspondence and related documents', in: *The Complete Works*, vol.
85-135 (1968-1977), D8287. Future references to Voltaire's correspondence will be
to this edition and will give the letter's reference code.
[50] Bray, 'Voltaire et la querelle du théâtre', vol. 1, pp. 137-147 (p. 139).
[51] D8903, 11 May 1760.
[52] Pomeau, *"Ecraser l'infâme", 1759-1770*, p. 97.
[53] Voltaire, *Tancrède*, p.11.
[54] Riley, *The Seven Years War*, p. 223.

certain model of Frenchness.[55] Aménaïde's speech in Act II, scene 2 sketches the characteristics of a French hero:

Ces généreux Français, ces illustres vainqueurs,
Subjuguaient l'Italie, et conquéraient des cœurs.
On aimait leur franchise, on redoutait leurs armes;
Les soupçons n'entraient point dans leurs esprits altiers
L'honneur avait uni tous ces grands chevaliers.

[These noble French, these illustrious conquerors
Subjugated Italy, and conquered hearts.
Their frankness was loved, their arms were dreaded;
Suspicion did not enter into their elevated minds
Honour had united all these great knights.]

The chivalric model is epitomised by the eponymous hero who embodies, as John Dunkley argues, 'the ideals of patriotism, bravery, military success, and devotion to a lady'.[56] Despite the fact that, properly speaking, the characters are not French but Norman, the play's dedication emphasises that its heroes are to be emulated.[57] The play has been considered, not least by Flaubert, as an early example of French national drama.[58]

Critical to the success of Voltaire's depiction of inspirational 'French' heroes is the sense of community fostered within the playhouse. Elsewhere he writes of the group effect within the playhouse; in the *Commentaires sur Corneille* (1765) he depicts a model of sociability whereby informed spectators of *Rodogune* correct those audience members who mistake the Syrian queen Cléopâtre for Caesar's mistress.[59] *Tancrède* bears witness to Voltaire's practical investment in this otherwise abstract belief in the theatre as a common place, and the play's subject matter encourages this emphatic materiality, as noted by the *Correspondance littéraire*, 'Les mœurs de la

---

[55] A note of caution should be sounded, for, as Edmond Dziembowski demonstrates, there are at least three Voltaires apparent in the published works and the correspondence; a patriotic Voltaire who openly prefers France to the enemy power, a rebellious Voltaire who is removed from the misfortunes affecting his country, and a cosmopolitan and anglophile Voltaire. See *Un nouveau patriotisme*, p. 133.

[56] Dunkley, 'Medieval heroes', p. 161. See also Karoui, 'Tancrède ou les valeurs chevaleresques', pp. 1320-1324.

[57] Voltaire, *Tancrède*, pp. 9-10.

[58] Flaubert, *Le Théâtre de Voltaire*, p. 307; see also Boës, *La Lanterne magique*, pp. 87-90.

[59] Voltaire, *Commentaires sur Corneille II*, ed. D. Williams, *The Complete Works of Voltaire*, vol. 54, p. 483.

chevalerie sont singulièrement théâtrales' (The customs of chivalry are singularly theatrical).[60] Rejecting Rousseau's criticism of spectacle, Voltaire creates a work that strikes new ground in its emphasis on visual pleasure, and it is telling that he began *Tancrède*'s composition the day after the Comédie-Française reopened with its stage rid of spectators. The necessity of clarifying the dramatic space had been a frequent topic in Voltaire's writings, notably in the 'Discours sur la tragédie à milord Bolingbrooke' (1731), in which he notes that the on-stage seating shrinks the performance space and renders action impracticable. *Tancrède* represents Voltaire's response to the challenges and opportunities, as made clear in the first allusion in his correspondence to the work, when he exclaims that tragedies will no longer be conversations in five acts at the end of which one learn that some blood has been spilt for the sake of tragic seemliness: 'On voudra de la pompe, du spectacle, du fracas' (We will want pomp, spectacle, crashing noise).[61] The play's dedication similarly stresses that French theatre lacks the pomp that Athenian tragedy employed.[62]

Available evidence confirms Voltaire's investment in the material performance of *Tancrède*. The Comédie-Française's archives hold Henri Lekain's manuscript register in which he notes the performance details of over thirty plays in which he acted. With no indication on the manuscript as to when these notes were originally made, when they were collated and transcribed, or indeed to which performances they refer, the information contained must be treated with some caution; nonetheless the register provides rare and valuable contemporary evidence by Voltaire's favourite actor as to how *Tancrède* might have been staged. In addition to the eight named characters, Lekain identifies a legion of other figures including nine knights, eight squires, twenty-four soldiers and thirty townspeople.[63] Henry Lancaster notes that at the first performance sixty-six soldiers were employed, dressed as knights, their followers or inhabitants of Syracuse, although in later performances this number fell to around thirty.[64] The rich variety of the production is evidenced by the description of the props, which include an elaborate stretcher on which to carry Tancrède, standards topped with crescents, and axes. The manuscript also includes instructions given to the *décorateur machiniste*:

---

[60] *Correspondance littéraire*, vol. 3, p. 299.
[61] D8249, 6 April 1759.
[62] Voltaire, *Tancrède*, pp. 7-8.
[63] Lekain, *Registre Lekain*, p. 159.
[64] Lancaster, *The Comédie Française 1701-1774*, p. 800. The discrepancy between Lancaster's calculation and Lekain's total of seventy-four assistants might be explained by the possibility that some soldiers may have performed more than one peripheral role, or a miscalculation on Lekain's part.

Tous les murs des bâtiments de la place sont garnis de trophées d'armes de chevalerie, qui sont des casques, des boucliers chargés de devises, et des lances. Il n'y a qu'un seul châssis de la décoration sur la droite de l'avant-scène qui ne soient pas ornés de ces trophées militaires.

[All the walls of the buildings in the square are covered in trophies of the knights' arms, which are helmets, shields decorated with emblems, and lances. There is only one single frame of the decoration on right of the forestage that is not adorned with these military trophies.]

Tancrède represents a massive investment in the material elements of production; as one contemporary notes, this tragedy and Voltaire's *Sémiramis* were the most spectacular of French plays.[65] The *mise-en-scène* consolidates the play's ideology, for it is particularly French in nature. Mlle Clairon, playing the lead role of Aménaïde, wanted a scaffold on stage in the third act, a proposal Voltaire rejected in strongly patriotic terms:

J'ai crié quarante ans pour avoir du spectacle, de l'appareil, de l'action tragique, mais domandavo aqua, no tempesta, et puis comment le public français peut-il adopter la barbarie anglaise, le viol anglais, la confession anglaise, la marche anglaise d'une pièce anglaise? Pauvres Français vous êtes dans la fange de toutes façons et j'en suis fâché.[66]

[For forty years I have been crying out for spectacle, machinery, tragic action, but *domandavo aqua, no tempesta*, and so how can the French public adopt English barbarity, English violation, English confession, the English operation of an English play? Poor Frenchmen, you are in the mire in all sorts of ways, and that aggrieves me.]

In one of his notebooks, the nearest thing Voltaire had to a traditional commonplace book, he wrote, 'Il en est du théâtre comme de la guerre' (In theatre as in war),[67] and given the political context of *Tancrède* creation, it is unsurprising that he should compare the fight to preserve France's cultural heritage to the country's military activities:

Mon ami, il faut battre les Anglais et ne pas imiter leur barbare scène.[68]

---

[65] La Noue, *Lettre critique à M***, pp. 27-28.
[66] D946115, December 1760.
[67] *Voltaire's Notebooks*, vol. 2, p. 312.
[68] D9358, 27 October 1760.

[My friend, we must beat the English and not imitate their barbaric stage.]

It is as if the Comédie-Française, officially part of the royal household, has become the last redoubt of French independence from English dominance:

> Si notre scène devient anglaise, nous sommes bien avilis. Nous ne sommes déjà que les traducteurs de leurs romans. N'avons-nous pas déjà baissé assez pavillon devant l'Angleterre? C'est peu d'être vaincus, Faut-il encore être copistes? Ô pauvre nation! [69]

> [If our stage becomes English, we are most demeaned. We are already nothing more than the translators of their novels. Have we not already shown the white flag quite enough to England? It is not enough to be beaten by them; must we yet be their copyists? O poor nation!].

In *Tancrède* Voltaire confirms the commonplace of the theatre as a shared school of virtue, and offers a lesson in national values in spectacular and nonetheless French fashion.

To emphasise the materiality of the theatrical experience is to accentuate the communion that occurs in that shared place, for this spectacular *mise-en-scène* creates a sense of pathos:

> Vous aurez sur le théâtre des drapeaux portés en triomphe, des armes suspendues à des colonnes, des processions de guerriers, une pauvre fille excessivement tendre et résolue et encore plus malheureuse, le plus grand des hommes et le plus infortuné, un père au désespoir; le 5e acte commence par un Te Deum et finit par un De profundis. [70]

> [You will have upon the stage flags carried in triumph, weapons suspended from the column, processions of warriors, a poor and exceedingly tender girl, resolute and yet more unhappy, the greatest and most unfortunate of men, a father in despair; the fifth act begins with a *Te Deum* and ends with a *De profundis*.]

This engineered pathos is instrumental to achieving the group effect:

> [Il] faut que cette machine soit brillante, pompeuse, que tout intéresse, que le cœur soit déchiré, que les larmes coulent, qu'un grand et tendre intérêt ne laisse

---

[69] D9327, 18 October 1760.
[70] D8305, 19 May 1759.

pas aux spectateurs le temps de la réflexion, et qu'ils ne songent aux poulies qu'après avoir essuyé leurs larmes.[71]

[It is vital that this machine be brilliant and full of pomp, that everything should engage the audience, that the heart be torn, that tears should flow, that a great and tender interest should leave the audience no time to reflect, and that they only think about the pulleys after wiping away their tears.]

Despite the lack of explicit reference to France's contemporary problems *Tancrède* responds to the political context in implicit and affective ways. It positively diverts (in a Pascalian sense) the spectator from the country's current misfortunes, and offers a consoling illusion of pathetic suffering.[72] It is in such terms that Voltaire refers to *Tancrède*, when he writes that he has performed the play 'pour nous consoler des malheurs de la France' (to console us for France's misfortunes),[73] and 'nous nous sommes amusés à Tourney pour nous dépiquer des malheurs publics' (we amused ourselves at Tourney to allay our anxieties at the public misfortunes).[74] The spectator may then participate vicariously in that suffering, and contemporary accounts repeat *Tancrède*'s emotional impact and cohesive effect; d'Alembert writes to Voltaire about seeing the play for the third time and notes that 'Tout le monde y fond en larmes, à commencer par moi, et la critique commence à se taire' (Everyone melted into floods of tears, starting with myself, and criticism of the play has begun to fall silent),[75] and d'Argental recounts that at a performance of the tragedy at Fontainebleau 'la salle fondoit en larmes' (the auditorium broke into a flood of tears).[76] Tears dissolve individual identity, and disparate spectators come to form a single weeping and virtuous group in the playhouse. In the words of one contemporary, 'Le théâtre de M. de Voltaire est une école de bienfaisance' (M. de Voltaire's theatre is a school of beneficence).[77]

The limits of the common place

Voltaire reinvigorates the commonplace of theatre as a school of virtue by investing heavily in the common place of theatre. The commonplace remains in currency not through ironic playfulness but through apparently

---

[71] D8363, 18 June 1759.
[72] On the theme of suffering in *Tancrède*, see Iotti, *Virtù e identità*, pp. 137-145.
[73] D8569, 5 November 1759.
[74] D8612, 24 November 1759.
[75] D9252, 22 September 1760.
[76] D15970, 24 October 1769.
[77] Thorel de Campigneulles, 'Lettre à M. Desprez de Boissy', p. 71.

sincere application. It retains its validity by being treated in literal rather than metaphorical terms; the lesson is effective when the students are assembled in a locatable space. Yet what becomes of that commonplace when the theatre is no longer a common place? Can the theatre be an effective school of virtue possible when that theatre becomes a virtual space, when the assembly in the playhouse is replaced by a disparate group of readers?

Voltaire's comment that *Tancrède* is worth more when performed than read is partly facetious,[78] for the play's publishing history reveals his preoccupation with the production of an authentic and reliable text.[79] Common sense and evidence alike suggest that a number of individuals would encounter *Tancrède* as text and not as performance; before the play was first performed at Voltaire's private theatre, a certain Antoine de Valette de Traversac writes:

> Il nous est indifférent qu'elle se joue, notre désir est qu'elle s'imprime; la lecture est tout notre théâtre.[80]

> [It is of no concern to us that it is performed, our desire is that it is printed; reading is all our theatre.]

The *Mercure de France* defends including lengthy extracts of *Tancrède* in its review of the work by noting that many readers live far from the capital and are therefore deprived of theatrical performances, sometimes even of printed copies of plays.[81] But do the lessons of national pride that are apparently so dependent on materialised performance remain effective in this immaterial encounter? To push the commonplace to the point of anachronistic conceit, can the school of virtue operate as a kind of Open University of long-distance learning?

In a sense *Tancrède*'s plot anticipates these questions of reading, for it hinges on the misuse of a text. Since the addressee of Aménaïde's letter to Tancrède is left nameless, the knights of Syracuse mistakenly believe that she is consorting with the Muslim enemy, and her request 'Régnez dans nos états' is treated as treason. Despite this trite plot device, criticized by Fréron and mocked in the parody *La Nouvelle Joute, ou Arlequin Tancrève*,[82] the fact that the work hangs on a misunderstood letter arguably betrays an anxiety that a text is susceptible to being misread by a wider readership. Just as

---

[78] D9696, 25 March 1761.
[79] Henderson, *Voltaire's Tancrède*.
[80] D8548, 20 October 1759.
[81] *Mercure de France*, March 1761, p. 188.
[82] *L'Année littéraire*, 1761, vol. 1, p. 302, and the *Mercure de France*, October 1760, vol. 2, pp. 1177-1178.

the 'lettre coupable' or 'lettre fatale'[83] demonstrates the perils of the un-planned (mis-)uses of a text, so the tragedy itself (like all texts) may function in a way different or indeed opposite to that intended by the author. The object of inquiry here is that of reading rather than performing the text, although one might pursue an analysis of representations that blunted the tragedy's moral or patriotic force, in which case one would start with its purported staging at Ferney; it apparently took place during festivities to celebrate the capture of Quebec by the English forces, and the stage carried the provocative inscription 'Libertati quieti / Musis Sacrum / Sp[ite] of the F[rench]'.[84] A lack of reliable evidence, however, makes the truth of this claim difficult to establish.

Although Voltaire intended his spectators to be so swept away by *Tancrède*'s pathetic representation of honour as to have no time to reflect upon the mechanisms that create such an effect, he notes that the reader may evaluate a play more judiciously in his study.[85] Indeed, whereas Diderot conceives of pathos as being expressed primarily through the body, Voltaire only legitimizes such appeals to the body by insisting on the primacy of language.[86] As a character remarks, however, in a meta-theatrical response to *Tancrède*:

> Je crains cependant que le grand jour de l'impression ne vous fasse du tort. Vous parlez bien, j'en conviens; mais la lecture ne présente pas aux yeux l'action comme la représentation. Au cabinet souvent on ne reconnaît pas.[87]

> [Nonetheless I fear that the clear light of publication will harm you. You speak well, I agree; but reading does not present action to the eyes as performance does. In the study one often fails to recognize.]

That *Tancrède* suffers from a lectorial rather than spectatorial experience is evidenced when Fréron declines to review the play upon first seeing it.[88] Rather than report on the tragedy's magnificent performance at the Comédie-Française, he chooses to wait until its publication:

---

[83] Voltaire, *Tancrède*, pp.27 and 74.
[84] See Rousseau, *L'Angleterre et Voltaire*, p.232.
[85] Voltaire, *Commentaires sur Corneille II*, ed. D. Williams, *The Complete Works of Voltaire*, vol. 54, p. 483, p. 513 and p. 556.
[86] Lagrave, 'Voltaire, Diderot et le "tableau scénique"', pp. 633-642; and Frantz, *L'Esthétique du tableau*, pp. 115-143.
[87] Cailleau, *Les Tragédies de M. de Voltaire*, p. 52.
[88] *L'Année littéraire*, 1760, vol. 6, p. 144.

Vous attendiez, Monsieur, avec impatience l'impression de cette tragédie; je ne sais si la lecture lui sera aussi favorable que la représentation; une pièce qu'on lit de sang-froid dans son cabinet est une femme qu'on peut juger avant sa toilette.[89]

[You were looking forward to this tragedy being printed; I do not know if reading will be as favourable to it as performance; a play that one reads with a level-head in one's study is like woman that one judges before her toilette.]

Although by no means representative of Voltaire's readers, it is striking that Fréron consciously extricates himself from the assembly in the playhouse, and retreats to a place of solitude from which to gauge the play's quality. What he finds there is remiss; he criticizes the hero's death, argues that his survival would have had a greater moral impact, decries Voltaire's use of *vers croisés* as being not sufficiently French, and fails to note any didactic value to the play. The *Correspondance littéraire* is less harsh, though similarly notes that the play's force owes much to the performance of Mlle Clairon:

Un parterre d'un goût plus sûr et plus sévère ne se fût pas laissé tromper par les poumons de l'actrice.

[A pit that had surer and more severe taste would not have been misled by the actress's lungs.]

In addition it condemns Voltaire's portrayal of the chivalric code, implying that the play lacks moral authority.[90]

Such responses reveal that the work's moral force greatly reduced when solitary readers supplant the assembled spectators. The theatre as a school of virtue is a commonplace whose effectiveness is founded upon the shared experiences of the spectators gathered within the playhouse. Once the play circulates in individual and private spaces, its moral impact appears to evaporate, and its lesson of national virtue that so appeals to the *parterre* is lost upon the dispersed readers in their *cabinets*. The case of *Tancrède* contradicts Anderson's and Wittman's account that the nation and public are conceived in terms of readers who virtually connect far beyond a spatially specific building. As Rousseau observes, 'si l'on prend des leçons de vertu sur la scène, on les va bien vite oublier dans les foyers' (If one takes lessons in virtue on the stage, one quickly forgets them in the foyers].[91]

---

[89] *Ibidem*, 1761, vol. 1, p. 289.
[90] *Correspondance littéraire*, vol. 4, p. 296 and p. 299.
[91] Rousseau, *Lettre à M. d'Alembert*, p.196.

IN PRAISE OF THE ENLIGHTENED RULER:
METASTASIO'S DRAMAS FOR THE COURT OF VIENNA, 1730-1740

Carlo Caruso

One may be allowed to speculate whether the eighteenth century saw a more universally acclaimed poet than Pietro Metastasio (Rome, 1698- Vienna, 1782). The list of subscribers appended to the edition in twelve volumes of his complete works, published by the widow Hérissant in Paris (1780-1782), included Louis XVI and Marie-Antoinette of France, George III and Sophie-Charlotte of England, Joseph II of Austria, Catherine II of Russia, the archbishop of Salzburg Mons. Colloredo, Condorcet, Friedrich Melchior Grimm, Goldoni, the *abbé* Prevost, Mary Wortley Montagu, Horace Walpole and Angelika Kauffmann.[1] Voltaire did not make it to 1782, but as one of Metastasio's greatest admirers he was credited with declaring that he would have liked to head any such list regardless of the alphabetical order.[2] The favourite poet of both princes and *philosophes*,[3] Metastasio seemed to embody like no other what once would have been called the spirit of the times. There was hardly a place where his 'drammi per musica' were not performed, provided there was a theatre, however small or malfunctioning, or even a simple yard – an astonished Louis-Antoine de Bougainville watched in 1767 a performance of *L'Olimpiade* on the green of a village near São Salvador de Bahia in Brasil, played by an orchestra of natives under the direction of an old missionary priest.[4] Metastasio's dramas were continuously staged for over a century until Romantic opera took off, and even then librettists could not easily get rid of his haunting presence. Well into the age of Verdi, Italian opera librettos are redolent of Metasta-

---

[1] Metastasio, *Opere*, vol. 12, pp. 415-432. See Carducci, 'Pietro Metastasio', pp. 68-69.
[2] Young, *Voltairiana. In Four Volumes*, vol. 1, pp. 199-200.
[3] Sozzi, ' *"Notre divin Métastase"'*, pp. 1-21.
[4] Carducci, 'Pietro Metastasio', p. 69; Brunelli's Introduction to Metastasio, *Tutte le opere*, vol. 1, p. xxxvii. See in general Chegai, *L'esilio di Metastasio*, and the recent monograph by Feldman, *Opera and Sovereignty*, in particular p. 231: 'Between 1723-24 and 1771, Metastasio codified a body of stories that embodied the fantasies of foundation, morality, and selfhood of European society like none other and were disseminated more widely than any other stories of their time'. I was only able to access Feldman's excellent book while revising my text for the press.

sian sentences and turns of phrase.[5] As an author of shorter and lighter texts for music (*canzonette*), Metastasio seems to have had no other rival than Anacreon himself.[6]

Metastasio's authoritative position was in no negligible part favoured by the vantage point he had chosen for himself early on in his career – the court of Vienna. He resided there for over fifty years, honoured like a living institution. His start in life, on the other hand, shows nothing that could even remotely suggest so great an achievement. He was born in Rome of humble condition, his real name being Pietro Trapassi. The benevolent assistance he received from his godfather, the influential cardinal Pietro Ottoboni, did not obtain him anything more than an apprenticeship in a goldsmith's workshop; so that it was not until he attracted the attention of Gian Vincenzo Gravina, professor of Civil Law in the Roman University 'La Sapienza' and co-founder of the literary Academy of Arcadia, that young Pietro would be offered a genuine opportunity to sport his talents. Gravina got permission to adopt him and take care of his education, and in truly Arcadian style 're-baptized' him by substituting his surname Trapassi for its hellenized equivalent Metastasio. He also introduced the promising pupil to the study of law and the philosophy of Descartes, while kindling in him an ardent passion for the Greek, Roman and Italian classics. When Gravina died in 1718, Metastasio, twenty years of age at the time, was made his universal heir. The young man moved to Naples, where he enjoyed his earliest triumphs. His very first 'dramma per musica', *Didone abbandonata* (Naples, 1724), literally took Europe by storm. In the course of the following hundred years the piece was set to music no less than sixty times, while by the end of the nineteenth century it would have been performed in one hundred and forty different theatres all over the world.[7] In 1728 Metastasio moved to Rome to obtain an even more resounding success, and in September 1729 received an invitation to Vienna with the prospect of being appointed Poet Laureate. On reaching the imperial capital on April 17, 1730, he dismounted at No 1182 (today Kohlmarkt 11), at the corner of the church of St. Michael. There he would spend the rest of his long and rather uneventful life. An inscription on the house corner reminds the modern visitor of his former lodgings, which he shared for some time with a good friend of his, Franz Joseph Haydn. He was finally laid at rest in the nearby church of

---

[5] Cf. Bellina, 'Zeno e Metastasio', p. 302.

[6] Fucilla, 'The European and American Vogue', pp. 13-33. By 'Anacreon' are of course meant the *Anacreontea*, the collection of Hellenistic drinking songs once believed to be by Anacreon and first published by Henri Estienne in 1556. For the standard modern edition see West, ed., *Anacreontea*.

[7] Bellina, 'Zeno e Metastasio', p. 300.

St. Michael, and a cenotaph was inscribed with the final, moving lines of his most famous sonnet.[8]

Staging opera for the Viennese court

At a rapid glance, Metastasio's activity in 1720s and 1730s, which may be regarded as his golden period,[9] appears to have been characterized by a considerable steadfastness of intent and creative output. Seven 'drammi per musica' were written by him while in Italy: *Didone abbandonata* (Naples, 1724), *Siroe re di Persia* (Venice, 1726), *Catone in Utica* (Rome, 1728), *Ezio* (Venice, 1728), *Semiramide riconosciuta* (Rome, 1729), *Alessandro nell'Indie* (Rome, 1730) and *Artaserse* (Rome, 1730). After his arrival in Vienna he produced ten further 'drammi': *Demetrio* (Vienna, 1731), *Issipile* (Vienna, 1732), *Adriano in Siria* (Vienna, 1732), *L'Olimpiade* (Vienna, 1733), *Demofoonte* (Vienna, 1733), *La clemenza di Tito* (Vienna, 1734), *Achille in Sciro* (Vienna, 1736), *Ciro riconosciuto* (Vienna, 1736), *Temistocle* (Vienna,1736) and *Zenobia* (Vienna, 1737). This uninterrupted flux of successful productions, apparently unaffected by the disruptions and distractions provoked by the poet's geographical wanderings, is in fact cut across by a clear dividing line, for the transfer to Vienna brought a radical change in Metastasio's compositional habits. On leaving Italy he had abandoned the busy world of impresario-led opera houses. Now, in his comfortable position as Poet Laureate, he found himself attached to the most prestigious court theatre in Europe and exclusively dependent on the gracious will of the emperor Charles VI and his spouse, the empress Elisabeth. They both loved their Poet Laureate dearly, who returned their affection with equal fondness and remained profoundly devout to their memory for his entire life.

The modes of production in Vienna's court theatre deserve a brief illustration. It was customary for the sovereigns to have their respective name-days and birthdays celebrated by the staging of a new piece for the opera theatre, which was presented by the husband to his wife, and vice versa, as a personal gift. On all such occasions the Poet Laureate was called forth to produce a new text to be set to music, which was either a 'dramma per mu-

---

[8] The final lines from the sonnet *Sogni e favole io fingo* read: 'Sogno della mia vita è il corso intero: / Deh tu, Signor, quando a destarmi arrivo, / Fa ch'io trovi riposo in sen del Vero.' (Metastasio, *Tutte le opere*, vol. 2, p. 939: 'My life's entire career is nothing but a dream: / my Lord, when I finally awaken, / let me rest in peace in the bosom of Truth').

[9] See however the recent monograph by Mellace, *L'autunno del Metastasio*, which sheds considerable light on the lesser-known final phase of his career, characterised by a productive collaboration with the composer Johann Adolph Hasse.

sica' or a less ambitious production ('festa teatrale', 'azione teatrale', 'componimento drammatico', cantata), according to the solemnity of the circumstance. The personal nature of the gift would be reflected in the carefully selected subjects, which would in turn be developed along the lines of well-established compositional canons with the aim of celebrating the imperial couple. In support of this rhetorical strategy, the use of commonplaces and other kinds of formulaic expressions played a prominent role.

Before turning to the specific nature of such texts, however, an examination of the external circumstances which occasioned their performance will be of assistance, as it is bound to reveal interesting patterns in the invention and sequencing of Metastasian subjects.[10] The principal occasion for the staging of new operas was the recurrence of the emperor's name-day, November 4, on which date the Roman Catholic Church celebrates St. Carlo Borromeo. On November 4 the first performances of *Demetrio* (1731), *Adriano in Siria* (1732), *Demofoonte* (1733), *La clemenza di Tito* (1734), and *Temistocle* (1736) took place. The titles denote a clear preference for heroic subjects, fit for the taste of an emperor. The empress's birthday (August 28), on the other hand, occasioned *L'Olimpiade* (1733), *Ciro riconosciuto* (1736), and *Zenobia* (1737), all characterised by a comparatively more romantic vein. Birthdays, traditionally less important than name-days, could occasionally be celebrated with a lower-ranked piece in the hierarchy of genres. Those produced for the empress include two 'feste teatrali', *Il tempio dell'eternità* (Vienna, 1731) and *L'asilo d'amore* (Linz, 1732), one 'azione teatrale', *Le grazie vendicate* (Vienna, 1735), and two 'componimenti drammatici', *Il Parnaso accusato e difeso* (Vienna, 1738) and *Astrea placata* (Vienna, 1739), all featuring female allegorical personifications and pagan deities: Eternity, Venus, the three Graces, Minerva, Astraea, etc. The pieces written for the emperor's birthday (October 1), all 'azioni teatrali', unsurprisingly present a more virile programme: *Il Palladio conservato* (Vienna, 1735), *Il sogno di Scipione* (Vienna, 1735) and *Il natal di Giove* (Vienna, 1740), where the courage of Metellus, the Choice of Scipio and the birth of Jupiter are the selected topics respectively. In 1738 the archduchess Maria Theresa's name-day (October 15) was celebrated with an allegorical 'azione teatrale' entitled *La pace fra la virtù e la bellezza*. At carnival, the height of all opera seasons in Europe, the Viennese court did not seem to expect much of its Poet Laureate. A 'dramma per musica' (*Issipile*) was produced for the carnival of 1732, while that of 1735 was celebrated with an 'azione teatrale' (*Le cinesi*), performed semi-

---

[10] Cf. Metastasio, *Tutte le opere*, vols 1 and 2, and Bellina's edition Metastasio, *Drammi per musica*, vol. 2, *Il regno di Carlo VI, 1730-1740* (Venice, 2003).

privately in the apartments of the archduchesses, presumably at the request of the younger members of the imperial family. *Achille in Sciro* was performed in Vienna on February 13, 1736, to celebrate the marriage of Maria Theresa with Francis Stephen of Lorraine and Tuscany, later Emperor Francis I. At Lent and during the Holy Week, when all forms of profane entertainment were suspended, 'azioni sacre' (i.e. oratorios) where performed in the imperial chapel.[11] The emperor's name-day was about to be honoured again on November 4, 1740, with one of Metastasio's masterpieces, *Attilio Regolo*, when all celebrations were hurriedly called off on October 20 after news that the emperor had been killed by a dish of poisonous mushrooms – a fateful event leading to the War of Austrian Succession and prompting Voltaire's famous comment 'et ce plat de champignons changea la destinée de l'Europe' (and this dish of mushroom changed the destiny of Europe).[12]

Rulers watching rulers perform on stage

Metastasio's Vienna productions offer an excellent example of the ways in which the imperial couple was exalted by the re-enactment of historical, mythical or religious events of exemplary value, all of which overtly allusive of their enlightened rule. It was the spectacularisation *of* the court *for* the court, which Jacques Joly analysed in detail in his monograph on Metastasio's 'feste teatrali' and their political significance.[13] In the context of the research on commonplaces, special attention will be here given to those 'drammi per musica' where exemplary figures of male rulers are portrayed, one of which, *La clemenza di Tito*, will demand closer inspection.[14]

The poet's objective was twofold: to make the message of the piece intelligible for any member of the audience, as well as to transport its significance on to a superior and truly universal level. In this respect, his responsibility was not limited to the selection of suitable topics. The way in which such topics should be formally presented was also relevant. A new feature, absent from all of Metastasio's 'drammi per musica' written in Naples or Rome, makes its appearance at the end of his very first Viennese drama, *Demetrio*: a final *licenza*, or envoi.[15] Like *Demetrio*, all subsequent Vien-

---

[11] Cf. Stroppa, *Fra notturni sereni.*

[12] Voltaire, *Mémoires*, p. 33. *Attilio Regolo* was performed for the first time in Dresden in 1750.

[13] Joly, *Les fêtes théâtrales.*

[14] For a wider-ranging, as well as detailed, analysis of such figures see now Feldman, *Opera and Sovereignty*, chapter 6 ('Myths of Sovereignty').

[15] Although modern editions of *Didone abbandonata* (1724) and *Semiramide* (1729) include final envois, they did not feature in the original performances of the 1720s. They were added by Metastasio in the 1750s, when he reworked both dramas for the

nese dramas of 1730s have a final *licenza*, with only two justifiable exceptions.[16] The *licenza* was a compliment paid to the sovereigns by the poet in recognition of their gracing the first performance with their presence; it responded to a requisite of court etiquette.[17] What is striking, in these *licenze*, is the peculiar nature of the language and style deployed for the task. In his Neapolitan and Roman years Metastasio had steered clear of the opulent ornamentations of Baroque verse in favour of a leaner and soberer diction, in line with a dramaturgy aiming at verisimilitude and linear progression in stage action. This was undoubtedly among the merits which had earned him the call to Vienna, where his predecessor, Apostolo Zeno, had already been credited for being one of the leaders of the classicizing reform of melodrama.[18] To such classicist ideals Metastasio subscribed with renewed conviction at his arrival in the imperial capital; yet it would be fair to say his *licenze* provide the reader (or the spectator) with a sensation of displacement, as if one had suddenly and unexpectedly been plunged into a world of elaborate Baroque antitheses, oxymora and conceits. The survival of such encomiastic formulae may ultimately derive from the influence exercised by the etiquette of the imperial court, which had been introduced at the time of the Spanish emperors and had gradually acquired a distinctive Baroque flavour.[19] It is significant that the contrast was immediately perceived by those readers who were by their own culture impervious to the charms of Baroque style. John Hoole, the first English translator of Metastasio's dramas, typically declared himself unable to turn such verses into acceptable English.

> Several of the dramas have, in the original, a kind of epilogue joined to them, which is indeed nothing more than a panegyric upon the Emperor or Empress: this being altogether local and temporary, and from its nature incapable of being made graceful in English, is left out in the present version.[20]

---

court theatre of Madrid. The Madrid versions were included in the definitive Hérissant edition of Paris 1780-1782 and from there reprinted in all the following editions.

[16] *Issipile* (1732) was a piece for the carnival, whereas *Achille in Sciro*, produced for the marriage of Maria Theresa with Francis Stephen, has no proper envoi but a dialogic cauda with three allegorical figures, Glory, Love and Time.

[17] Final *licenze* also appear in the 'drammi per musica' for the imperial court by Metastasio's predecessors (Apostolo Zeno, Pietro Pariati, Silvio Stampiglia).

[18] Fehr, *Apostolo Zeno*. On the actual extent of the so-called 'reform', cf. Bellina, 'Zeno e Metastasio', pp. 280-281.

[19] Metastasio himself, though genuinely devoted to the classicist cause, was a fond reader of the Mannerist and Baroque poets, and held Torquato Tasso and Giovan Battista Marino among his most cherished authors. Cf. De Sanctis, *Storia della letteratura italiana*, pp. 749-750.

[20] *The Works of Metastasio*, vol. 1, pp. ix-x.

The envois are, however, something more than redundant appendices. In fact, their primary function is to provide a clue that would let the august spectators, as well as the rest of the audience, make sense of the performed action. The dignified silence and forbearance characterising Demetrio's demeanour, for instance, prompts the poet to pay a graceful compliment to the emperor by contrasting the opposite virtues of admired silence and altisonant praise.[21] A more elaborate point is driven home in the *licenza* of *Adriano in Siria*. Elected to the empire in Antioch at the end of his victorious campaign against the Parthians, Hadrian proves unable to resist the temptation of indulging his lust for beautiful Emirena. His whimsical and at times undignified behaviour reverts to imperial soberness and reasonableness no sooner than the final scene, as his loyal *fiancée* Sabina dutifully remarks ('Ecco il vero Adriano: or lo ravviso', *Adriano in Siria*, III, last: 'Now I recognize the real Hadrian'). The motif is an old one, and a favourite of opera librettists, for it could also be tailored to other great men of the ancient past that European audiences loved watching in similar straits, Scipio the conqueror of Spain and Alexander the conqueror of India.[22] Metastasio even allowed himself to portray in the final lines a still upset Hadrian, not yet fully in control of himself and struggling to keep faith to his resolution. At this point the *licenza* is deployed before any misunderstanding might occur.

> Cesare, non turbarti. A te non osa
> somigliarsi Adrian. Quando al tuo sguardo
> le sue vicende espone,
> fa spettacol di sé, non paragone.
> Troppo minor del vero
> l'immagine sarebbe; e troppo chiare,
> Signor, fra voi le differenze sono.
> Fu grande e giusto
> ei talvolta, e tu sempre.

[Do not get upset, Caesar. Hadrian does not dare compare himself to you. When he offers his vicissitudes to your sight, he is just making a show of himself, no comparison. Too inferior to truth would that image be, Sire, as too evi-

---

[21] Metastasio, *Demetrio*, in: Metastasio, *Tutte le opere*, vol. 1, pp. 476-477.
[22] The romantic versions of Scipio's conquest of Spain are loosely based on Livy, Book 26. On Metastasio's *Alessandro nell'Indie* (Rome, 1730), see Feldman, *Opera and Sovereignty*, pp. 258-265.

dent are the differences between Hadrian and yourself. Only occasionally was
he great and fair, while you always are.]

In the *licenza* of *Demofoonte* the misfortunes suffered by Timante are presented to the audience as a vivid reminder of the privilege of being subjects
of Charles – because 'the comparison makes one tell apart the opposites
more clearly', and 'whatever excess may be put on stage', the opposite virtue will be admired in Charles.[23] Likewise, 'the hand of an ingenious painter
knows how to alternate light and shade to good effect', or 'a skilled goldsmith to exalt [the splendour of] a lucid, gold-mounted gem by setting it
against a darker colour'.[24] In the envoi of *Temistocle*, the poet turns apolo-
getic about the foolish illusion that he could have formed the idea of
Charles' great spirit by assembling the scattered virtues of the heroes of old,
just as the Greek painter Zeuxis had aimed to portray the perfect beauty of
Venus by selecting and uniting the separate beauties of five girls in one single figure.[25]

Virtues and faults

As repositories of laudatory commonplaces, Metastasio's *licenze* are ordi-
narily constructed according to an antiphrastic pattern, engineered in such a
way as to let the figure of Charles shine by contrast against the background
of the vicissitudes and partial failings of the heroes acting on stage.

    This raises a further and wider question, which pertains to the domain
of dramaturgy. Like many other eighteenth-century poets and critics, Metastasio considered the 'dramma per musica' the natural heir of Greek tragedy.
He supported this view principally by relying on the authority of Aristotle's
Poetics, about which he produced a series of penetrating observations, and
by avoiding to engage in any theoretical discussion – let alone a comparison
with his own work – of the tradition of the musical theatre: his courteous
but firm refusal to write the entry 'Opéra' for the *Encyclopédie* is in this respect eloquent enough.[26] He would not on the other hand subscribe to Aris-

---

[23] '(…) Gli opposti oggetti / Rende più chiari il paragon'; '(…) Qualunque eccesso /
Rappresentin le scene, in te ne scopre / La contraria virtù'.
[24] 'Così artefice industre, / Qualor lucida gemma in oro accoglie, / Fosco color le
sottopone (...)' – an old *topos*, which in Italian literature dates back to the late
thirteenth-century collection of short stories known as *Novellino*: see Lo Nigro, ed.,
Novellino, p. 63. One might even wonder whether Metastasio's apprenticeship as a
goldsmith in his young age helped inspire this image.
[25] An ancient *topos*: cf. Cicero, *De inventione*, 2, 1, 1 (where the beautiful figure that
serves as model is not Venus's but Helen's); Pliny, *Historia naturalis*, 35, 64.
[26] Metastasio, *Estratto dell'Arte poetica di Aristotile*, chapters IV and XII, in:

totle's words blindly as if they were eternal truths, certainly not without attempting to qualify and adapt them to the changed circumstances of the modern stage. One of the points at issue was the well-known Aristotelian statement according to which tragedy should primarily involve characters of high estate (*Poetics*, 5, 1448b, 1449a). While acceptable in principle, this requisite could not by itself offer any guarantee of success for the staging of a piece. The point was forcefully and impatiently made by Metastasio in a lively letter addressed to his brother, who had offered him a set of somewhat dull suggestions for new theatrical subjects.

> Che mi dite mai, accennandomi: io ci ho *Silla*, io ci ho *Cesare*, io ci ho *Pompeo*? Gran mercé del regalo: questi ce li ho ancor io, e gli ha ognuno che sappia leggere. Bisogna dirmi: nella vita di Silla mi pare che si potrebbe rappresentare la tale azione, perché interessa per tal motivo; perché dà luogo a tali episodi; perché sorprende per tal ragione. Io ci ho il *Silla*! oh bontà di Dio! E che vorreste voi? che io ne scrivessi la vita? Non mi mancherebbe altro! [27]

> What do you mean when you say 'I have a Sulla, a Caesar, a Pompey for you'? Many thanks for that! I, too, have those, and so has any one else who can read. You should rather have told me: It seems to me that out of Sulla's life one could [extract and] put on stage such and such deed, as it would elicit interest for such and such reason – as it would prompt such and such episode – as it would cause surprise for such and such motive. 'I have a Sulla for you!' For goodness' sake! And what would you expect of me? That I narrated his life? I'd really need that!

According to Metastasio's convictions, which reflected those of his mentor Gravina, a poet writing for the stage was expected to put narration at the service of representation.[28] It follows that it is not so much the biography of

---

Metastasio, *Tutte le opere*, vol. 2, respectively pp. 975-990 and pp. 1068-1069. The invitation to write the entry 'Opéra' had been made by Louis de Cahusac, one of Rameau's librettists and the author of *La danse ancienne et moderne ou Traité historique de la danse* (1754). For Metastasio's reply see the letter dated Vienna, August 12, 1751, *ibidem*, vol. 3, p. 665. Cf. also the letter to Antonio Maria Zanetti, dated Vienna, August 21, 1751, *ibidem*, vol. 3, p. 670.

[27] Vienna, June 25, 1735, in: Metastasio, *Tutte le opere*, vol. 3, p, 128.

[28] Cf. Gravina, *Della tragedia*, in: Gravina, *Scritti critici e teorici*, p. 515: '(...) to show off their ingenuity, [modern playwrights] lose their plot in producing labyrinths rather than tragedies, while stolidly putting on stage the entire life of a character and the duration of a century' ('[...] per ostentare l'ingegno, [i moderni tragediografi] perdono il giudizio ed ordiscono più labirinti che tragedie: rappresentando ancora stolidamente l'intera vita d'un personaggio e 'l corso d'un secolo'). *Ibidem*, p. 509: 'As one is supposed to narrate for the sake of the

the ruler but rather some unusual or even quirky aspect of his personality which will function as the propeller of the main action. A 'dramma per musica' would automatically be sentenced to failure if deprived of that special something that, in Metastasio's own words, 'stimulates and keeps [the audience] hanging, and excites curiosity'.[29] Without any such stimuli, the spectators could not 'either fear or hope, or else crave for something', because their attention would be allowed to wander without direction or focus.[30] The poet was therefore expected to induce in his audience 'the necessary unsettling suspension'[31] allowing 'a spectator's spirit to be removed from its natural tranquillity'.[32]

An approach like this involved the deliberate selection and adaptation of episodes where a prince had shown himself a lesser, viz., a morally weaker, ruler – even in those cases where the piece was meant for the august eyes and ears of those sovereigns who considered themselves the scion of the Roman emperors they watched being re-enacted in their own theatre. This dexterous solution, lucidly illustrated by Metastasio but as a matter of fact already practiced by his French models (notably Corneille and Racine), achieved a twofold goal. By exposing the faults of the ancient rulers against the virtues of his own monarch, Metastasio automatically marked an advantage for the moderns over the ancients; yet in doing so he would still abide to Aristotle's teachings, whose ideal tragic hero was supposed to be someone 'not pre-eminent in moral virtue' (*Poetics*, 13, 1453a).

The emperor's clemency

Among Metastasio's productions for the Vienna court, *La clemenza di Tito* stands in a class of its own. Topical modesty prevented the poet from declaring his portrait of Emperor Titus to be an adequate mirror-image of Charles VI – hence the poet's excuse in the *licenza*.

---

representation, and not vice versa' ('Imperoché si narra per rappresentare, non si rappresenta per narrare'). Both Gravina and Metastasio expand here on Aristotle, *Poetics*, 6, 1449b.

[29] Vienna, December 30, 1747, to Calzabigi, in: Metastasio, *Tutte le opere*, vol. 3, pp. 331-332: '(...) che stimoli, che sospenda, che determini la curiosità dello spettatore (...)'.

[30] Vienna, December 30, 1747, to Calzabigi, in: Metastasio, *Tutte le opere*, vol. 3, pp. 331-332: '(...) non teme questi, non ispera, non desidera cosa alcuna; sempre è dissipata e vagante e non mai riunita la sua attenzione (...)'.

[31] *Ibidem*: 'la necessaria inquieta sospensione'.

[32] Vienna, July 22, 1747, to Giovanni Claudio Pasquini, in: Metastasio, *Tutte le opere*, vol. 3, p. 312: 'rimuovere l'animo dell'uditore dalla naturale sua tranquillità'.

Non crederlo, signor; te non pretesi
Ritrarre in Tito. Il rispettoso ingegno
Sa le sue forze appieno.

[Do not believe it, Sire – in portraying Titus I did not aspire to offer a portrait of yours. My respectful wit knows the limitations of its strengths.]

Nevertheless the comparison did not appear to him entirely inappropriate, as it had the support of both the common view and Charles's own self-perception.

Veggo ben che ciascuno
Ti riconobbe in lui. So che tu stesso
Quegli affetti clementi,
Che in sen Tito sentiva, in sen ti senti.

[I can see all too well that everyone recognized you in him; and I know you feel inside yourself the same sense of clemency that Titus felt.]

Metastasio's Tito endures all sorts of ordeals – the departure of Queen Berenice, whose love he renounces for the undivided care of his empire; a conspiracy of his beloved subjects organized by jealous Vitellia; the betrayal of his friend and confidant Sesto, who out of love for Vitellia joins the conspirators. Despite all this, Tito shows clemency and understanding to such an extent that even his closest supporters and advisors are taken by surprise at each new decision of his.

Titus is thus presented as a wholly virtuous character – in theatrical terms, not unlike another character of modern tragedy Metastasio knew very well, Corneille's *Polyeucte*. As a martyr saint, Polyeuctus appeared devoid of that *hamartia* ('fault'), which according to Aristotle was the primal cause of the catastrophe (*Poetics*, 13, 1453a). Polyeuctus could therefore be regarded by some as an unsuitable protagonist for a tragic piece.[33] Metastasio was aware of this potential problem, and in his *Estratto dell'Arte poetica di Aristotile* defended Corneille's *Polyeucte* against the strictures of André Dacier.[34] True, a Roman emperor was not expected to equal a Christian martyr, and Titus as a historical character had not been without blame, especially when considered in the light of the deeds he had performed before

---

[33] See for all Dacier, *La Poétique d'Aristote*, pp. 200-205.

[34] *Estratto dell'Arte poetica di Aristotile*, chapter XIII, in: Metastasio, *Tutte le opere*, vol. 2, pp. 1070-1072. On the debate on Aristotle's *hamartia* in eighteenth-century Italian theatre see Mattioda, *Teorie della tragedia*, chapter 3.

his election to the principate – ruthless deeds, which had made people fear he could repeat Nero's excesses.[35] The action of the metastasian Tito are all, without exception, dictated by a strong sense of civic duty tempered by profound humanity and generosity, which a series of heavy blows does not manage to shake. Moreover, although the plot hardly presents any love complications, as Berenice is announced as already departed near the beginning of the drama (I ii) and Tito is only given three lines to lament the loss (I v), yet there is no doubt as to the influence exercised by the romantic Tituses of Racine's *Bérénice* and Corneille's *Tite et Bérénice* in helping shape Metastasio's highly sensitive Tito. Finally, Corneille's *Cinna ou La clémence d'Auguste*, while it referred to Cinna's conspiracy under Augustus, presents more than one point of contact with Metastasio's *Tito*, especially in the handling of those scenes where the emperor tries to make sense of his friend's unacceptable conduct.[36]

From the outset, *La clemenza di Tito* looks like a programmatic piece. The main biographical source, Suetonius' *Titi Vita*, is employed to sketch the character's profile by the quotation of famous *dicta*.[37] His definition of Titus as *deliciae generis humani* (Suet. *Titi Vita*, 1), for example, is recalled in the Argument preceding the text.

> Non ha conosciuto l'antichità né migliore né più amato principe di Tito Vespasiano. Le sue virtù lo resero a tutti sì caro, che fu chiamato 'la delizia del genere umano'.

> The ancient world did not know a better and more beloved prince than Titus Vespasianus. His virtues so endeared him to everybody that he was called 'the delight of the human race'.

---

[35] As testified by the ancient biographers – see in particular Suetonius, *Vita Titi*, 6-7.

[36] Cf. A. Scuppa's annotations in his edition of *La clemenza di Tito* (Modena, 1930), and also Brunelli's commentary in Metastasio, *Tutte le opere*, vol. 1, pp. 1499-1501. The relationship between the two texts once led Voltaire to misquote Metastasio's drama as *La clémence d'Auguste*: see Voltaire to Francesco Albergati Capacelli, Ferney, December 23, 1760: 'J'ai vu un prince pardonner une injure, après une représentation de la *Clémence d'Auguste*' ('I once witnessed a prince forgiving an offence after watching a performance of *The Clemency of Augustus*'), in: Voltaire, *Correspondence*, vol. 44, p. 263, n. 8722.

[37] According to common practice, the ancient sources are declared in the 'Argument' prefixed to the text of the libretto: Suetonius, Aurelius Victor, Cassius Dio, Zonaras, followed by an 'etc'. As a matter of fact, Suetonius is the only author among these to have been extensively used by Metastasio.

The same point is made by Sesto in the first scene when he tries to counter Vitellia's arguments for having Tito murdered.

> Sesto (…) Ah, non togliamo, in Tito,
> La sua delizia al mondo, il padre a Roma,
> L'amico a noi. (I i)

> [Sextus (…) Ah! Let us not, in Titus, deprive the world of its delight, and take from ourselves a friend, from Rome its father!]

Later on Sesto speaks through another Suetonian dictum referred to Titus, the famous *Amici, diem perdidi* (Suet. *Titi Vita*, 8).

> Sesto (…) Inutil chiama,
> perduto il giorno ei dice,
> in cui fatto non ha qualcun felice. (I i)

> [Sextus (…) And [Titus] thinks the day is purposeless and lost, that has not made someone happy.]

Suetonius is not the only author who offered adequate words for the praise of Titus. When Annio exhorts Tito to accept a public declaration of his divine status,

> Annio (...) Più che mortale
> Giacché altrui ti dimostri, a' voti altrui
> Comincia ad avvezzarti. (I v)

> [Annius (...) Since you have shown your subjects your immortal nature, you will have to accept your subjects' invocations.]

he does so by rephrasing Virgil's address to Augustus in *Georgics*, 1, 42, 'and even now [i.e. before your deification] grow used to be invoked in prayers' (*et votis iam nunc adsuesce vocari*).[38] The Augustus of Corneille's *Cinna* offered further materials that could easily be adapted by Metastasio for the glorification of Titus[39] – though not without a competitive intent, as a revealing scene suggests. While in anguish about the incumbent need of using severity against the conspirator Sesto, Tito is suddenly worried by the thought of his legacy.

---

[38] See Brunelli's commentary, in Metastasio, *Tutte le opere*, vol. 1, p. 1500.
[39] *Ibidem*, pp. 1501-1502.

(…) Or che diranno
I posteri di noi? Diran che in Tito
Si stancò la clemenza,
Come in Silla e in Augusto
La crudeltà. (III vii)

[What will posterity say? They will say that clemency in Titus wearied out, as cruelty had in Sulla and Augustus.]

That Sulla should be remembered as the tyrant who had grown tired of his own countless atrocities was fair enough. To associate with his name that of Augustus, on the other hand, could not but be a premeditated attempt to remove a potential threat to Titus' primacy. After all, Titus' progress had not been much different from that of Augustus – both had paved their way to imperial rule with the corpses of their enemies.[40] In Metastasio's portrait of the clement ruler Titus was supposed to stand alone and unrivalled.

Political maxims and stage action

The most influential sub-text for Metastasio's treatment of Titus is however Seneca's *De clementia* ('On Mercy'). It is perhaps not irrelevant to note that the joint comment on Sulla's and Augustus' cruelty was probably inspired by Seneca's essay.[41]

In an article published in 1994, L. Sannia Nowé thoroughly investigated the character of the clement sovereign in seventeenth- and eighteenth-century French and Italian theatre.[42] The Senecan text was standard reading for the supporters of enlightened rule, and it is safe to assume that Metastasio must have taken direct cognizance of it. One should add that the editions

---

[40] Cf. Suetonius, *Augusti Vita*, 13-15, 27 and *idem, Titi Vita*, 6.

[41] Cf. Seneca, *De clementia*, 1, 12, 1: 'Sullam (…) cui occidendi finem fecit inopia hostium' ('Sulla (...) whose assassinations were only put to an end by a dearth of enemies'); 1, 9, 1: 'Cum [Augustus] hoc aetatis esset, quod tu nunc es, duodevicensimum egressus annum, iam pugiones in sinum amicorum absconderat (...)' (When [Augustus] was at your [Nero's] present age, having just passed his eighteenth year, he had already buried his dagger in the bosom of friends […]).

[42] Sannia Nowé, 'Epifanie e metamorfosi', pp. 171-196. Cf. also Joly, 'Metastasio e l'ideologia', pp. 9-40, reprinted (with changes) in J. Joly, *Dagli Elisi all'Inferno. Il melodramma tra Italia e Francia dal 1730 al 1850* (Florence, 1990), chapter 2; Seidel, 'Seneca-Corneille-Mozart', pp. 345-66; Gioviale, 'La *Clemenza di Tito* da Metastasio a Mozart', pp. 117-142; Angelini, '*La clemenza di Tito*', vol. 2, pp. 1039-1053; Bellina, 'Zeno e Metastasio', p. 289; Feldman, *Opera and Sovereignty*, pp. 226-267.

of Corneille's *Cinna*, since the appearance of the first (Paris, 1643), had the dedicatory epistle to M. de Montoron followed by the long passage from Seneca's *De clementia* (1, 9) where Titus deals directly with the conspirator Cinna, often accompanied by Montaigne's translation (*Essais*, I, 23).[43]

'Of all men none is better graced by mercy than a king or a prince'.[44] Seneca's words, thought by him to be fitting for Nero as a promising young emperor, turned out to be a perfect token of utterly misplaced confidence. But the ideal lived on, and could be applied to more suitable individuals like Titus. Most of the principles discussed by Seneca in his essay and introduced by Metastasio in his drama have been identified by Sannia Nowé. They all present the typical characteristic of commonplaces solidified by centuries of political discourse – the king is like a father to his nation (I v; *De clem.* 1, 12, 2); gods must be imitated, not emulated, by rulers (I v; *De clem.* 1, 3, 7); the frequency of punishments only goes to the detriment of authority (I viii; *De clem.* 1, 20, 2; 1, 22, 1-2); regal dignity brings anxiety and special obligations towards one's own reputation (III, vii; *De clem.* 1, 8); before sentencing someone to death kings must exercise patience, like wise farmers strive to save the unsound branch of a tree before sacrificing it (III vii; *De clem.* 2, 7, 4).

Metastasio's ways of turning Seneca's argument into effective theatrical lines may be appreciated from the following examples. Tito's comment against the rigours of excessively severe justice,

> Tito Se la giustizia usasse
> Di tutto il suo rigor, sarebbe presto
> Un deserto la terra. (I ix)

> [Titus If justice should exert its utmost rigour, the earth would soon be turned into a desert.]

clearly echoes Seneca's *De clementia*, 1, 6, 1.

> (...) consider how great would be the loneliness and the desolation of it [i.e. of Rome] if none should be left but those whom a strict judge would acquit.[45]

---

[43] Corneille, *Cinna ou La Clémence d'Auguste*, sign. ē ii *recto*-[ē ii *verso*]. The famous dialogue between Augustus and Cinna served as model for the dialogue between Tito and Sesto in *La clemenza di Tito*, III, vi.

[44] Seneca, *De clementia*, 1, 3, 3: 'Nullum tamen clementia ex omnibus magis quam regem aut principem decet'. All quotations are from Seneca, *Moral Essays*, vol. 1.

[45] *Ibidem*, 1, 6, 1: '(...) quanta solitudo ac vastitas futura sit, si nihil relinquitur, nisi quod iudex severus absolverit'.

The lines that immediately follow

> Ove si trova [i.e. a man]
> Che una colpa non abbia, o grande o lieve?
> Noi stessi esaminiam. Credimi: è raro
> Un giudice innocente
> Dell'error che punisce. (I ix)

[Where shall we find a man without fault, either light or grave? Let us but view ourselves. Believe me, seldom is a judge free from the crime with which he has charged the offender.]

neatly correspond to another Senecan reflection:

> How few prosecutors there are who would escape conviction under the very law which they cite for the prosecution; how few accusers are free from blame.[46]

When the supreme moment has come and Tito, made certain of Sesto's culpability, has nearly resolved to send him to the block, the thought of giving in to the base desire of personal revenge holds back his hand.

> Tito Vendetta! Ah! Tito, e tu sarai capace
> D'un sì basso desio, che rende uguale
> L'offeso all'offensor? Merita in vero
> Gran lode una vendetta, ove non costi
> Più che il volerla. Il torre altrui la vita
> È facoltà comune
> Al più vil della terra: il darla è solo
> De' numi e de' regnanti. (III vii)

[Titus Revenge! Ah! Titus, and will you then descend so low, and harbour such a base desire, that makes the offended and the offender equal? Indeed a mighty praise deserve those who take revenge at no greater cost than their own whim. To take one man's life is the prerogative of the lowliest member of mankind; to give it, is the privilege of gods and kings alone.]

Seneca had already expressed the same notion.

---

[46] *Ibidem*, 1, 6, 2: 'Quotus quisque ex quaesitoribus est, qui non ex ipsa ea lege teneatur, qua querit? quotus quisque accusator vacat culpa?'.

But the man for whom vengeance is easy, by disregarding it, gains assured praise for clemency. Those placed in lowly station are more free to use force, to quarrel, to rush into a brawl, and to indulge their wrath; when the odds are matched, blows fall light; but in a king, even loud speech and unbridled words ill accord with his majesty.[47]

The noble words whereby Tito rejects his vengeful instinct as unworthy of a ruler sparked the enthusiasm of Voltaire. He considered them 'l'éternelle leçon de tous les Rois, & le charme de tous les hommes' (an eternal lesson for all kings, and a delight for the human race), and the two pivotal scenes of Metastasio's drama (III vi and vii) seemed to him

> comparables à tout ce que la Grece a eu de plus beau, si elle ne sont pas supérieures; ces deux scenes dignes de Corneille, quand il n'est pas déclamateur, & de Racine, quand il n'est pas faible; ces deux scenes qui ne sont pas fondées sur un amour d'opera; mais sur les plus nobles sentimens du cœur humain, ont une durée trois fois plus longue au moins que les scenes les plus étendues de nos Tragédies en musique. De pareils morceaux ne seraient pas supportés sur notre théâtre lyrique, qui ne se soutient guéres que par des maximes de galanterie, & par des passions manquées, à l'exception d'Armide, & de belles scenes d'Iphigénie, ouvrages plus admirables qu'imités.[48]

> [comparable, when not superior, to the finest ever produced in ancient Greece. Those two scenes are worthy of Corneille when he is not declamatory or of Racine when he is not feeble. Those two scenes do not rely upon the usual operatic love intrigues, but on the noblest feelings of a human heart. Their duration is at least three times as long as the longest scenes in our *tragédies en musique*. Nothing of that sort would be appreciated in our music theatre, where pleasantries and unsatisfied passions are the only imaginable themes. *Armide* and some scenes from *Iphigénie* are the only exceptions – but these are works that one tends to admire rather than imitate.]

---

[47] *Ibidem*, 1, 7, 4: '(...) at cui ultio in facili est, is omissa eam certam laudem mansuetudinis consequitur. Humili loco positis exercere manum, litigare, in rixam procurrere ac morem irae suae gerere liberius est; leves inter paria ictus sunt; regi vociferatio quoque verborumque intemperantia non ex maiestate est'. Cf. also *Ibidem*, 1, 5, 4-7; 1, 20-22.

[48] [Voltaire], *La tragédie de Sémiramis*, pp. 7-8. I reproduce Voltaire's spelling as it appears in the 1750 edition. The two *tragédies en musique* cited by Voltaire are presumably Jean-Baptiste de Lully's *Armide* (Paris, 1686) and Henri Desmarets' *Iphigénie en Tauride* (Paris, 1704). The latter's score was completed by André Campra.

Love for an author can alter one's judgment, but it can also sharpen it by making the judge more perceptive. Voltaire may have got carried away by his predilection for Metastasio when he claimed that Corneille and Racine and all of Greece hardly had anything to offer that could be compared to those two memorable scenes. But he was sufficiently expert in literary matters to realise that no sentiment, however noble, could have been so successfully conveyed without Metastasio's consummate art – that is, no commonplace, however powerful and persuasive, could have achieved such an effective result without an adequate translation into dramatic diction and action.

By claiming that the sustainability of such scenes (and the message thereof) would have been unthinkable in any other operatic piece, Voltaire was paying homage to a specific feature of metastasian style. This consisted of something that came to be illustrated more fully in later years, after the critical literature on Italian opera had grown in both size and depth. In his work *Le rivoluzioni del teatro musicale italiano* (1783-1788), Stefano Arteaga described as typically metastasian the ability to make sententious speech sound natural – that is, speech in which maxims had been inserted (*sentenziare*).[49] It was, he observed, nothing like the pedantic style of Seneca's tragedies, nor the style of those French authors plagued by the unhealthy habit of making 'lengthy inserts on insipid metaphysical questions'.[50] It was rather the result of *brevitas* conjugated with an ability to let 'the action come alive' by 'truncating many circumstances' and 'letting the plot move rapidly from one situation to another'.[51]

Arteaga's emphasis on Metastasio's sophisticated strategy, which coherently involved all the compositional elements of a drama to the minutest detail, still stands today as the most persuasive vindication of the poet's achievement. Less acute critics, unable to get the broader picture when trying to explain the enchanting effectiveness of metastasian style, have tended to deal with such features as plot, characterization, scene sequencing, stage action, poetic diction (and so forth) separately, without making at any point any serious attempt to produce a general consideration and evaluation of the whole in non-anachronistic terms. The foreseeable result has been that, in referring to diction in particular, most of them misinterpreted (and some keep misinterpreting) Metastasio's aim towards 'naturality' as excessive

---

[49] Hence the habit of extracting 'sentences and maxims' from Metastasio's works and arraging them thematically: cf. e.g. 'Sentenze, e massime estratte dalle Opere del Metastasio', in: *Opere del Signor Ab. Pietro Metastasio*, vol. 15, pp. 1-132.

[50] Arteaga, *Le rivoluzioni del teatro*, vol. 1, p. 361: 'Riflettasi quanto sia naturale il suo sentenziare, e non pedantesco ... lunghi squarcj d'insipida metafisica'.

[51] *Ibidem*, p. 350: '... troncar molte circostanze, passar in somma rapidamente da una situazione in un'altra, acciochè si renda più brillante, e più viva l'azione'.

proneness to facility and 'musicality'.[52] If one turns on the other hand to Arteaga, one realizes how, in his view, *that* specific diction naturally complemented the dynamics of *that* specific kind of theatrical representation, while successfully delivering a message that was supposed to be of ethical and political significance – in the spirit of Horace's suggestion to mix *utile* with *dulce*, an underlying tenet for all forms of art production until the Romantic Age.[53] In such a context, Metastasio could with good reason be praised for his unrivalled skill in making solemn formulations sound as natural and accessible as plain speech, and as plausible as common wisdom or – indeed – commonplaces.

---

[52] See in particular the objections moved by Saverio Bettinelli in his *Discorso sopra la poesia italiana* (1781), in: Bettinelli, *Lettere virgiliane*, pp. 218-219.
[53] Arteaga, *Le rivoluzioni del teatro*, vol. 1, pp. 345-361.

STAGING COMMONPLACES IN *CHEFS D'ŒUVRE*

MOZART'S DA PONTE OPERAS

Ståle Wikshåland

Emperor Joseph II articulated much of his own critique of Mozart, as well that of immediate posterity, in his famous remark on *The Abduction from the Seraglio*: 'Too many notes, and too beautiful for our ears, my dear Mozart' – an anecdote too good not to be true. The same can also be said of Mozart's reply, in all its hair-raising impudence: 'Exactly as many as needed, Your Majesty!'[1] The words resonate in numerous versions of subsequent – and precedent – complaints about a genre containing too much music and too little action. According to the playwright Beaumarchais for example, French opera is overburdened with *trop de musique*, and he quotes the *expression naïve* of his mentor, the opera composer Gluck, for whom opera in the French manner 'stinks of music'.[2]

Here we are confronted with a commonplace reaction, all the more confronting as it was articulated by a patron concerning a music market, or more precisely, an arena of entertainment, which was about to dissolve the existing feudal master-servant relationship between the musician-composer and a principal who reigned with absolute power, as was the situation in Vienna during the 1780s. We also encounter a highly untypical answer from someone who is still a subject of Joseph II, his sovereign – though on the brink of not being so any longer – and in this respect it is a highly impertinent and self-conscious remark. As we will see, this exchange marks a very tense and challenging situation indeed.

Viva la liberta!

However, let us move on to the music, where we find another example of Mozart's attitude, hopefully not too oft-used for the occasion, namely his *Don Giovanni*, in particular, the ending of Act I, No. 13 Finale, which covers Scenes XVI-XX.

---

[1] See Niemetschek's biography from 1798, *Leben des K.K. Kapellmeisters Wolfgang Gottlieb Mozart*.
[2] Howarth, *Beaumarchais*, p. 197.

With the assistance of Leporello, Don Giovanni is about to organise a ball at his own estate, with the aim of getting the peasants drunk and dancing and carrying off Zerlina during the confusion. Here, we enter the Finale in Scene XX.[3] Don Giovanni arrives after the finale has begun and starts to organise affairs by once again trying to separate Zerlina from Masetto. However, at this point, Don Ottavio, Donna Anna and Donna Elvira enter, masked, with the intention of participating in the party incognito. Leporello invites them in.[4]

The scene changes to a large illuminated ballroom with multiple dances playing at once. In this melée, Don Giovanni manages to drag Zerlina away, and her screams are heard as he assaults her. As the door is knocked down by Don Ottavio, Don Giovanni produces Leporello as the criminal, although the guests continue to believe that Don Giovanni is guilty. The finale ends in turmoil, within and without.

This ending of the first act depicts – immediately after a resounding *Viva la liberta!* – class society through the simultaneous play, in elaborate counterpoint, of three different genres aligned to the three classes of feudal society: a courtly minuet for the nobles, a less noble contredanse for the middle ranks and a rustic Teutscher for the peasants.[5] In short, we are confronted with a virtuoso musical representation of the reigning class structure.

The question is whether this setting of '*Viva la libertà*' ('Hooray for liberty') in *Don Giovanni* has a secret political meaning or not. It is true that the overt significance of the words uttered at Don Giovanni's party echo with libertine ideas, that is, they plain and simply invite the guests to enjoy themselves and have a good time. However, Mozart's setting is clearly martial and stirring. With trumpets and drums, the music resonates like a call to arms.

Several commentators have dismissed such an overtly political interpretation, such as for example Robert Marshall:

> Don Giovanni's declaration of 'Viva la libertà' was indeed nothing less than subversive. The guiding spirit of the seducer's political message, however, is not Thomas Jefferson but the Marquis de Sade. Don Giovanni is clearly calling not for political democracy but for the liberty of the libertine. At this point, at least, one can only hope that Mozart is in fact not 'expressing himself'.[6]

---

[3] Mozart, *Don Giovanni*, pp. 204-264.
[4] *Ibidem*, p. 212.
[5] *Ibidem*, pp. 219-227.
[6] Marshall, 'What Mozart Meant'.

There are no obvious arguments that can be voiced against Marshall's point, no reconstruction of the meaning in general to which we can appeal. We simply have to concentrate on what is going on in the music. When we do so – and in spite of the cheers in the midst of a heavily sexually laden scene being played out on a larger scale within a clearly libertine plot – there is no reason to doubt that this scene is political. Even if the meaning of the words *Viva la libertà* is certainly 'Have a good time and enjoy yourselves', the music is ostentatiously militaristic and rousing, with trumpets and drums reappearing in the score for the first time since the overture, and in brilliant and resonant C major.

As such, this is clearly political. Ideas of political liberty were very much in the air right after the American Revolution. As pointed out by Marshall, political liberty and libertinism have generally been associated – and for good reason; it was sometimes thought that when the revolutionaries gained power, wives and daughters would inevitably be raped or debauched. Furthermore, in the most influential of the Marquis de Sade's writings, *La philosophie dans le boudoir*, sexual liberty is presented as the logical and necessary culmination of the French Revolution.[7]

However, an interpretation along these lines does not hit the mark, because Mozart's music at this *specific* point in *Don Giovanni* is not in the least erotic but utterly political and military in character. Mozart is certainly *also* leaning on the popular belief that revolutionary politics and libertinism were closely bound together, as they were, indeed, constantly from the seventeenth century until the twentieth. Which does not, however, mean that either Mozart or *Don Giovanni* were propagandists for 'democracy', but only that an audience in 1780 would have understood the allusion.

Staging social topoi

Does all this have any bearing on our topic, the role of commonplaces with respect to the legitimation of authority in the eighteenth century, as is the main theme of this volume?

Let us take the matter a little further by focusing specifically on the subject of commonplaces in connection with *chefs d'œuvre*, or art for the elite. As noted in the introduction to this volume, the project to which the volume contributes was not primarily concerned with the analysis of so-called masterpieces or how these might function in public debates or in the communication of – or the persuasion concerning – authority. The focus and point of departure for this project rather has been cultural production, less appreciated in arts discourses, which was meant to reach, convince and se-

---

[7] See De Sade, *La philosophie dans le boudoir*, originally published in 1795.

duce the masses or specific groups. Although the notion of commonplaces is not irrelevant to much of that which is considered to belong to the higher arts – this will also be made clear in the following concerning Mozart's operas – it remains reasonable to assert that such forms as the texts, music and images directly produced to convince or influence large groups in society are generally more dependent on the use of commonplaces than complex works of art where the 'message' would normally be less unequivocal and the employed means much more refined. However, employed in very individual ways, commonplaces are not at all absent in artistic masterpieces. Indeed, my topic, the staging of commonplaces in Mozart's Da Ponte operas – indisputable masterpieces to say the least – makes it urgent to thematise commonplaces insofar as they *are* at play in these *chefs d'œuvre*, but not only – and perhaps not even first and foremost – in the overtly political way we have just seen exemplified in *Don Giovanni.*

Thus, if commonplaces in general denominate formulas and artefacts in standard usage, sometimes even verging on banalities, commonplaces in music, for example, are of another order. As I will try to point out in this paper, it both comprises standard elements of an opera plot, and also, in a more limited musical context, turns out to be closely related to musical conventions.

On a more general level, we might say that Mozart's Da Ponte operas stage their own time and social relationships at all levels. From this perspective, the exchanges on the opera stage play games with the legitimacy of their own time, and this is particularly the case for *The Marriage of Figaro.* The arena for this play with reality is not limited to the stage in a narrow sense, but also comprises the relationships between opera stage and *salon*, between actors and spectators.

We are dealing with a staging of power, where power and authority are dramatised, simulated and displayed in situations where something important, at a theatrical as well as a social level, is at stake. The stage in the literal sense is located in a broader social context, which includes the audiences of Vienna and Prague, who, when the show is over, walk home and put to practice the same games amongst themselves that they have just witnessed on stage in the opera house. There, these games can gain from the power of fascination associated with fiction, expressing a dizzying kaleidoscope of relationships.

From this perspective, with *The Marriage of Figaro*, Mozart is at the very threshold of his full development of the art of musical characterisation: the ability to portray people in the process of change. The characters are portrayed through conflicts that are fundamentally social and political. The preconditions for being able to portray people through social and political conflicts turn out to be closely linked to the changing forms of a motif in the sonata style. This not only gives a logical coherence to the music, but allows it to express emotions that change before our eyes, from menace to triumph. Take the Countess, for example, who lives in a world of comedy and carries the court's mask of conversation and intrigue. In her soliloquies, however, we see her as a real woman. The court also sees her when she lowers her mask, in the context of reconciliation and forgiveness in the finale of the very last, that is the fourth, act. We not only see behind her mask, we see her very unmasking, her transformation.[8]

We will pursue this theme through a closer look at the finale to the fourth act of *Figaro*, the scene that concludes the opera as a whole. In a dark garden with two handy niches we see Barberina rush through before Figaro, Bartolo and Basilio arrive in preparation to accost the Count as he approaches Susanna. Basilio describes the perils of confronting those in power using a fable about a donkey-skin cape. Figaro vents his fury at the female sex and Susanna realises that Figaro has heard about the assignation and has misinterpreted it. She decides to tease him by singing a serenade, ostensibly to the Count, but actually to Figaro. Cherubino arrives, mistakes the Countess for Susanna and flirts with her. The Count arrives to meet Susanna, and just as Cherubino is about to give the disguised Countess a kiss, the Count interposes himself and (once again) sends Cherubino away.

The Count starts to woo 'Susanna', with Figaro and the real Susanna commenting separately from the sidelines until the Count takes 'Susanna' into a private garden house. Figaro starts to tell the 'Countess' (actually Susanna) about the Count's misdeeds, but recognises Susanna's voice, and starts to woo her as if she really was the Countess. Susanna cannot bear this, reveals herself, slaps Figaro and they are blissfully reunited. The Count enters this conundrum, looking for 'Susanna', who has evidently slipped away. The real Susanna and Figaro continue the pretence that Figaro is wooing the Countess. The commotion brings everyone out, last of all, the real Countess. The Count reacts to the appearance of the Countess in her own person by surprisingly asking her for forgiveness, in a most sincere tone of voice. The Countess responds in a manner that distinguishes the renowned recognition scene, one of *Figaro*'s single most famous scenes, by nobly and unconditionally accepting the Count's humble apology. Thus, the opera's *folle journée* ends in rejoicing.

This concluding section depends for its efficacy upon the finale being viewed as a whole in all its hilarity, while at the same time the situation outgrows it. Music not only provides decorum to a drama already depicted, it creates drama of a depth that would not have existed through the libretto alone. Mozart transgresses the standards of the genre and establishes a new

---

[8] Nagel, *Autononomy & Mercy: Reflections on Mozart's Opera*, p. 32.

level of characterisation and thus becomes the actual dramatist of the opera. He is also able to portray a subversion or destabilisation of the structure of class society by means of a seduction that also implies a seducing of the seducer. Along these lines, *The Marriage of Figaro* stages an almost unheard of political situation, attaining power through its musical and formal potential.

This example shows us how Mozart does not confine himself to relating to a given world of musical forms in the abstract, but elucidates how the dramatic and the musical become one and the same, where the drama in each single case portrays and legitimises its point through the verisimilitude of its dramaturgy – Mozart's musical staging, so to speak. At the same time, within this particular integrated musical, the dramaturgical staging articulates the critical portrayal of the times' most pressing social conflicts. The new tone of voice in Mozart's music, occurring as the Count asks for and is granted forgiveness, intervenes in the story and gives it a new dimension in a way that alludes to what we, with Adorno, might call music's *Einspruchsrecht*.

Here, the arena of entertainment is in the new context of opera, markedly different from the situation surrounding *opera seria*. The latter appears as the projection of a sphere of public representation onto and for the audience, as subjugates of a medium strongly regulated by rules of genre and conventions. This transformation, moving from the political authority of the old order linked to the public sphere of *opera seria*, marks a situation where the uncontested stability of traditional authority was no longer unequivocally acceptable. This can be observed variously but very generally in the late eighteenth century through the rise of new political groups and the political influence of intellectual discussions which questioned traditional commonplace wisdom and authority with notable destabilising effects.[9] Moreover, due to the increasing influence of different means of communication, increasing numbers of people entered the public debate. In this general situation, which of course would vary from place to place, the authorities needed a change in strategy in order to gain and maintain continuous control.

From my point of view, and in accordance with the example cited from *Figaro*, I will emphasise that the relevance of this problematic in the context of the Mozart Da Ponte operas above all concerns the transition from one public order to a new and different one, with new rules – a situation in which no particular event has the privilege of being foremost. What we are dealing with is the establishment of an entertainment market of an entirely

---

[9] See also the introduction to this volume, p. xii.

new kind.[10] Here the entertainment effect is as crucial as it is hard to control. It is an effect, however, that always attracts the greatest interest.

Take the uses of the so-called *droit de seigneur*, which plays an important role in both *Figaro* and *Don Giovanni*. Politics had always played an important role in *opera seria*, but the political impact of *Figaro* and *Don Giovanni* is mainly grounded in the popular conception of the aristocracy's corruptness and sexual exploitation of others. This attitude may appear superficial in light of the situation current in the Vienna of the 1780s, but a closer look reveals the deeper emotions touched upon by this topos.

In Mozart's time, the phenomenon of *droit de seigneur* itself had already become an anachronism, merely a vulgar myth. In fact, according to recent research, it was probably never more than a myth and measured against any actual, contemporary situation was fictitious from the outset.[11] However, bringing this fiction into operatic plots as a familiar topos, invigorates the play with relationships of authority and power and the erotics entangled in this game which make it possible to challenge the ruling power. Bringing it onto the stage quite simply creates a genuine anti-aristocratic resonance in the plot as such – an atmosphere which evokes the audience's spontaneous laughter at the aristocracy. It makes the aristocracy subject to ridicule, as part of the entertainment, which in this manner opens a new space and a new repertoire of possible utterances.

Such is the advantage of fiction, and the exploitation by both operas of the phenomenon of the *droit de seigneur* underlines this, just as it facilitates a certain way of challenging power. In this manner, comic opera, *opera buffa,* became more serious politically than *opera seria* ever managed to be – even if *opera seria* clearly is the more strategic of the two due to its task of representing power and, as such, contributing to its maintenance.

In general, we must be aware of how Mozart's operas stage their elements – how they put them into play. Considering them merely as 'reality represented' provides a limited perspective. This point touches upon the aesthetic dimension, the privilege of art to act in a subversive way towards the elements it stages – a dimension that both prevents the operas from becoming worn through over-use and helps them create their own tradition.

The point also touches upon the way music conveys meaning. Almost all of the musical elements in Mozart's musical world do *not* act as 'signs'. They do not suggest meaning, but rather stimulate emotion. In short, they do not signify, they excite. This is the basic difference between the way that, for example, Bach and Rameau deal with sentiment and the way that Mozart approaches it. Representing or signifying emotion in music works

---

[10] See the seminal study by Hunter, *The Culture of Opera Buffa.*
[11] Till, *Mozart and the Enlightenment*, p. 148; Boureau, *The Lord's First Night.*

through metaphor or imitation. Stimulating or provoking, it may have metaphorical roots that have helped develop and elaborate the technique, but the
metaphors are no longer immediately recognisable. The music accompanying the entrance of the Statue in *Don Giovanni* does not portray fear and
does not *signify* fear, *it strikes fear into our hearts*.

Mozart's music works directly upon our nervous systems. So, of course,
does the music of, let us say, Handel or Jomelli, that is, the music of *opera
seria*, but it is not their principal way of conveying emotion. The creation
and conveyance of extra-musical meaning in the later eighteenth century
moves away from the conventional representation of coded meaning which
needs an insider's knowledge, towards the sheer effect of music upon the
listeners in a concert hall or opera house. This is what looms large in the
new arena of entertainment, and it is inextricably linked to the new music
market which was about to supplant the power relations of the old order.

Commonplaces at play

Thus, do commonplaces exist in this context? They are in fact a very important dimension of Mozart's art, though largely underplayed in its interpretation history, according to which commonplaces are generally considered to
be among elements that great composers would rather shun than embrace.

We will highlight the issue with an example, approaching the problem
via a detour through *Figaro*'s libretto (thereby also hopefully shedding
some light on the importance of Da Ponte), and leave aside the musical issues for a while. In accordance with Jessica Waldoff,[12] I will focus on the
function of recognition scenes in *Figaro*'s plot, bearing in mind that these
scenes not only mark moments of resolution and completion, but also strain
belief and call attention to the contrivance and quality of artifice inherent to
fictional plots.

I will begin my discussion by summarising Jessica Waldoff's recent
discussion of one of Mozart's favourite scenes,[13] when in the third act the
discovery of a spatula-shaped birthmark on Figaro's arm reveals him to be
the long-lost son of his archenemies Marcellina and Bartolo. This recognition scene marks a crucial reversal in the plot. It releases Figaro from the
contract that binds him to either repay the money he owes Marcellina or to
marry her, for, as the lawyer Don Curzio is the first to observe, Figaro cannot marry his own mother. It transforms Marcellina and Bartolo into doting

---

[12] Waldoff, *Recognition in Mozart's Operas*, pp. 10-15.
[13] According to Michael Kelly, who created the roles of Basilio and Don Curzio in
the first *mise en scène* of *Le nozze di Figaro*. Cf. Waldoff, *Recognition in Mozart's
Operas*, pp. 10-14.

parents who are now glad to forgive their newly rediscovered son his outstanding debt and to embrace Susanna as a daughter. Finally, to the Count's
dismay, it removes the last obstacle in the way of Figaro's marriage to
Susanna.

It is difficult to imagine a coincidence more fortuitous – or more
unlikely. It is as if this recognition scene was designed to call attention to
the construction of the plot and the implausibility of its fiction; to the fact of
one's participation in a comedy. Furthermore, it does so by making deliberate sport of the conventions of recognition.

Completely in accordance with Beaumarchais, the scene combines aspects of two well-known recognition scenes from the classical period, both
treated as paradigmatic in Aristotle's *Poetics*. The spatula-shaped birthmark
is modelled on Odysseus' scar, the mark by which his old nurse recognises
him on his return to Ithaca. At the same time, the comic discovery of identity by means of this scar, fortunately indeed for Figaro, occurs in time to
prevent him from marrying his mother and enduring the tragic fate of Oedi-
pus. Thus, fused by the librettist into one scene, we are presented with the
two scenes that Aristotle marks out as respectively the finest and the weakest examples of his five types of recognition.

Such a moment as occurs in *Figaro* may be enjoyed as much for its ingenious construction as for the happy reconciliation it makes possible on
stage. However, Mozart uses this means twice, with Susanna entering soon
after during the Sextet, Scene V, No. 19, to discover Figaro in Marcellina's
arms. Confusion, discovery and reconciliation are immediately replayed to
create a second recognition scene for Susanna. This complex and critically
self-reflective recognition illustrates how recognition can problematise the
very sense of closure it attempts to bring about. It is literally a scene that is
too good to be true, simultaneously rounding off the plot and highlighting
its own artifice.

Here Mozart and Da Ponte combine long stretches into one continuous
action, making the plot coherent by way of dramaturgical means. However,
by appearing too good to be true, their effect is as much to draw attention to
its fictional character as it is to directing attention towards the story that
makes us all draw a deep sigh of relief at its happy resolution. In all its dramatic verisimilitude, moments such as these also always reminds us that we
are in the world of the theatre. We partake in *Figaro*'s entertaining games of
fiction because the plot becomes credible in the very moment and by the
very means that also point to its own character of artifice, making the impossible and unlikely both possible and likely – though only on stage. Thus
we may indulge in the pleasure of the performance, letting ourselves be ap-
palled and delighted in turn without being hindered by reservations.

The use of conventions

Conventions in Mozart demonstrate his reliance on formulas that are almost meaningless in themselves. We are dealing with expressive motifs, the expressive content of which remains vague and diffuse, so that significance would have to be drawn – in a specific way – from each new work and from each and every passage as it renders itself concrete as a musical event. What we wish to achieve is to avoid hearing Mozart filtered through a finicky set of references to the melodic formula. Rather, we should be aware of how these formulas – very often banal, conventional and commonplace, even if there are remarkable exceptions – work within a larger harmonic movement to allow the dramatic action to unfold, to establish the most extraordinary dramatic strokes by rapid changes of harmony and texture, and to allow both the passion and the irony of the music to move easily within the spacious frame created by Mozart's manipulation and transformation of conventional form. According to Charles Rosen, 'Mozart displays the conventions nakedly: his radical ideas coexist side by side with the most commonplace ones, the latter transformed only by his exquisite workmanship'.[14]

Mozart's melodic shapes are almost never as idiosyncratic as Haydn's, and his passage work is almost always banal. Beethoven knew how to make the most ordinary tonal formulas appear idiosyncratic, like Haydn's more individualised motifs, *grosso modo* – by way of rough use of accent, marked reiteration and dynamics. Mozart needed his motifs to sound ordinary; it allowed him to release the latent expressiveness of tonal language with ease, so that moments of concentrated energy could act as a shock. His accidental borrowings from Gluck, Paisiello and Piccinni do not establish him as a borrower of meaning. It rather shows us how commonplace these formulas were, as ingredients of the style of the period, and the examples could be multiplied, not least by searching for musical quotations from Johann Christian Bach.

Any attempt to realise the old musicological dream of giving music a distinct, referential power, thus enabling it to act like a language, bypasses the large scale on which Mozart works. He does not represent feelings through insignificant motifs, just as he never characterises the hero in passing using four or five notes. The shudder felt by Donna Elvira is indicated through her musical gesture in very few notes in the Sextet, but Mozart needs a whole aria, transformed into a trio by Leporello's and Don Giovanni's sardonic comments, in order to take on her characterisation.

---

[14] Rosen, 'Radical, Conventional Mozart', p. 90.

Mozart's motifs are not at all as unique as many presume. This can also be said of the cases where it is not wrong to point to ideas in Mozart that we cannot relate intertextually to other composers. These ideas nonetheless find their place within the style of the time in a completely uncontroversial way. Mozart works on, unwearyingly, within a style permeated by conventions.

This style has something to do with perspective and focus. Most importantly, and perhaps most characteristically for Mozart's operatic style, no-one else was able to control music over such long musical spans, not even Beethoven, who nevertheless did not rely as much on single motifs as on blocks of tonality, and articulated his points more through rhythm and texture. Altogether, Mozart's feeling for long-range movement was unsurpassed.

The point is that in spite of his radical experiments, Mozart as a composer appeared to rely heavily on the musical conventions of his day, exploiting the musical commonplaces of reigning styles bluntly – apart from the very fact that no-one but Mozart was able to handle these basic conventions with similar skill and completely naturally.

Apart from Mozart's exceptional talents, there are also good historical reasons for this, connected to the specific character of Mozart's musical education and to its historical context. He travelled around Europe for years, visiting most of the important occidental musical centres, often for months at a time. We are not speaking of short concert visits, but of sojourns that often lasted months. This gave him the opportunity to gain first-hand acquaintance with all the contemporary styles in the Europe of his day, a situation which he made the most of with his exceptional talent for imitation. No other composer-in-the-making was ever offered such riches of perspective on their chosen art.

In addition to developing a completely unrestrained use of conventions, another aspect of this perspective can be formulated in relation to one of his almost contemporary colleagues, namely Beethoven. Not only was Mozart the last composer to compose as if Beethoven had not yet been born, he composed as if Beethoven would never come into existence. As Scott Burnham has shown so brilliantly in his seminal study, *Beethoven Hero*, Beethoven was not only 'a good composer', he very soon set the standard for what being 'a good composer' actually meant. He set the standards by which, fairly soon, all of Europe would be measured, and accordingly would listen. Transgression, the renunciation of conventions and genres, the notion of musical uproar, the doting upon conflict and resolution – in short the whole package of *per aspera ad astra* and the demand for originality in a formally revolutionary way – were non-existent ideals for Mozart. He did not relate to the Beethovenian standard at all.[15]

One of the consequences of this was that quite a few of Mozart's own musical topoi could be transferred into the new romantic aesthetic and musical arenas completely unmediated by any Beethovenian ideals and standards. We see this, for example, in the reception of Mozart by S. Kierkegaard, E.T.A. Hoffmann, G.B. Shaw and H. Abert – a reception of his work that runs contrary to a more general domestication of Mozart into a composer primarily of *schöne Klänge*. It also outdistances the growing perception of Mozart as a composer who incomprehensibly made the mistake of setting beautiful music to sham librettos such as Da Ponte's *Così fan tutte*, an attitude that culminated in Richard Wagner's comments.[16]

The fact is that Mozart's music radiated, not only through its potential to shock, but as much through its – seemingly effortless – ability to produce conventions with a corresponding ease and lightness. Charles Rosen has pointed out how long phrases with decidedly conventional figuring and banal motifs shape the ending of long stretches and give the structure a new clarity:

> Writing about Mozart, we are always tempted to dwell on the extraordinary purple passages without noticing that in every case they are followed or preceded by the most conventional devices. They complement and support each other.[17]

To be precise, Mozart was not radical or transgressive in his musical language, as, for example, was Beethoven. He was, however, able to compose within and with conventions, in this way staging commonplaces.

Final call

Here we may have located the conventions in their right place, not as part of persuasive strategies working on the behalf of power, but merely strategies for creating musical fictions. As such, music becomes able to seduce us into believing and involving ourselves in what is being played out in front of us, and without forcing us in any way to turn our backs on the knowledge that we still are in the theatre.

---

[15] Burnham, *Beethoven Hero*, pp. 29-65.
[16] Wagner, 'Oper und Drama', p. 37; Kierkegaard, 'The Immediate Erotic Stages', pp. 59-136; Hoffmann, *Schriften zur Musik*; Abert, *W.A. Mozart*.
[17] Rosen, 'Mozart at 250', section 3. Shaw, *Shaw on Music*, pp. 67-82.

The trick is to listen to Mozart without attaching a specific set of references to the melodic formulas. Instead, we should be aware of how these
formulas – often banal, conventional and commonplace, even if there are
indeed remarkable exceptions – operate within a larger harmonic movement
that enables the dramatic action to unfold so that it may produce the most
extraordinary outcome through rapid harmonic and textural changes. This to
allow both music's irony and passion to move unrestrained within the airy
frame created by Mozart's manipulation and transformation of conventional
form.

This is what we witness unfolding in the reunion scene of Pamina and
Tamino, one of *The Magic Flute*'s most moving single numbers.[18] The
scene is an inversion of the common myth of man's initiation by way of becoming the woman's saviour: here the woman in distress becomes the res-
cuer.

Tamino is about to go through his final trials and suddenly hears Pamina's voice. He is granted permission to speak to her and consequently to
pass through the trials with Pamina by his side. Pamina declares in front of
Tamino, who has arrived at Sarastro's palace with the sole purpose of sav-
ing her, that she will stand by him throughout his ordeal. The scene is part
of the finale of the second, that is, the last act.

The opening of this reunion scene is electrifyingly simple. In turn, the
loving couple sings only a small scale and a short cadence. There is not a
trace of original melody, everything is according to musical convention.
Yet, we are confronted with a passage that overflows with happiness, and as
such even surpasses the above-mentioned grand Sextet of *Figaro* (where
Susanna discovers that Figaro has found his true parents, so that nothing
stands between them and marriage).

The music here is seemingly very simple: a figure is repeated while the
harmonic rocks to and fro on the basic harmonies, that is, the tonic and the
dominant, where it seems to halt for half a minute or so. At the same time
we perceive a sudden background calm, a drastic shift of tonality, soft,
transparent instrumentation and a growing steady pulse in the orchestra that
flows into Mozart's melodic invention as a subtle form of declamation. All
the elements are commonplace, and the sum of them outstanding and
unique. As is Mozart himself.

---

[18] Mozart, *The Magic Flute*, pp. 299-104.

BIBLIOGRAPHY

Aan het volk van Nederland. Het democratisch manifest van Joan Derk van der Capellen tot den Pol 1781, eds W.F. Wertheim and A.H. Wertheim-Gijse Weenink (Weesp, 1981).

Abert, H., *W.A. Mozart* (New Haven, 2007).

Amdisen, A., *Til nytte og fornøjelse. Johann Friedrich Struensee (1737-1772)* (Copenhagen, 2002)

Anderson, B., *Imagined Communities. Reflections on the Origin and Spread of Nationalism* (London/New York, 2006).

Angelini, F., '*La clemenza di Tito*', in: Asor Rosa, A., ed., *Letteratura italiana. Le opere. L'età moderna, 1580-1800*, vol. 2 (Turin, 1993), pp. 1039-1053.

Arteaga, S., *Le rivoluzioni del teatro musicale italiano dalla sua origine fino al presente*, 3 vols. (Bologna, 1783-1788).

Aubignac, F.H., abbé de, *La Pratique du théâtre*, ed. P. Martino (Algiers, 1927).

Baeumer, M.L., 'Vorwort', in: Baeumer, M.L., ed., *Toposforschung* (Darmstadt, 1973).

Banks, K. and Bossier, P.G., eds, *Commonplace Culture in Western Europe in the Early Modern Period II. Consolidation of God-Given Power* (Leuven/Paris/Walpole, MA, 2010).

Barras, M., *The Stage Controversy from Corneille to Rousseau* (New York, 1933).

Beaumarchais, P.-A.C. de, *Œuvres*, Larthomas, P., ed., (Paris, 1988).

Bell, C., *Ritual Theory. Ritual Practice* (Oxford, 1992).

Bellina, A.L., 'Zeno e Metastasio: la riforma del melodramma', in: Malato, E., ed., *Storia della letteratura italiana*, vol. 5, *Il Settecento* (Rome, 1998), pp. 274-302, 311-312.

Benedetto, L.F., 'Jean-Jacques Rousseau tassofilo', in: *Uomini e tempi. Pagine varie di critica e di storia* (Naples, 1953), pp. 217-238.

Bergman, G.M., *Lighting in the Theatre* (Stockholm, 1977).

Bettinelli, S., *Lettere virgiliane e inglesi e altri scritti critici*, ed. Vittorio Enzo Alfieri (Bari, 1930).

Black, J., *The English Press in the Eighteenth Century* (London/Sydney, 1987).

———, *The English Press, 1621-1861* (Sutton, 2001).

Bloch, M., *Les rois thaumaturges* (Paris, 1924).

Blok, P.J., *Geschiedenis van het Nederlandsche volk*, vol. 2 (3rd rev. ed.; Leiden, 1924).

Boës, A., *La Lanterne magique de l'histoire. Essai sur le théâtre historique en France de 1750 à 1789*, *Studies on Voltaire and the Eighteenth Century* 213 (1982).

Boileau, N., *Satires, Epîtres, Art poétique*, ed. J.-P. Collinet (Paris, 1985).

Bossuet, J.B., *Maximes et réflexions sur la comédie* (Paris, 1928).

Bouhours, D., *La Manière de bien penser dans les ouvrages d'esprit* (Paris, 1705).

Boureau, A., *The Lord's First Night: The Myth of the Droit de Cuissage* (Chicago, 1998).

Boyce, G., 'The Fourth Estate: the reappraisal of a concept', in: Curran, J., Boyce, G. and Wingate, P., eds, *Newspaper History from the seventeenth century to the present day* (London, 1978), pp. 19-40.

Bradshaw, L.E., 'Ephraim Chambers' *Cyclopaedia*', in: Kafker, F., ed., *Notable Encyclopaedias of the Seventeenth and Eighteenth Centuries: Nine Predecessors of the "Encyclopédie", Studies on Voltaire and the Eighteenth Century* 194 (1981), pp. 123-140.

Bray, B., 'Voltaire et la querelle du théâtre en 1761: la *Conversation de M. l'intendant des menus en exercice avec M. l'abbé Grizel*', in: Mervaud, C., and Menant, S., eds, *Le Siècle de Voltaire. Hommage à René Pomeau*, vol. 1 (Oxford, 1987), pp. 137-147.

Bregnsbo, M., *Caroline Mathilde. Magt og skæbne* (Copenhagen, 2007).

Brewer, D., 'Constructing Philosophers', in: Brewer, D. and Hayes, J.C., eds, *Using the "Encyclopédie": Ways of Knowing, Ways of Reading, Studies on Voltaire and the Eighteenth Century* 2002:5, pp. 21-36.

Broersma, M., *Beschaafde vooruitgang. De wereld van de Leeuwarder Courant, 1752-2002* (Leeuwarden, 2002).

———, 'Constructing public opinion. Dutch newspapers on the eve of a revolution (1780-1795)', in: Koopmans, J.W., ed., *News and Politics in Early Modern Europe* (Leuven/ Paris/Dudley, MA, 2005), pp. 219-235.

———, 'Journalism as performative discourse. Why form and style matter', in: Rupar, V., ed., *Journalism and Meaning-making: Reading the Newspaper* (Cresskill, N.J.), pp. 15-35.

Burke, P., *The Fabrication of Louis XIV* (New Haven, 1992).

———, *A Social History of Knowledge. From Gutenberg to Diderot* (Cambridge, 2000).

Burnham, S., *Beethoven Hero* (New Jersey, 1995).

Burrows, S., 'The cosmopolitan press', in: Barker, H. and Burrows, S., eds, *Press, Politics and the Public Sphere in Europe and North-America 1760-1820* (Cambridge, 2002), pp. 23-47

Caffaro, F., *Lettre d'un théologien illustre par sa qualité et par son mérite, consulté par l'auteur pour savoir si la Comédie peut être mise, ou doit être absolument défendue*, in: *Œuvres de M. Boursault*, vol. 1 (Amsterdam, 1721), pp. 7-70.

Cailhava d'Estendoux, J.-F., *De l'Art de la comédie, nouvelle édition*, 2 vols. (Paris, 1786).

Cailleau, A.-C., *Les Tragédies de M. de Voltaire, ou Tancrède jugée par ses sœurs* (Paris, 1760)

Carducci, G., 'Pietro Metastasio' (1882), in: Carducci, G., *Opere*, vol. 19 (Bologna, 1908), pp. 63-93.

Cartmill, C., 'Madame de Sévigné, lectrice de Pierre Nicole. La lettre à l'épreuve de l'essai', in: Brouard-Arends, I., ed., *Lectrices d'Ancien Régime* (Rennes, 2003), pp. 351-359.

Chambers, E., *Cyclopedia; or, An Universal Dictionary of the arts and sciences* (London, 1728).

Charrier, C., *Héloïse dans l'histoire et dans la légende* (Paris, 1933).

Chartier, R., *On the Edge of the Cliff. History, Language, and Practices* (Baltimore, 1997).

Châtelain, J.-M., 'La fréquentation des livres et l'usage du monde', in: Châtelain, J.-M., *La bibliothèque de l'honnête homme: livres, lectures et collections en France à l'âge classique (1630-1730)* (Paris, 2003), pp. 9-47.

Chegai, A., *L'esilio di Metastasio. Forme e riforme dello spettacolo d'opera fra Sette e Ottocento* (Florence, 1998).

Christiaans, P.A., 'De Mandeville', *Jaarboek Centraal Bureau voor Genealogie* 33 (1979), pp. 118-125.

Clutius, Theodorus, *Van de bijen, haar wonderlijke oorspronk, natuer, eygenschap, krachtighe, onghehoorde seltsame werken (...)* (Amsterdam, 1705).

Corneille, P., *Cinna ou La Clémence d'Auguste* (Paris, 1643).

Correspondance littéraire, philosophique et critique par Grimm, Diderot, Raynal, Meister etc., ed. M. Tourneux, 12 vols. (Paris, 1877-1880).

Cowling, D., 'Introduction', in: Cowling, D. and Bruun, M.B., eds, *Commonplace Culture in Western Europe in the Early Modern Period I. Reformation, Counter-Reformation and Revolt* (Leuven/Paris/Walpole, MA, 2010), pp. ix-xvii.

Cowling, D. and Bruun, M.B., eds, *Commonplace Culture in Western Europe in the Early Modern Period I. Reformation, Counter-Reformation and Revolt* (Leuven/Paris/Walpole, MA, 2010).

Cranfield, G.A., *The Development of the Provincial Newspaper 1700-1760* (Oxford, 1962).

Curtius, E.R., 'Topik als Heuristik', *Zeitschrift für romanische Philologie* 58 (1938) pp. 197-199.

———, 'Beiträge zur Topik der mittellateinischen Literatur', in: *Corona Querna. Festgabe Karl Strecker zum 80. Geburtstages dargebracht* (Leipzig, 1941).

———, *European Literature and the Latin Middle Ages* (New York/Evanston, 1953).

D'Alembert, J. le Rond, *Oeuvres complétes*, vol. 4 (Geneva, 1967).

Dacier, A., *La Poétique d'Aristote, contenant Les Règles les plus exactes pour juger du Poëme Héroïque, & des Pieces de Théâtre, la Tragedie & la Comedie. Traduite en françois, avec des Remarques Critiques sur tout l'Ouvrage par Mr. Dacier. Nouvelle Edition* (Amsterdam, 1733).

De Méré, A.G., *Les Oeuvres de Monsieur le Chevalier de Méré*, 2 vols. (Amsterdam, 1692).

De Sanctis, F., *Storia della letteratura italiana*, ed. G. Contini (Turin, 1968).

De Vries, M., *Beschaven! Letterkundige genootschappen in Nederland 1750-1800* (Nijmegen, 2001).

Dekker, R., '"Private vices, public virtues" revisited: the Dutch background of Bernard Mandeville', *History of European Ideas* 14 (1992), pp. 481-498.

———, '"Schijnheilig atheïst." Bernard Mandeville als pamflettist tijdens het Costerman-oproer in Rotterdam in 1690', *Holland* 26 (1994), pp. 1-17.

Der kleine Pauly. Lexicon der Antike (...), vol. 1 (Munich, 1979).

Derrida, J., *De la grammotologie* (Paris, 1967).

Descartes, R., *Discours de la méthode* (Leiden, 1637).

———, *Discours de la méthode*, ed. E. Gilson (Paris, 1925).

Dictionnaire de l'Académie française (Paris, 1762).

Diderot, D., and d'Alembert, J. Le Rond, eds, *Encyclopédie; ou, Dictionnaire raisonné des sciences, des arts et des métiers*, 28 vols (Paris, 1749-1772).

——, eds, *Encyclopédie, ou Dictionnaire raisonné des sciences, des arts et des métiers, par une société de gens de lettres*, 17 vols. (Paris/Neufchâtel, 1751-1765).

Diderot, D., *The nun* (London, 1797).

——, *Œuvres esthétiques*, ed. P. Vernière (Paris, 1968).

——, *La Religieuse*, in: Diderot, D., *Œuvres complètes*, vol. XI, présentation Georges May ed. (Paris, 1975), pp. 281-282.

——, *Lettre sur les aveugles à l'usage de ceux qui voient*, eds M. Hobson and S. Harvey (Paris, 2000).

Domenech, J., 'Saint-Preux et Julie lecteurs du Tasse. Connivence érotique et spiritualité amoureuse dans *La Nouvelle Héloïse*', *Annales Jean-Jacques Rousseau*, 44 (2002), pp. 119-147.

Dooley, B., *The Social History of Skepticism. Experience and Doubt in early Modern Culture* (Baltimore/London, 1999).

——, 'News and doubt in early modern culture; or are we having a public shere yet?', in: Dooley, B. and Baron, S., eds, *The Politics of Information in Early Modern Europe* (London/New York, 2001), pp. 275-290.

Duindam, J., *Myths of Power. Norbert Elias and the Early Modern European Court* (Amsterdam, 1996).

Dunkley, J., 'Medieval heroes in Enlightenment disguises. Figures from Voltaire and De Belloy', in: Damian-Grint, P., ed., *Medievalism and manière gothique in Enlightenment France, Studies on Voltaire and the Eighteenth Century* 2006:5, pp. 152-180.

Dunthorne, H., 'Dramatizing the Dutch Revolt. Romantic history and its sixteenth-century antecedents', in: Pollmann, J. and Spicer, A., eds, *Public Opinion and Changing Identities in the Early Modern Netherlands. Essays in Honour of Alastair Duke* (Leiden/Boston, 2007), pp. 11-31.

Dziembowski, E., *Un nouveau patriotisme français 1750-1770. La France face à la puissance anglaise à l'époque de la guerre de Sept Ans, Studies on Voltaire and the Eighteenth Century* 365 (1998).

Fehr, M., *Apostolo Zeno und seine Reform des Operntextes* (Zurich, 1912).

Feldman, M., *Opera and Sovereignty: Transforming Myths in Eighteenth-century Italy* (Chicago, 2007).

Fenouillot de Falbaire, C.G., *L'Honnête Criminel* (Paris, 1767).

Flaubert, G., *Le Théâtre de Voltaire*, ed. T. Besterman, *Studies on Voltaire and the Eighteenth Century* 50 (1967).

Fougeret de Montbron, J. L., *Margot la ravaudeuse* (Hamburg, 1773).

Frantz, P., 'Schule, Kirche und Radau', in: Pelzer, E. and Wagner, M., eds, *Die Französische Revolution als Bruch des gesellschaftlichen Bewusstseins* (Munich, 1988), pp. 258-269.

——, *L'Esthétique du tableau dans le théâtre du XVIIIe siècle* (Paris, 1998).

Friedland, P., *Political Actors. Representative Bodies and Theatricality in the Age of the French Revolution* (Ithaca, 2002).

Friis, A., *Bernstorffske Papirer*, vol. 1 (Copenhagen, 1904).

Fuchs, M., *La Vie théâtrale en province au XVIIIe siècle* (Paris, 1986).

Fucilla, J.C., 'The European and American Vogue of Metastasio's Shorter Poems', *Italica* 29 (1952), pp. 13-33.

Furbank, P., *Diderot: A Critical Biography* (New York, 1992).

Furetière, A., *Le Roman bourgeois* (Paris, 2001).

[Gervaise, A.-F., ed.], *Les veritables lettres d'Abeillard et d'Heloise* (Paris, 1723).

Giesey, R.E., 'Models of Rulership in French Royal Ceremonial', in: Wilentz, S., ed., *Rites of Power* (Philadelfia, 1985).

―――, 'The King Imagined', in: Baker, K.M., ed., *The Political Culture of the Old Regime, The French Revolution and the Creation of Modern Political Culture*, vol. 1 (Oxford, 1987).

Gioviale, F., 'La *Clemenza di Tito* da Metastasio a Mozart', in: Gioviale, F., *Intermezzi serio-comici e idilli imperfetti* (Rovito, 1992), pp. 117-142

Goethe, J.W. von, *Die Leiden des jungen Werther* (Munich, 1978).

―――, *The Sorrows of Young Werther* (Oxford, 2006).

Grant, J., *The Newspaper Press. Its Origin, Progress and Present Position*, vol. 1 (London, 1871).

Gravina, G.V., *Scritti critici e teorici*, ed. A. Quondam (Bari, 1973).

Griffiths, D., *Fleet Street. Five Hundred Years of the Press* (London, 2006).

Grimm, F.M., *Correspondance littéraire, philosophique et critique, 1. partie, 1-6 (1753-1769)* (Paris, 1813).

Guldberg, O., *Tale til sine Landsmænd, ved Anledning af Hans Kongelige Høiheds Vor Naadigste Kronprintses Confirmation* (Copenhagen, 1765).

Hagen, E., *'Een min of meer doodlyken haat.' Antipapisme en cultureel natiebesef in Nederland rond 1800* (Nijmegen, 2008).

Hammann, C., 'Rousseau citant le Tasse, ou les séductions de l'artifice', *Dix-huitième siècle* 38 (2006), pp. 511-528.

―――, 'La vie de Jean-Jacques Rousseau ou l'éternel retour du Tasse', *Revue d'histoire littéraire de la France* 106, 4 (2006), pp. 859-883.

Hanou, A., ed., *Nijmeegse mutsen. Een satire uit 1792. E.J.B. Schonck, De Bonheurs uit de mode. Heldenzang* (Leuth, 2006).

Harboe, L., *En hellig og høitidelig Bekiendelse aflagt af Hans Kongelige Høihed Kron-Prinds Christian* (Copenhagen 1765).

Henderson, J.S., *Voltaire's* Tancrède. *Author and publisher*, *Studies on Voltaire and the Eighteenth Century* 61 (1968).

Henkel, A. and Schöne, A., *Emblemata. Handbuch zur Sinnbildkunst des XVI. und XVII. Jahrhunderts* (Stuttgart, 1976).

Highet, *The classical tradition. Greek and Roman influences on western literature.* (Oxford, 1949).

Hoffmann, E.T.A., *Schriften zur Musik. Nachlese* (Munich, 1963).

Holbach, P.T., *Le Bon-Sens: ou, Idées naturelles opposées aux idées surnaturelles* (London, 1772).

Holm, E., *Danmark-Norges Historie fra Den store Nordiske Krigs Afslutning til Rigernes Adskillelse*, vol. 4 (Copenhagen 1901).

Horace, *On the Art of Poetry*, in: Dorsch, T.S., ed. *Classical Literary Criticism*, (London, 1965), pp. 77-95.

Høst, J.K., *Geheimekabinetsminister Grev Johann Friedrich Struensee og hans Ministerium samt de det nærmest foregaaende og efterfølgende Tildragelser i Danmark*, vol. 1 (Copenhagen, 1824).

Howarth, W., *Beaumarchais* (New York, 1995).

Hunter, M., *The Culture of Opera Buffa in Mozart's Vienna. A poetics of Entertainment* (Princeton, 1999).

Iotti, G., *Virtù e identità nella tragedia di Voltaire* (Paris, 1995).

Israel, J., *Radical Enlightenment. Philosophy and the making of Modernity 1650-1750* (Oxford, 2001).

———, *Enlightenment Contested. Philosophy, Modernity, and the Emancipation of Man 1670-1752* (New York, 2006).

Jackson, R.A., *Vive le Roi! A History of the French Coronation from Charles V to Charles X* (London, 1984).

Jansen, A.C., 'Vondst in de bibliotheek van de Maatschappij. Twee Nederlandstalige gedichten van Bernard Mandeville', *Nieuw Letterkundig Magazijn* 23 (2005), pp. 2-8.

———, 'Het leven van Bernard Mandeville', in: Mandeville, Bernard, *De wereld gaat aan deugd ten onder. Verzameld werk, deel I (...)*, ed. A.C. Jansen (Rotterdam, 2006), pp. 329-257.

Javitch, D., *Proclaiming a Classic: The Canonization of Orlando Furioso* (Princeton, 1991).

Johansen, D., *Den skiftende maktrepresentasjon i herskerportrettet i helstaten under Christian VIIs regjeringstid (1766-1808)* (Trondheim, unpublished thesis, 2007).

Joly, J., *Les fêtes théâtrales de Métastase à la cour de Vienne (1731-1767)* (Clermont-Ferrand, 1978).

———, 'Metastasio e l'ideologia del sovrano virtuoso', in: Nicastro, G., ed., *Istituzioni culturali e sceniche* (Milan, 1986), pp. 9-40.

Jongenelen, T., 'De Ouderwetse Nederlandsche patriot', in: Van Wissing, P., ed., *Stookschriften. Pers en politiek tussen 1780 en 1800* (Nijmegen, 2008), pp. 19-36.

Jonson, B., *The Staple of News*, A. Parr ed. (1625; Manchester, 1988).

Kafker, F.A., and Kafker, S.L., *The Encyclopedists as Individuals: A Biographical Dictionary of the Authors of the "Encyclopédie"*, Studies on Voltaire and the Eighteenth Century 257 (1988).

Kalff, G., 'Jan Nomsz', in: Kalff, G., *Geschiedenis der Nederlandsche letterkunde*, vol. 6 (Groningen, 1910), pp. 476-484.

Kantorowicz, E.H., *The Kings Two Bodies. A Study in Mediaeval Political Theology* (Princeton, N.J., 1957).

Karoui, A., '*Tancrède* ou les valeurs chevaleresques revues par Voltaire', *Studies on Voltaire and the Eighteenth Century* 304 (1992), pp. 1320-1324.

Kaye, F.B. [Frederick B. Kugelman] ed., *The Fable of the Bees or Private Vices, Publick Benefits. By Bernard Mandeville. With a commentary critical, historical, and explanatory*, vol. 1 (Oxford, 1924).

Kerkhof, A.J., *De mens is een angstig dier. Adam Smith' theorie van de morele gevoelens* (Meppel, 1992).

Kierkegaard, S., 'The Immediate Erotic Stages or the Musical Erotic', in: Kierkegaard, S., *Either/Or* (London, 1992), pp. 59-136.

Klei, E., '"Notre Wilkes": de theatraal tegendraadse stijl van optreden van Joan Derk van der Cappellen tot den Pol', *Overijsselse historische bijdragen* 120 (2005), pp. 104-127.

Klein, S.R.E., *Patriots republikanisme. Politieke cultuur in Nederland (1766-1787)* (Amsterdam, 1995).

Kloek, E., 'Moons, Magdalena', in: *Digitaal Vrouwenlexicon van Nederland.* URL: http:// www.inghist.nl/Onderzoek/Projecten/DVN/lemmata/data/moons [28/02/2008].

Kluit, A., *Inwijingsrede over 't recht, 't welk de Nederlanders gehad hebben, om hunnen wettigen vorst en heer, Philips, koning van Spanje, aftezweren* (Leiden, 1779).

Knoop, J.H., *Kort onderwys, hoedanig men de couranten best lezen en gebruiken kan* (Leeuwarden, 1758).

Knuttel, W.P.C., *Verboden boeken in de Republiek der Vereenigde Nederlanden. Beredeneerde catalogus* (The Hague, 1914).

Koepp, C.J., 'Making Money: Artisans and Entrepreneurs in Diderot's *Encyclopédie*', in: Brewer, D. and Hayes, J.C., eds, *Using the "Encyclopédie": Ways of Knowing, Ways of Reading, Studies on Voltaire and the Eighteenth Century* 2002:5, pp. 99-118.

Koopmans, J.W., 'Oorlogen in het vroegmoderne nieuws. Nederlandse nieuwsbronnen over militaire confrontaties', *Leidschrift. Historisch tijdschrift* 22 (2007), pp. 103-121.

Kuijper, G., 'Van voorbeeld tot vergetelheid. Amerika in Nederlandse publicaties', *Mededelingen van de Stichting Jacob Campo Weyerman* 26 (2003), pp. 158-166.

La Harpe, J.-F. de, *Éloge de Racine* (Amsterdam/Paris, 1772).

La Noue, J.-B.S. *Lettre critique à M**, sur la tragédie de Tancrède* (Paris, 1760).

Lagrave, H., 'Voltaire, Diderot et le "tableau scénique". Le malentendu de *Tancrède*', in: Mervaud, C., and Menant, S., eds, *Le Siècle de Voltaire. Hommage à René Pomeau*, vol. 2 (Oxford, 1987), pp. 569-575.

Lancaster, H. C., *The Comédie Française 1701-1774: Plays, Actors, Spectators, Finances* (Philadelphia, 1951).

Langen, U., *Den afmacgtige. En biografi om Christian 7.* (Copenhagen, 2008).

Lavoisier, A., 'Mémoire sur la manière d'éclairer les salles de spectacle', in: *Œuvres*, vol. 3 (Paris, 1865), pp. 91-102.

Le Francq van Berkhey, J., *Het verheerlijkt Leyden, bij het tweede eeuwgetijde van deszelfs heuchlijk ontzet etc.* (Leiden, 1774).

Lekain, H., *Registre Lekain*, Bibliothèque de la Comédie-Française, ms. 25035.

Libourel, J.-L., *Voitures hippomobiles. Vocabulaire typologyique et technique* (Paris, 2005).

Lo Nigro, S., ed., *Novellino e Conti del Duecento* (Turin, 1989).

Loaisel de Tréogate, J., *Dolbreuse ou l'Homme du siècle ramené à la vérité par le sentiment de la raison*, 2 vols. (Paris, 1785).

Longino Farrell, M., *Performing Motherhood: The Sévigné Correspondence* (Hanover, 1991).

Lough, J., *The "Encyclopédie"* (Harlow, 1970).

Macaulay, T.B., *Essays, critical and miscellaneous* (rev.ed.; Boston, 1858).

Mandeville, B., *A Letter to Dion*, ed. B. Dobrée (Liverpool, 1954).

———, *De fabel van de bijen*, ed. and transl. A.C. Jansen (Rotterdam, 2008).

Marivaux, M. de, *Le Paysan parvenu* (The Hague, 1734).

Marshall, R, 'What Mozart Meant', *The New York Review of Books* 54, nr. 19 (2007).

Maslan, S., *Revolutionary Acts. Theater, Democracy and the French Revolution* (Baltimore, 2005).

Mason, H., 'Diderot critic of Voltaire's theatre', in: Mervaud, C., and Menant, S., eds, *Le Siècle de Voltaire. Hommage à René Pomeau*, vol. 2 (Oxford, 1987), pp. 633-642.

Mattheij, T.M.M., *Waardering en kritiek. Johannes Nomsz en de Amsterdamse Schouwburg* (Amsterdam, 1980).

Matthisson, F., *Briefe von Friedrich Matthisson* (Zurich, 1802).

Mattioda, E., *Teorie della tragedia nel Settecento* (Modena, 1994).

McManners, J., *Church and Society in Eighteenth-Century France*, 2 vols. (Oxford, 1998).

Mellace, R., *L'autunno del Metastasio: gli ultimi drammi per musica di Johann A-dolph Hasse* (Florence, 2007).

'Memorie, gedaen maken, en overgegeeven aen de Edele Groot Achtbaere Heeren, die van den gerechte der Stad Leyden, door ofte van wegens Cornelis van Hoogeveen junior, en Pieter van der Eyk en Daniel Vygh, tot apui van 't verzoek, door hun by Requeste aen hunne Edele Groot Achtbaerheeden ge-daen, omme te obtineeren, dat hun Edele Groot Achtbaerheeden gelieven the coöpereeren, ten einde het nader geredresseerd Concept-Placaet tegen Godslasterlyke Boeken en Geschriften by de Edele Groot Mogende Hee-ren Staeten van Holland en Westfriesland werde gedeclineerd', *Nieuwe Nederlandsche Jaerboeken, of vervolg der merkwaerdigste geschiedenis-sen, die voorgevallen zijn in de Vereenigde Provincien, de Generaliteits landen en de volksplantingen van den staet*, vol. 5, 2nd part (1770), pp. 808-896.

Metastasio, P., *Opere*, 12 vols. (Paris, 1780-1782).

——, *Opere del Signor Ab. Pietro Metastasio Poeta Cesareo*, 15 vols. (Venice, 1783).

——, *La clemenza di Tito*, ed. A. Scuppa (Modena, 1930).

——, *Tutte le opere*, ed. B. Brunelli, 5 vols. (Milan, 1943-1954).

——, *Drammi per musica*, ed. A. L. Bellina, 3 vols. (Venice, 2002-2004) [vol. 1, *Il periodo italiano 1724-1730*; vol. 2, *Il regno di Carlo VI, 1730-1740*; vol. 3, *L'età teresiana, 1740-1771*].

Mézières, E.-É. de Béthisy, marquis de, *Critique d'un livre contre les spectacles in-titulé J.J. Rousseau, citoyen de Genève, à M. d'Alembert* (Paris, 1760).

Miedema, H., *Beeldespraeck. Register op D.P. Pers' uitgave van Cesare Ripa's Iconologia (1644)* (Doornspijk, 1987),

Mittman, B.G., *Spectators on the Paris Stage in the Seventeenth and Eighteenth Centuries* (Ann Arbor, 1984).

Moss, A., *Printed Commonplace-Books and the Structuring of Renaissance Thought* (Oxford, 1996).

——, 'Power and Persuasion: Commonplace Culture in Early Modern Europe', in: Cowling, D. and Bruun, M.B., eds, *Commonplace Culture in Western Europe in the Early Modern Period I. Reformation, Counter-Reformation and Revolt* (Leuven/Paris/Walpole, MA, 2010), pp. 1-17.

Mozart, W.A., *Don Giovanni. Urtextausgabe aus Wolfgang Amadeus Mozart. Neue Ausgabe sämtlicher Werke* (Kassel, 2005).
———, *The Magic Flute. Urtextausgabe aus Wolfgang Amadeus Mozart. Neue Ausgabe sämtlicher Werke* (Kassel, 2005).
Munby, J., 'Les Origines du coche', in: Roche, D. and Reytier, D., eds., *Voitures, chevaux et attelages. Du XVIe au XIX siècle* (Paris, 2000).
Nagel, I., *Autononomy & Mercy. Reflectons on Mozart's Operas* (Cambridge, 1991).
Nellen, H., *Hugo de Groot. Een leven in strijd om de vrede 1583-1645* (Amsterdam, 2007).
Nicole, P., *Traité de la comédie et autres pièces d'un procès du théâtre*, ed. L. Thirouin (Paris, 1998).
Nielsen, G., *Abriss der Sittenlehre. Zum Gebrauch des Unterrichts Seiner Königlichen Hoheit der Kronprinzen Christianus* (Copenhagen, 1760).
Niemetscheks, F.X., *Leben des K.K. Kappelmeisters Wolfgang Gottlieb Mozart* (Prag, 1798).
Nies, F., *Les lettres de Madame de Sévigné: conventions du genre et sociologie des publics*, transl. M. Creff (Paris, 2001).
Nomsz, J., *Vaderlandsche brieven*, 2 vols. (Amsterdam, 1785).
Norman, B., *Touched by the Graces: The Libretti of Philippe Quinault in the Context of French Classicism* (Birmingham, Alabama, 2001).
Obermayer, A., 'Zum Toposbegriff der modernen Literaturwissenschaft' in: Baeumer, M.L., ed., *Toposforschung* (Darmstadt, 1973).
Parr, A., 'Introduction', in: Jonson, B., *The Staple of News*, ed. A. Parr (1625; Manchester, 1988).
Patte, P., *Essai sur l'architecture théâtrale* (Paris, 1782).
Payne, H.C., *The Philosophes and the People* (London, 1976).
Petit de Bachaumont, L., *Mémoires secrets pour servir a l'historie de la république des letters en France depuis MDCCLXII jusq'a nos jours* (London, 1777).
Phillips, H., *The Theatre and its Critics in Seventeenth-Century France* (Oxford, 1980).
Phillips, J., '"Vox populi, vox dei": Baudelaire's Uncommon Use of Commonplace in the Salon de 1846', *French Forum* 31 (2006), pp. 21-39.
Pollmann, J., *Het oorlogsverleden van de Gouden Eeuw. Oratie uitgesproken bij de aanvaarding van het ambt van bijzonder hoogleraar op het gebied van de Geschiedenis en Cultuur van de Republiek der Verenigde Nederlanden aan de Universiteit Leiden vanwege de Stichting Legatum Perizonianum op vrijdag 27 juni 2008* (Leiden, 2008).
Pomeau, R., *"Ecraser l'infâme", 1759-1770, Voltaire en son temps*, vol. 4 (Oxford, 1994).
Popkin, J.D., *News and Politics in the Age of Revolution. Jean Luzac's Gazette de Leyde* (Ithaca/London, 1989).
———, 'Periodical publication and the nature of knowledge in eigtteenth-century Europe', in: Kelley D.R. and Popkin, R.H., eds, *The Shapes of Knowledge from the Renaissance to the Enlightenment* (Dordrecht/Boston/London, 1991), pp. 203-213.
———, 'New Perspectives on the Early Modern European Press', in: Koopmans, J.W., ed., *News and Politics in Early Modern Europe* (Leuven/Paris/Dudley, MA, 2005), pp. 1-27.

Porée, C., *L'homme instruit par le spectacle, ou le Théâtre changé en école de vertu* (Paris, 1726).

———, *An Oration in which an Enquiry is made whether the Stage is, or can be made a School for forming the Mind to Virtue*, transl. J. Lockman (London, 1734).

Prak, 'M., 'Citizen Radicalism and Democracy in the Dutch Republic: The Patriot Movement in the 1780s', *Theory and Society* 20 (1991), pp. 73-102.

Prévost d'Exiles, A.-F., *Histoire du chevalier des Grieux et de Manon Lescaut*, ed. H. Coulet (Paris, 1967).

Proust, J., *L'"Encyclopédie"* (Paris, 1965).

———, *Diderot et l'"Encyclopédie"* (Paris, [3]1995).

Racine, J., *Œuvres complètes*, ed. R. Picard (Paris, 1950).

Ravel, J.S., *The Contested Parterre. Public Theatre and French Political Culture, 1680-1791* (Ithaca, 1999).

Riccoboni, L., *De la réformation du théâtre* (Paris, 1743).

Riccoboni, M.J., *Lettres d'Adélaïde de Dammartin, comtresse de Sancerre*, 2 vols. (Paris, 1767).

Riley, J.C., *The Seven Years War and the Old Regime in France. The economic and financial toll* (Princeton, 1986).

Rockwood, C., '"Know Thy Side." Propaganda and Parody in Jonson's *Staple of News*', *ELH: A Journal of English Literary History* 75 (2008), pp. 135-149.

Rosen, C., 'Radical, Conventional Mozart', in: Rosen, C., *Critical Entertainments: Music Old and New* (Cambridge, 2000), pp. 85-104.

———, 'Mozart at 250', *The New York Review of Books* 9, section 3 (2006).

Rosenblum, R., ed., *Citizens and Kings. Portraits in the Age of Revolution 1760-1830* (London, 2007).

Rothstein, M., *Reading in the Renaissance:* Amadis de Gaule *and the Lessons of Memory* (Newark, 1999).

Rousseau, A.M., *L'Angleterre et Voltaire, Studies on Voltaire and the Eighteenth Century* 145 (1976).

Rousseau, J.-J., *Écrits sur l'abbé de Saint-Pierre*, in: *Œuvres complètes*, ed. B. Gagnebin and M. Raymond, vol. 3 (Paris, 1964), pp. 563-682.

———, *Emile ou de l'éducation*, ed. M. Launay (Paris, 1966).

———, *Les Rêveries du promeneur solitaire* (Paris, 1972).

———, *Lettre à M. d'Alembert*, in: *Du contrat social et autres œuvres politiques*, ed. J. Ehrard (Paris, 1975), pp. 123-234.

———, *Correspondance complète de Jean-Jacques Rousseau*, ed. R.A. Leigh, vol. 39 (Oxford, 1981).

———, *Essai sur l'origine des langues*, ed. J. Starobinski (Paris, 1990).

———, *The Reveries of the Solitary Walker* (Indianapolis, 1992).

———, *La Nouvelle Héloïse*, ed. H. Coulet, 2 vols. (Paris, 1993).

———, *Dictionnaire de musique*, in: Rousseau, J.-J., *Œuvres complètes*, ed. B. Gagnebin and M. Raymond, vol. 5 (Paris, 1995).

Sade, [D.A.F.], marquis de, *La philosophie dans le boudoir, Oeuvres Completes*, vol. 25 (Paris, 1972).

———, *Œuvres*, ed. M. Delon, 3 vols. (Paris, 1990-1998).

Sannia Nowé, L., 'Epifanie e metamorfosi della clemenza nella letteratura dramma-
    turgica del Settecento', in: Sala di Felice, E. and Sannia Nowé, L., eds, *La
    cultura fra Sei e Settecento* (Modena, 1994), pp. 171-196.
Sbarra, F., *Tieranny van eigenbaat. Toneel als wapen tegen Oranje*, ed. T. Holzhey
    and K. van der Haven (Zoeterwoude, 2008).
Schneider, M., 'Hoe de krant lezen. Kanttekeningen bij een pershistorisch hand-
    boekje' in: Daudt, H., *et al.*, eds, *Selectiviteit in de massacommunicatie*
    (Deventer, 1971), pp. 127-145.
Schutte, G.J., 'Van grondslag tot breidel der vrijheid. Opvattingen over de Unie van
    Utrecht in het laatste kwart van de achttiende eeuw', in: Groenveld, S. and
    Leeuwenberg, H.L.Ph., eds, *De Unie van Utrecht. Wording en werking
    van een verbond en een verbondsacte* (Den Haag, 1979), pp. 199-225.
Seeber, H.U., 'Von den Wordsworths zu De Quincey: Gehen und Kutschenfahren in
    der englischen Romantik oder die Entdeckung der Gewalt der Geschwin-
    digkeit', in: Alexander, V. and Fludernik, M., eds, *Romantik* (Trier, 2000),
    pp. 7-32.
Seidel, W., 'Seneca-Corneille-Mozart. Questioni di storia delle idee e dei generi nel-
    la *Clemenza di Tito*', in: Durante, S., ed., *Mozart* (Bologna, 1991), pp.
    345-366
Seneca, *Moral Essays*, ed. and transl. J.W. Basore, 3 vols. (London/New York,
    1928).
Sévigné, M. de Rabutin-Chantal, *Correspondance*, ed. R. Duchêne, 3 vols. (Paris,
    1972-1978).
Shapiro, B.J., *A culture of fact. England, 1550-1720* (Ithaca/London, 2000).
Shaw, B., *Shaw on Music*, ed. E. Bentley (London, 1955).
Sherman, S., 'Eyes and ears, news and plays: the argument of Ben Jonson's *Staple*',
    in: Dooley, B. and Baron, S., eds, *The Politics of Information in Early
    Modern Europe* (London/New York, 2001), pp. 23-40.
Simpson, J.G., *Le Tasse et la littérature et l'art baroque en France* (Paris, 1962).
Smit, F.R.H., 'Mijnheer de Friessche Patriot! De politieke pers in Friesland 1780-
    1787', in: Bergsma, W., *et al.*, eds, *For uwz lân, wyv en bern. De patriot-
    tentijd in Friesland* (Leeuwarden, 1987), pp. 111-126.
Smit, W.A.P., 'De vaderlandse epen van Johannes Nomsz 1779; 1789', in: Smit,
    W.A.P., *Kalliope in de Nederlanden. Het Renaissancistisch-klassicistisch
    epos van 1550 tot 1850*, vol. 2 (Assen, 1983), pp. 775-803.
Smith, A., 'The long road to objectivity and back again: the kinds of truth we get in
    journalism', in: Curran, J., Boyce, G. and Wingate, P., eds, *Newspaper
    History from the seventeenth century to the present day* (London, 1978),
    pp. 153-171.
Sozzi, L., '"*Notre divin Métastase*"', in: Sozzi, L., *Da Metastasio a Leopardi. Ar-
    monie e dissonanze letterarie italo-francesi* (Florence, 2007), pp. 1-21.
Starobinski, J., 'L'imitation du Tasse', *Annales Jean-Jacques Rousseau* 40 (1992),
    pp. 265-297.
Stieler, K., *Zeitungs Lust und Nutz*, G. Hagelweide ed. (1695; Bremen, 1969).
Stroppa, S., *Fra notturni sereni. Le azioni sacre del Metastasio* (Florence, 1993).
Suhm, P.F., *Hemmelige Efterretninger on de danske Konger efter Souverainiteten*
    (Copenhagen 1918)
    Système de la nature (London, 1770).

Theeuwen, P.J.H.M., *Pieter 't Hoen en De Post van den Neder-Rhijn (1781-1787)* (Hilversum, 2002).

Thomas, A.-L., *Essai sur les éloges, suivi de l'Éloge de Marc-Aurèle*, 2 vols. (Toulouse, 1819).

Thorel de Campigneulles, C.-C.-F. de, 'Lettre à M. Desprez de Boissy, avocat au parlement de Paris, sur les spectacles', in: *Nouveaux essais en différents genres de littérature* (Geneva, 1765), pp. 49-86.

Till, N., *Mozart and the Enlightenment* (London, 1992).

[Van der Capellen tot den Pol, Joan Derk], *An Address to the People of the Netherlands, on the Present Alarming and most Dangerous Situation: Showing the True Motives of the most Unpardonable Delays of the Executive Power in Putting the Republic into a Proper State of Defence, and the Advantages of an Alliance with Holland, France and America* (London, 1782).

Van der Capellen tot den Pol, Joan Derk, *Aan het volk van Nederland. Het patriottisch program uit 1781*, ed. H.L. Zwitzer (Amsterdam, 1987).

Van der Meulen, R., *De Courant. Geschiedkundig en vergelijkend overzicht der nieuwsbladen van alle landen* (Leiden, [1858]).

Van Dijk, E.A., *et al.*, eds, *De wekker van de Nederlandse natie. Joan Derk van der Capellen 1741-1784* (Zwolle, 1984).

Van Sas, N.C.F., 'De vaderlandse imperatief. Begripsverandering en politieke conjunctuur, 1763-1813', in: Van Sas, N.C.F., ed., *Vaderland. Een geschiedenis vanaf de vijftiende eeuw tot 1940* (Amsterdam, 1999), pp. 275-308.

Van Vliet, R., *Elie Luzac (1721-1796). Boekverkoper van de Verlichting* (Nijmegen, 2005).

———, 'Leiden and censorship during the 1780s. The Overraam affair and Elie Luzac on the freedom of the press', in: Koopmans, J.W., ed., *News and Politics in Early Modern Europe (1500-1800)* (Leuven/Paris/Dudley, MA, 2005), pp. 203-217.

Van Wissing, P., *Stokebrand Janus 1787* (Nijmegen, 2003).

———, 'De Post naar den Neder-Rhijn: een "mission impossible"?', in: Van Wissing, P., ed., *Stookschriften. Pers en politiek tussen 1780 en 1800* (Nijmegen, 2008), pp. 37-58.

Velema, W.R.E., *Enlightenment and conservatism in the Dutch Republic. The political thoughts of Elie Luac (1721-1796)* (Assen/Maastricht, 1993).

Vles, E.J., *Pieter Paulus (1753-1769). Patriot en staatsman* (Amsterdam, 2004).

[Voltaire (F.-M. Arouet)], *La tragédie de Sémiramis, et quelques autres Piéces de Littérature* (Paris, 1750).

Voltaire [F.-M. Arouet], *Tancrède* (Paris, 1761).

———, *Œuvres completes*, ed. L. Moland, 54 vols. (Paris, 1877-1885).

———, *Voltaire's Notebooks*, ed. T. Besterman, 2 vols. (Geneva, 1952).

———, *The Complete Works of Voltaire* (Oxford, 1968-).

———, *Correspondence and Related Documents*, ed. Th. Besterman, 51 vols. (Geneva, 1968-1977).

———, *Mémoires: texte intégral*, ed. L. Lecomte (Paris, 1993).

Von der Marwitz, F.A.L., *Friedrich August Ludwig v.d. Marwitz, ein Edelmann im Zeitalter der Befreiungskriege*, vol. 1 (Berlin, 1908).

Von Holten, C.H., *Af en gammel Hofmands Mindeblade. Konferenceraad Carl Henrik Holtens Optegnelser* (Copenhagen, 1909).

Von Raumer, F., *Europa vom Ende des siebenjährigen bis zum Ende des amerikanischen Krieges (1763-1783). Nach dem Quellen im britischen und französischen Reicharchive*, vol. 1-3 (Leipzig, 1839).

Von Schmettau, S.L., 'Kammerherre, Amtmand Samuel Leopold von Schmettaus Selvbiografi', *Personalhistorisk Tidsskrift* 4/4 (1901), pp. 135-156.

Wagner, R., 'Oper und Drama (1851)', in: *Richard Wagner: Prose Works*, vol. 2 (London, 1970), pp. 72-380.

Waldoff, J., *Recognition in Mozart's Operas* (Oxford, 2006).

Ward, S.J., *The Invention of Journalism Ethics. The Path to Objectivity and Beyond* (Montreal/Kingston, 2004).

Weekhout, I., *Boekencensuur in de Noordelijke Nederlanden. De vrijheid van drukpers in de zeventiende eeuw* (The Hague, 1998).

West, M.L., ed., *Anacreontea* (Leipzig, 1984).

Wittich, K., *Struensee* (Copenhagen, 1887).

Wittman, R., *Architecture, Print Culture, and the Public Sphere in Eighteenth-Century France* (New York/London, 2007).

Woolf, D., 'News, history and the construction of the present in early modern England', in: Dooley, B. and Baron, S., eds, *The Politics of Information in Early Modern Europe* (London/New York, 2001), pp. 80-118.

Woordenboek der Nederlandsche taal, vol. 6 (The Hague/Leiden, 1912).

Works of Metastasio, translated from the Italian, The, transl. J. Hoole (London, 1767).

Yeo, R., 'Reading Encyclopaedias: Science and the Organisation of Knowledge in British Dictionaries of Arts and Sciences, 1750-1830', *Isis* 82 (1991), pp. 24-49.

————, 'Ephraim Chambers' *Cyclopaedia* (1728) and the Tradition of Commonplaces', *Journal of the History of Ideas*, 57 (1996), pp. 157-175.

Young, M.J., *Voltairiana. In Four Volumes. Selected and Translated from the French*, 4 vols. (London, 1805). Baker, K.M., 'Public opinion as political invention', in: Young, M.J., *Inventing the French Revolution. Essays on French political culture in the Eighteenth Century* (Cambridge, 1990), pp. 167-199.

INDEX

PRINTED ON PERMANENT PAPER • IMPRIME SUR PAPIER PERMANENT • GEDRUKT OP DUURZAAM PAPIER - ISO 9706

N.V. PEETERS S.A., WAROTSTRAAT 50, B-3020 HERENT